Pregnant Darkness

Pregnant Darkness

Alchemy and the Rebirth of Consciousness

Monika Wikman

Nicolas-Hays, Inc.
Berwick, Maine

First published in 2004 by
Nicolas-Hays, Inc.
P. O. Box 1126
Berwick, ME 03901-1126
www.nicolashays.com

Distributed to the trade by
Red Wheel/Weiser, LLC
P. O. Box 612
York Beach, ME 03910-0612
www.redwheelweiser.com

Client privacy was ensured as all names and circumstantial details have been changed on dreams and other client material. Thanks to all who generously shared their lives and dreams for the purpose of this work.

Library of Congress Cataloging-in-Publication Data available on request.

VG

Cover and text design by Phillip Augusta.
Cover: "Stars, Moon, and Hand from Crypt at Chartres" photograph by Melina Leodas Whelan, copyright © 2002, used by permission of photographer.
Typeset in Minion
Printed in the United States of America
10 09 08 07 06 05 04
7 6 5 4 3 2 1

The paper used in this publication meets the minimum requirements of the American National Standard for Information Sciences—Permanence of Paper for Printed Library Materials Z39.48–1992 (R1997).

For Marcie
For Ray
And the living waters of change.

Contents

Illustrations

Acknowledgments

The sources for the epigraphs on part title pages and chapter title pages are:

Part I title page: Robert Duncan, "Osiris and Set," final stanza, from *Roots and Branches* (New York: Charles Scribners Sons, 1964), p. 69. Copyright © 1964 by Robert Duncan, reprinted by permission of New Directions Publishing Corp.

Chapter 1: Monika Wikman, excerpt from "This Being of Midnight," first stanza, in *Psychological Perspectives* 45 (2003): 154–155, used by permission of *Psychological Perspectives.*

Chapter 2: Rainer Maria Rilke, excerpt from "I Have Many Brothers," from *Selected Poems of Rainer Maria Rilke*, edited and translated by Robert Bly (New York: Harper Colophon, 1982), p. 15. Copyright © 1981 by Robert Bly. Reprinted by permission of HarperCollins Publishers, Inc.

Chapter 3: Jalal Al-din Rumi, "What Hurts the Soul," from *The Soul of Rumi: A New Collection of Ecstatic Poems*, Coleman Barks, trans. (San Francisco: HarperSanFrancisco, 2002), p. 126. Copyright © 2001 by Coleman Barks. Reprinted with permission of HarperCollins, Coleman Barks, and Maypop Books, Athens GA.

Chapter 4: C. G. Jung, *The Collected Works of C. G. Jung, vol. 14, Mysterium Coniunctionis*, ¶ 193.

Chapter 5: Jalal Al-Din Rumi, "There Is Some Kiss We Want," excerpt from *Like This*, Coleman Barks, trans. (Athens, GA: Maypop Books, 1990), p. 16. Copyright © by Coleman Barks. Reprinted with permission of Coleman Barks and Maypop Books.

Chapter 6: Marie-Louise von Franz, *The Golden Ass of Apuleius: The Liberation of the Feminine in Man* (Boston: Shambhala, 2001), pp. 186-187.

Part II title page: Lisel Mueller, "Spell for a Traveler," excerpt from *The Private Life: Poems by Lisel Mueller* (Baton Rouge: Louisiana State University Press, 1976), p. 18. Copyright © 1976 by Lisel Mueller. Reprinted by permission of Louisiana State University Press.

Chapter 7: C. G. Jung, *C. G. Jung Letters, Volume 1,* Gerhard Adler and Aniela Jaffé, eds., R.F.C. Hull, trans. (Princeton: Princeton University Press, 1992), p. 19.

I am also grateful for permission to use the following material:

W. H. Auden, "Autumn Song" excerpt on page 24, copyright 1937 and renewed 1965 by W. H. Auden, from *Collected Poems* by W. H. Auden (New York: Random House, 1976). Reprinted by permission of Random House, Inc.

Liam Blake, photograph of a jackass on p. 91, Bray Co., Wicklow, Ireland, Real Island Design Limited, Ref: SP 52, copyright © 2002.

C. G. Jung, quote on p. 227, from *The Collected Works of C. G. Jung,* Princeton University Press, 1977. Reprinted by permission of Princeton University Press.

Kabir, poem 25 excerpt on p. 95 from *Kabir: Ecstatic Poems*, Robert Bly, trans. (Boston: Beacon Press, 2004), p. 33. Copyright © 2004 by Robert Bly.

Jalal Al-Din Rumi, "What Is the Path?" excerpt on page xxiv from *One-Handed Basket Weaving* (Athens, GA: Maypop Books, 1991), p. 112. Copyright © Coleman Barks. Reprinted by permission of Coleman Barks and Maypop Books.

Jalal Al-Din Rumi, "The Dream That Must Be Interpreted," excerpt on p. 196 from *The Essential Rumi*, Coleman Barks with John Moyne, trans. (San Francisco: HarperSanFrancisco, 1997), p. 113. Copyright © Coleman Barks. Reprinted by permission of Coleman Barks, Maypop Books, and HarperCollins.

Marie-Louise von Franz, quote on p. 157, from *Alchemy* (Toronto: Inner City Books, 1981) p. 166, reprinted by permission of Inner City Books.

David Whyte, "Faces at Braga," excerpt on page 169 from *Where Many Rivers Meet* by David Whyte. Copyright © 1990 David Whyte. Used by permission of the author and Many Rivers Press (*www.davidwhyte.com*).

Monika Relph Wikman, "Up Rustler's Gulch: A Winter Solstice Offering," on page 286 from *Psychological Perspectives* 45 (2003):11; and "Inner Music, Living Water," in *Psychological Perspectives* 44 (2002):98–113. Used by permission of *Psychological Perspectives.*

Monika Relph Wikman, "Human Connection and Community Mysteries in the Jungian Lineage," from *Quadrant* 33, no. 2, 2003. Used by permission of *Quadrant.*

W. B. Yeats, "The Song of the Wandering Aengus," page 75, reprinted with permission of Scribner, an imprint of Simon & Schuster Adult Publishing Group and A. P. Watt Ltd., on behalf of Michael B. Yeats, from *The Collected Poems of W. B. Yeats, Volume 1: The Poems, Revised*, edited by Richard Finneran (New York: Scribner, 1997), pp. 59–60.

This project has come into being with support and guidance from a number of individuals. I would like to thank Valerie Cooper at Nicolas-Hays. Her vision and expertise helped shape and birth this work in countless ways.

I extend gratitude to the analysts at the Center in Switzerland whose courage, profound depth, and creativity organically generates a rare star I am grateful to have been near: Theo Abt, Hansueli Etter, Gothilf Isler, Brigitte Jacobs, Regina Schweizer, and Eva Wertenschlag. Their own individual work with alchemy and the religious attitude toward the psyche filters into their various creations and teachings. For the years of exposure to both their work and way of life with the objective psyche I will always be gratefully indebted.

I would also like to thank Jeff Raff for his seminal work with alchemy. In Jeff Raff's earliest work, *Jung and the Alchemical Imagination*, and in Dr. von Franz's book, *Alchemy,* I found the initial trails into the wilderness of psyche exploring the mysteries of how the latent Self comes into the manifest Self in human life. Jeff Raff also encouraged me over the years to look deeper into the specific processes of the incarnation mysteries appearing in dreams, in life, and in the alchemical emblems, and to the appearance, via active imagination, of the inner companion, the ally.

Gratitude goes to Ralph Metzner. Among many of Ralph's practical meditations and tools for expanding consciousness and experiencing the activation of the realms, here I owe specific gratitude to him for exposure to the use of the Buddhist medicine wheel. It is one of the tools applied to dream and life experiences in the last chapter of this book on the processes of the *rubedo*.

I also thank the people with whom, in various ways, I have had the fortune of sharing life's depths and complexities: Ray Hillis, Marcie Telander, Jacqueline West, Lucy Sikes, Kathleen Burt, Patrick Whelan, Don Eulert, Pui Harvey, Regina Abt, Jack Sanford, Leslie Hammel-Turk, Susie and Gayther Gonzales, Grazia Calza, Julian David, Barbara Getz, and my family, friends, and clients who have generously offered to share their dreams and life stories for the purpose of this work. Also thanks to Margaret O'Ryan and Kate Talbot for their kind assistance with the manuscript at the beginning of the process.

Introduction

In the early 1980s, my body was over-run with an aggressive stage IV ovarian cancer that had spread throughout various organs. After working with the illness for four years and seeing the illness rise and fall within a range in which I could just about eek out a life, suddenly the illness and its effects rocketed and I was told I had a few weeks to live. After years of working with the illness, and then being given the terrible two-week prognosis, I was entirely exhausted, and finally gave up. In the instant that I confessed my exhaustion to myself, and was ready to accept death, windows onto the psychoid (a transpersonal realm of autonomous energy beyond the personal psyche) spontaneously opened and I experienced a series of visions. Afterward, there was no sign of cancer anywhere in my body. I took medical tests the next day and for many consecutive weeks after in awe as the tests that measured for active ovarian cancer that were previously sky high, were now below the normal range. All the symptoms had vanished as well. "Spontaneous remission," the doctors said, and closed my file. Meanwhile, my heart, mind, and life were doing the opposite. They began to open, increasingly moved with gratitude and awe to the mysteries and the map and the grace between us and the autonomous energies living in the psyche and psychoid beyond ordinary consciousness. C. G. Jung's work gave me the lens that enabled me to see these mysteries at work.

Later, I returned to the same medical center in San Diego where I was treated to do research under the guidance of Marie-Louise von Franz's work on the dreams of the dying. Over the years I have gathered evidence of something beyond ordinary consciousness coming into people's lives, helping them into an unexpected state of grace, transformation, and rebirth. Our deepest darknesses are pregnant with incredible life energy.

Cultivating a living relationship with the mysteries of psyche and psychoid depends on our ability to go into the darkness, dim the light of the ego, and attend to what appears. We descend into darkness voluntarily when we meditate or engage in any kind of spiritual practice, dream work, active imagination, shamanic journeying, creative endeavor, and so on. We descend *involuntarily* through depression and crises, such as health problems, loss of love, loss of position, and so on. When we go to meet the unconscious halfway, we make our best attempt to give the dialogue with the unconscious another channel of communication, besides crisis and depression. It is my hope that the stories and ideas in this book will show you many ways this dialogue can begin and be supported.

Sometimes we willingly court the darkness and help create the third mystical center—our relationship with the eternal mysteries embodied in the manifestion of the Self. Sometimes the center, *in potentia*, comes in search of us through crisis and difficulty as we learn to tend to its presence. Usually, both of these paths, the active one where we court the soul, and the one in which crisis pulls us into the psyche, can lead us to the source of transformation and renewal. Indeed, these two paths often converge. Courting the soul and holding a sacred place for the ways we suffer and are blocked, wounded, one-sided, or stunted, brings needed contact with this healing source.

Jung said that his work was one of melting down the fixed thought-forms of world religions and pouring this melted substance into the molds of individual experience.[1] Jung showed how what we have ascribed to the gods—or God—can be found inside human experience and related to in a fresh and immediate way, unobstructed by the fixed thought-forms of dogma. This active dynamism, this living force of the god within is what Jung termed the *religious function*. Of its value, Jung says, "The individual who is not anchored in God can offer no resistance on his own resources to the physical and moral blandishments of the world. For this he needs the evidence of inner transcendent experience, which alone can protect him from the otherwise inevitable submersion in the mass."[2]

When we lose connection with the spirit in the core of all beings, our consciousness becomes one-sided, dry, and cut off from the natural sources of renewal in the psyche. This severance is a modern condition from which few are immune. After all, it is in the very nature of ego functioning to defend against the dynamic fluidity of the psyche and the mysteries of which we are all a part. This modern condition can be addressed by the religious function that is activated in work with the psyche. The religious function can bring us into contact with the *numen*—the original spirit informing all life—and can create bridges between the realms of existence that help to heal this schism. Then the "crack between the worlds" becomes a fruitful field of initiation where our human participation matters. Here, spirit, soul, and our consciousness work together as splits heal between the visible and invisible worlds, between the known and unknown, between spirit and matter, between heaven and earth, human and divine, conscious and unconscious fields of awareness and between all polarities.

We all have the capacity to experience the numinous, that which connects us with transcendent dimensions of reality that are beyond the ego and ordinary states of consciousness. When we are stuck in any arena of life, we can tap into inner realms that may guide us toward change and growth, toward new adaptations that are life serving, even life saving at times. These realms include experience of the chthonic regions of the alchemists, of all world religions, and of the pagan deities. And certainly not all contact with the numinous is pleasant or easy. For in contact with the numinous we encounter the opposites as well—the heavenly and hellish, the celestial and demonic, inner darkness, and processes of enlightenment. With such experience of the numinous may come activation in the psyche of unique guiding and protecting forces. Then we have the chance of discovering a fruitful relationship with psyche and psychoid. As we learn the way of the religious or transcendent function, life's very crises can bring us toward renewal.

Authentic relationship with darkness and unknowing usually brings about a shamanic death (the alchemical *nigredo*). It is not for the fainthearted, and it is way beyond the ego's fantasies, attachments, or ideas of grandeur. It includes experiences of "hell," as well as "heaven," as we attempt to find the optimal relationship with the flame. Jung found that a victory for the Self always included a defeat for the ego, an experience we are sure to have if seeking alchemical renewal.[3]

Relating with this part of the psyche usually means that we must encounter feeling lost, empty, bereft, or simply unable to go on the way we have been living. If we turn toward the psyche and psychoid during these spiritual crises, we may find an honest, humble way to discover this source of renewal. Crisis contains a fire capable of clearing the attitudes that blind us to the mysteries, if we will but allow the reality of our inner death to the old ways. The dark night of the soul may then bring us into contact with the inner light that expands our mortal lives through connection with the eternal essence dwelling in each of us.

In psychological terms, the light of consciousness is grown from the primal darkness by the Self. It is an element of Self used, as Jung points out, like a mirror, in which the unconscious becomes aware: "The ego, ostensibly the thing we know the most about, is in fact a highly complex affair full of unfathomable obscurities. Indeed one could even define it as a relatively constant personification of the unconscious itself, or as the Schopenhauerian mirror in which the unconscious becomes aware of its own face."[4]

The need to be in contact with mystery, unknowingness, and darkness is as crucial to the soul's life as any gains in consciousness. What are gains in consciousness worth if we lose our rooting in the chaotic unknown, the erotic wilderness of the psyche that brings renewal of consciousness in the first place? Without experiential roots in the wilderness of psyche, we lose connection with the original living spirit that is the healer, the uniter of opposites of which Jung and the alchemists spoke.

Gustav Dreifuss recounts an encounter in which Jung was asked by new analysts who had just graduated from the Jung Institute in Kusnacht, Switzerland, "What is the meaning or value of consciousness?":

> I vividly remember Jung's answer with regard to the meaning of consciousness. Then he added: But a still bigger problem is unconsciousness. How can man time and again become unconscious in order to unite with the depth of his soul and drink from the deepest well?[5]

How *can* we become unconscious again and again to drink from that deepest well of our being? Herein lies the heart of spiritual practice. In any spiritual tradition or lineage, dedication to a living practice is essential. Spiritual practice entails performing acts that assist us in dipping into, or immersing ourselves in, lunar consciousness, the unconscious, for renewal of consciousness. The shadow side of our modern spiritual eclecticism is that we risk not committing ourselves to spiritual practice, to daily dialogue with the numinous. Any technique that opens us to the irrational (for example, active imagination, meditation, dance, dreaming and dream work, chanting, drumming, yoga, exercise, sexuality, art, music), anything that helps us root in existence beyond the rational, has potential as spiritual practice.

Without experiences beyond the tiny mind, how isolated we become, how utterly dried up consciousness and culture become—cut off from the living root of our existence. Through reconnection with the *numinosum*, we can recover. It is up to us. These instinctual religious patterns living in us can search out the mysteries, find nourishment in the numinosum, and then replenish the soul, body, psyche, personality, relational life, and the planet itself.

In this book, we shall explore how we connect with forces in the psyche and psychoid that reach into our lives through our dreams and the life situations in which we find ourselves. It is a process begun by a longing. C. G. Jung wrote, "In the unconscious are hidden those 'sparks of light' (*scintillae*), the archetypes, from which a higher meaning can be "extracted." . . . The 'magnet' that attracts the hidden thing is the self, or in this case the 'theoria' or the symbol representing it, which the adept uses as an instrument."[6] We can become "the adept," and engage in using symbols to draw out the wisdom inherently present in the psyche. As I was working on this idea, I dreamed the following dream:

> Someone was showing me something important. It was said that theoria is like a fishing line cast into the sea. The image of someone casting a line in the sea then accompanied this voice. The theoria was the lure and the hook on which to catch the fish or beast that swims up to one. Specific theoria attract specific fish.

According to this dream message and image, our particular theoria attracts certain constellations in the unconscious, so in "fishing," we hook up with what is called by what we cast out. If conscious of this dynamic, we can use our theoria as a "magnet of the wise," as the alchemists tell us. Flexible then, and in conscious relationship with the felt presences, we move toward working with the psyche as it becomes manifest. We must be conscious of which theoria we cast out and what our point of view attracts in the vast sea of the unconscious. Personal theoria affects all we do and, most importantly, our depth work with others. Remaining receptive to what constellates in work with others, and why, is key. Psyche must be worked with where and how she alights, so the ego cannot become too attached to ideations or hierarchies of importance in the work. That attachment stifles the soul. Taking the living spirit and attempting to force it into "theories" creates false gold. In contrast, theoria as the magnet of the wise serves to bring us fresh, experiential contact with the living spirit of the imagination, with the numen. As we enter the darkness, if a new light is born it illuminates the heights and depths of the human soul. Jung saw the development of the religious function as learning the art of seeing, not as creating religious truths and dogma. Thus the theoria of the adept helps him or her refine this art of seeing into the mysteries.

Alchemical symbolism is particularly useful for illustrating the consciousness transformation that results from our interaction with the numinous, and through the many examples I provide, you will see the ancient alchemical process at work in modern life. This symbolism provides a map of the transformational journey, and if you can understand the alchemy operating in your life, you may learn to avoid many pitfalls inherent in working with the psyche and you may learn to gather wisdom and soul from difficulties you encounter.

The organizing principle of the psyche is inherent in every human being, and when we live close to it and develop relationship with it, we can discover immense peace and awareness about what needs our attention and what is flourishing. When we become ill, or lose jobs, or relationships are on the brink and we turn toward the arena we are stuck in, and with concern try to free up the block, then we are practicing alchemy. We are seeking, with the help of the psyche, to penetrate into the heart of the matter, gain insight, free spirit and find renewal—the fundamentals of alchemy. To have the help of the dream spirit, active imagination, and another human being in the process can make all the difference, otherwise the ego may just go on projecting its ideals and not enter into the round of death and rebirth necessary for change to happen. Listening to the subtle movement of the Self from within is key.

Part I is a journey toward the source of the living waters where we find renewal and redemption. Through alchemical metaphor, myth, and dream imagery, you will witness the creation and cultivation of the living religious attitude—the inner, individually honed, active force of receptivity toward darkness and unknowing, toward emptying and opening to the mysteries. But the work is not done once we have reconnected with the source; we need to enter into and refine a dialogue with the divine on a daily basis. Part II describes this process at work in ordinary individuals' lives. In the refinement of this dialogue, there are pitfalls as well as ecstatic heights, and you'll learn ways to recognize and deal with these. You will also come to understand that inner work is as important for the transformation of the divine as it is for us. When we give the work our attention, we receive help, or divine grace, because through our efforts the divine experiences renewal as well.

In Greek mythology, Pegasus, upon taking to the air, pushed hard with a back hoof and penetrated the earth. A spring rose up where his hoof dashed the earth, and in this hole—at the font of the Hippocrenes—the muses reside. One role of the religious function is to bring us toward that inner spring of the muses where something numinous—beyond the ego—resides, instructs, and inspires. Like the hole created from Pegasus's propelling foot, contact with this inner spring often entails a crack in our field of ordinary consciousness, giving access to the *numinosum* and the possibility of a renewing drink of those waters.

In the inner world, the spring of living symbols and accompanying presences is the source of dreams and visions, as well as the fountain of inspiration at the heart of poetry, art, ritual, mythology, and even religions. If you learn to tend the source and drink from these living waters you may experience redemption, a renewal of being. This psychic reality of redemption and renewal is mirrored in many legends, one of which is the Irish legend of St. Asurnai. Upon her retirement to the island of Innishmor, off the Connemara coast of Ireland, St. Asurnai lived a life so close to the heart of the divine that the well water became sweet in smell and taste and brought healing and vision to those who drank from it. Indeed, pilgrims came from hundreds of miles around to partake of the well's healing properties. In tending the source, you also may become an inspiration for others on their own healing journey, for as the alchemists saw it, this wisdom has a way of multiplying of its own accord as it becomes grounded in our lives.

None of this comes about without a confrontation with darkness. When it comes down to dealing with real human darkness, Jung found human contact to be more important than fixed theoretical constructs. This following remark is primarily advice for analysts, but non-analysts can apply it to their conscious orientation toward their inner work:

> Of course, if you begin the analysis with a fixed belief in some theory which purports to know all about the nature of neurosis, you apparently make your task very much easier; but you are nevertheless in danger of riding roughshod over the real psychology of your patient and of disregarding his individuality. I have seen any number of cases where the cure was hindered by theoretical considerations. Without exception the failure was due to lack of contact. It is only the most scrupulous observation of this rule that can prevent unforeseen catastrophes. So long as you feel the human contact, the atmosphere of mutual confidence, there is no danger; and even if you have to face the terrors of insanity, or the shadowy menace of suicide, there is still that area of human faith, that certainty of understanding and of being understood, no matter how black the night.[7]

As we gather evidence of the divine in our lives, we also learn from and with one another. Sharing meditations on the divine mysteries and images and processes of the incarnating Self guides us to open our consciousness to what is possible. Human contact and shared wisdom have their place in the journey. We cannot "borrow," by unconscious identification, the gold of Jung, or of anyone else; we can only discover fully the mysteries unfolding within our own being. Yet, the emanations of others may inspire us on our own trails, pointing to what is possible and teaching us ways to work with what appears in our fields of being. And gold does multiply. As Lucy Sikes, an analyst from the Midwest puts it, it is like a good yeast for bread—it can go on creating its unique recipe in the lives of others, if it is brought to a welcoming, capable kitchen.[8]

The Sufi poet and mystic Rumi speaks to the need for true connection, for a community, of specific souls with whom to travel so that we do not become lost in the desert. He locates the caravan among those who "have come before," pointing to the reality that our community of souls—those who can help constellate the meditations of the divine—is not contained within the limits of time and space. He also heralds a sharp warning as to how the soul is tested, as a sieve sifts and separates genuine from fake, which calls up the compelling need for true connections:

What Is the Path?

A self-sacrificing way,
but also a warrior's way, and not
for brittle, easily-broken, glass bottle people.

The soul is tested here by sheer terror,
as a sieve sifts and separates
genuine from fake.

And this road is full of footprints!
Companions have come before.
They are your ladder.
Use them!

Without them you won't have the spirit-quickness
you need. Even a dumb donkey
crossing a desert becomes nimble footed
with others of its kind.

Stay with a caravan. By yourself
you'll get a hundred times more tired
and fall behind.[9]

Rumi's images of the caravan of souls remind us of how ancient a truth it is to have soul companions on our journey. Also, the caravan image has a linking quality. Souls who travel similar paths are linked with one another. If we consider the links and the lineage, we would track back not only to Jung, but also to the alchemists, the shaman, and to Hermes, the father of alchemy, himself. For this reality to be active in us, we must serve the unfolding development of the Self mysteries in our own lives. From here, the value of "the footsteps of companions who have come before" (regardless of time and space) becomes clear. Without enough of an anchor to the mysteries from within our own individual experience—without substantial individual work to create this mystical new center of consciousness—the caravan image means nothing. The dreams, alchemical mysteries, myths, and life stories that follow portray the work of building this new center. The calling to our path can be answered only from inside our heart, our life and work, experienced and expressed in all we love and do. Work with the imagination, if we choose to participate, helps us individually answer the call and discover means toward cultivating the Philosopher's Stone—a living mystery capable of growing in the human soul.

Part I

The *Nigredo* and the Rising of Lunar Consciousness

Hail! forgotten and withered souls!
Our Mother comes with us to gather her children!

Now is the time for Hell
to nurse at the teats of Heaven.

Dark sucks at the white milk.
Stars flow out into the deserted souls.

In our dreams we are drawn towards day once more.
—Robert Duncan

1

The Psyche's Alchemical Language

In the dead of night
something with wings comes
from out of the darkness
toward your single flame, and
toward the smell of sulfur burning
drawn irresistibly.

The transformational processes in the alchemical rounds of renewal have been depicted through the ages of humankind and in all cultures in some manner, and remain alive and available in the depths of psyche. The call for the birth of the new light out of the dark comes to us any time we encounter something new that requires development beyond our current capacities. For example, many changes occurring in love relationships require transformations in both parties. Every long-term couple experiences marriage crises. The couple's consciousness of the relationship patterns must change in order to nourish the changing individuals over time. One such couple came for counseling at the nadir of despair. Both parties' "good intentions" were getting them nowhere. Struggle, criticism, and trouble riddled their interpersonal field. After ten years, the old constellation of the marriage, with all its merger qualities, was breaking up. The depth of the darkness they experienced as this seismic shift hit was enormous. At the crux of the crisis, the woman had a dream that illustrates in modern terms the ancient principles of the alchemical cycle:

> Downstairs, in the lowest floor of our retreat home, I meet my mate in the dark. The feeling of the tremendous crisis we are in fills the dark house. We are instructed by an over-voice in the dream to go into the bathroom. Here we see a small, dark-blue light that has just appeared and is dancing in the darkness over the toilet. Then we are instructed to go to the laundry room together. The doors are open on the washer and dryer, and the laundry is there, too. Here we are told that the future depends upon our attention, that we each must work with our own "seven devils" in the darkness.
>
> Then I see him go from the laundry room into the living room. The coming of new light in the house depends upon how each of us deals with his or her devils. It feels like the devils will be manifesting to each of us separately, and our own private attention to them and how we deal with them is crucial.

Part of what is so moving about this dream is its portrayal of the psychic reality that the birth of the new way, the new light in the darkness, depends on the work of ego consciousness in turning toward the darkness and the conflict—entering the *nigredo*, the first stage of the alchemical round. In the beginning of this dream, there is no light source, no consciousness yet sufficient to light the new way; how it will be worked out is not known. With the two figures turning toward the darkness, the first dark light appears, and there is the promise of more light as the masculine and feminine work with their respective "seven devils." This is also a subjective mirror, where her inner counterpart and she must go through a *separatio*, which is another alchemical operation at the beginning of the work. It was clear that they needed to separate out their own elements from their tangled complexes and interpersonal patterns or the repetitive patterns of suffering would lead one of them to end the relationship.

That each partner is seen as having "seven devils" is interesting. Mary Magdalene is reported to have had seven devils. In ancient astrology, the texts speak of seven lords, each with a planetary being, who also have devilish sides with which human beings must deal. Each individual must come into relationship with each lord (each archetype) and create an inner harmony, an inner music of the seven lords, as they imprint upon the individual's life and personality. The dreamer reported that, during an active imagination she subsequently entered, the seven devils showed up in the seven chakras, the (body's primary energetic centers). In ancient Eastern traditions, the seven chakras of the body correspond to various archetypal energy configurations. In Chinese alchemical astrological texts, the chakras correspond to the seven rungs of the planetary ladder. It seems that this dream image refers to a process of embodying relationship with the archetypes and the shadow manifestations inherent in each center of being—a prescription for individuation, and no small task. Indeed, it is an ongoing life task.

The black light birth, this dream points out, can also mean seeing into the mysterious centers of personality, including our embodied relationships with the archetypes—the light and dark sides. The "seven devils" suggest a need to *imagine into* the different personifications of these centers. Most likely, this dream image refers to the constellations we must learn to master in our life, constellations that can wreak devilish havoc with life and relationship. As this dream points out, relationship life can mirror the need for more light in the dark, more consciousness.

"Devilish" energy—fear, insecurity-power problems, addiction, compulsivity, mania, crippling inner-critic thought patterns, and self-denigration—appears in our lives when unconscious dynamics take hold and threaten our essence. These patterns require the light of consciousness to loosen their hold. Then the "devils" potentially become initiatory allies. They change as well, to some degree, in their manifesting nature and in their degree of autonomy from the overall unity of the personality. Anything, of course, can become devilish. Discovering the devils and being willing to suffer them in the *nigredo*, in the darkness, and await the transformation are the dream's guidance. Then new freedom of essence may come.

This same woman also dreamed, around this time, that a male lover said, "I am so torn this night, I don't believe in redemption." This anguish is the reality of darkness. This dream brings the perspective of the inner one who is torn by the night, and brings to the fore the cry from the depths, expressing how he sees and feels the inner night. When it is that black, there is no sense of, no link to, nor any comfort in "redemption," in change and transformation. When it is that black, what the hell does *redemption* even mean?! The dream voice wants her to hear the reality of the inner darkness, wants her consciousness to be penetrated by the cry. The inner lover tells her that he is so *torn* this night. *Torn* is a powerful word and denotes such feeling. We use being "torn" to express deep inner pain. "I am torn between this and that," "I am torn in half," "I have a tear in me so great." It is a pure cry out of the depths. Darkness like this means that we really do not see a way. Our bereft cry from such depths expresses an honest human standpoint. At times, only that honesty from the depths of our experiences of utter darkness penetrates the barrier between our humanity and the divine within. Only this outcry gets us into dialogue with the divine powers so that help can arrive.

Another angle to this potent dream line comes in as we view the word *believe*. A crisis of faith arrives sooner or later when our connection to the mysteries relies on belief. Believing is nothing more than a childlike projection or wishful thought-form. Discovering from inner experience what might be "redemption" is another matter. Opening to the mystery of the night—to all that is beyond solar or ego consciousness—we discover interplay, dialogue, subtlety, ambiguity, relationship with the *mysterium*, where belief in anything is of little consequence. Instead, responsibility is placed in the growing inner body of wisdom, which requires experience—the gathering of evidence in our lives—combined with reflective processes of differentiation and then embodied via fruitful living.

Returning to the dream of the seven devils, the images of the bathroom and laundry room shed light on the alchemical bridges the dream world offers between the pain and chaos and the hope for transformation. The bathroom is, of course, the room in all of our homes dedicated to what the alchemists called *prima materia*, the "shit." In an experience of facing the darkness and the place of the usually devalued shit—the psychological stuckness and emotional tangle or suffering—the first hope of the dark light is born. The new dawning of consciousness in the dark situation begins with facing the darkness, the shit. Regarding the value of facing psychological darkness, an alchemical text says, "When you see your matter going black, rejoice: for that is the beginning of the work."[1] As in this dream, conscious endurance of darkness potentially nourishes the Self.

The dream instructs her to go to the laundry room. After the first dawning of consciousness in the dark situation, the dreamer must learn to do the "laundry." Alchemists saw this stage of the process as one of *distillation* and *circulation*. The fire of transformation heats up the water and the contents in the water. It cooks, cleans, and whitens. In alchemical texts, the flame of *calcinatio* purges and whitens. In psychological terms, this valuable inner psychic heat of struggle or pain becomes the flame of transformation via our attention to the inner darkness. Contact with the inner darkness and unknowing brings an experience of "purgatory," wherein we consciously suffer the lostness but also—with grace—a new

Fig. 1. ". . . [T]he water washes the precipitation of the black body away,"[2] Atalanta Fugiens, *Emblem III from de Jong,* Michael Maier's *Atalanta Fugiens, p. 379.*

way out of this state. Then the *nigredo* brings about the *albedo*; that is, the washing of the old, dark, unconscious state brings about a whitening as new illumination is discovered. The dreamer must begin the sorting, heating, soaking, rinsing, and drying processes of the dirty laundry, the *prima materia*, the chaos of the stuck complexes, for a new spirit to alight in her life.

Thinking of her dream in the context of relationship work, soaking the problem in the heating water could be like consciously feeling into the nature of the emotional tangles or complexes. Washing dissolves dirt; dirt is of the earth. The earthy fixity of the situation, the old form of the problem, dissolves. Perhaps by looking into the earthy, sensation-level facts involved in a given problem, she can liberate the spirit of relatedness and dissolve the old, fixed pattern. The drying also removes the old emotional qualities, perhaps by taking out the old energy. The whitening, the alchemists say, brings the caught spirit, the tangled psychic pattern, into freedom, back to its pure essence, where it unites with source—the moon—which brings "clarity and perfection," insight and freedom from the old pattern.

This process includes what the alchemists called the "whitening work of the moon." As the alchemists pictured this process, in "doing the work of the washerwoman" (see figure 1 on page 7), the whitening of illumination takes place.

With this imagery, the alchemists pointed to the renewing phases of the moon as she cycles through her twenty-eight-day round of death and rebirth. The new moon signifies the *nigredo*, and the full moon, the *albedo*, the whitening rebirth. Thus, another way in which light appears in the darkness is by our engaging in the alchemical operation of circulation and distillation leading to rebirth. To take something to its lunar state is to cleanse it of its earthly fixity and see into its original essence. By attending to the dream spirit's instructions, and to our own experience of what is stuck, pained, or caught, the specific elements that require these processes become clear. There are many means of achieving circulation and distillation. Circulating awareness through each element (earth, air, fire, and water) or each psychological function (sensation, thinking, intuition, and feeling) distills insight that frees the essence into the intermediary place that exists between opposites.

Curiously, at the end of the dream, the male figure walks from the laundry room into the living room, which suggests the integration of the cleansing experience into the living situation. In a way, the three rooms depicted in the dream process show the three ravens, the three phases of the transformative work that are said to compose alchemy. One text says alchemy is made of three ravens: One is black, one white, and one red: "the black which is the head of the art, the white which is the middle, and the red which brings things to an end."[3] The bathroom, as the container of waste, points to the black raven—the *nigredo* or blackening. The laundry room, with its soaking, washing, and drying, points to the white raven—the *albedo* or whitening rebirth. The living room points to the red raven—the *rubedo* or reddening—the reanimation of fresh spirit by the red blood of experience, in the living of human life. Importantly for the dreamer's situation, the reddening process associated with the living room represents the integration of the devils into the larger psyche, thereby ending their autonomous reign. About the reddening process, Jung says, "Blood alone can reanimate a glorious state of consciousness in which the last state of blackness is dissolved, in which the devil no longer has an autonomous existence but rejoins the profound unity of the psyche. Then the *opus magnum* is finished and the *human soul* is completely integrated."[4]

Thus, the dream spirit sees the whole round of the work and prescribes conscious participation in the processes necessary to transform the pain the dreamer was experiencing at this stage in life. It seems to prescribe a deep *nigredo* experience of honest confrontation with her old patterns and a straightforward cleansing process.

If the *nigredo* goes so dark, sometimes it is not a theory that helps orient us, or even vision or the *theoria* of the adept, but a simple human presence and warmth that reaches us and connects with our humanity in the darkness. As a young man, Andrew entered medical school in the 1970s with a freight-load of family expectations on him to become a doctor, like one of his parents. He went straight from college to medical school, unlike many of the other students. The difficulty of the family expectations and the intensity of the work, added to his being young and without much adult identity formed yet, led him to a breakdown. The divorce of his parents when he was younger also had terribly split the family, and he suffered trying to keep love going with both of them. When he got to medical school the pressure without the foundation of love and steadiness in his life pushed him near the abyss and when fell, he fell hard and ended up in a psychiatric clinic for a time.

Having lost all words and registering nothing, he fell into an enormous silence. One of the social workers there, who had tremendous heart and soul, kept a special eye on this young man. When he began to speak in unintelligible "word salad" without coming back to normal connection and conversation, the red flags went up. Would he ever make it back to himself and his life? The social worker took him outside for walks, kindly taking Andrew by the arm and walking with him along the garden path surrounding the facility. Late one night they went for a walk in the dark to a spot overlooking the freeway. Andrew remembers the social worker telling him, "Andrew, there is something I have been wanting to show you. Here you see, we do things strangely, and when you return, you will as well. See the lights that go in lines, one after another, following the way of the road? The red lights form a line of the cars going that way, and the white lights form a line of the cars going this way. This is how thoughts work here among us humans; they go in lines, just like this, and follow a single road. When you come back, you will learn to do this, too. It is not necessarily better than where you are; in fact it may be less interesting. It is just something that happens here."

Later that week, Andrew was in his bed when the team of psychiatrists and social workers stopped to visit. He had a pad of paper and wanted very badly to communicate. He began to write in word salad in a desperate attempt to communicate. The social worker picked it up, with the team present, and said, "I can't understand a word you are saying, but Andrew, you sure have great handwriting!" With that embracing comment, the team laughed out loud, and as Andrew laughed out loud, too, and joined in with them, the spell broke, and his linear thoughts returned. He has communicated just fine ever since. Besides becoming a doctor, he developed a tremendous love for music and plays professionally—communicating movingly out of the nonlinear, passionate side of himself. He continued over the years to work with a caring psychologist to integrate his experiences and heal.

This moment in the *nigredo*—when the social worker's bare-bones relatedness carrying the facts of the psychic situation reached into the psychic constellation that held Andrew captive—became the bridge for Andrew's return. The social worker's inner knowing of the difference between where this young man was residing, and where ordinary consciousness resides did create a bridge, but that bridge was created due to this social worker's honesty and *embodiment* of this knowing, and his ability to communicate from that embodied wisdom. In alchemical terms, we could say that the social worker embodied the living stone of the Self in such a way that he could reach and communicate from this wholeness in himself. This broke the spell and created the eros and humor bridge upon which Andrew returned.

THE ACTIVATION OF MERCURIUS

The experience of the *nigredo* may also take us toward the mysterious root at the core of the psyche, the *radix ipsius*, the uncreated *increatum*, into an experience of the void beneath all forms and beneath all words and images. Hermes/Mercurius, the alchemical god of transformation, is pictured in figure 2 (page 11) urging silence. Mercurius's eloquence belongs to the "revealed world of appearances," to the "phenomenal periphery." Here the "experience of the effects of the spiritual center (the Unit or

Fig. 2. Hermes/Mercurius. From Achilles Bocchius, Symbolicarum quaestionum . . . , *Bologna, 1555, in Alexander Roob,* Alchemy and Mysticism, *p. 13.*

Monas shown above his head) is inaccessible to the expressive possibilities of language." [5] The experiential effect of this dimension of being is so profound, Mercurius seems to tell us, that silence in its presence is all that is possible.

Honoring the stillness, the wordless, imageless, the silence, the space between thoughts—honoring the great emptiness from which we are born—leaves room for the numinous to touch us anew during a *nigredo*. The healing vastness of psychic space can be discovered in the *nigredo*, creating a "sky of mind" experience. The fruit of the *nigredo*, with its inherent psychological release of old forms and psychic investments, is the eventual quieting of complexes and the tiny mind, allowing connection to universal mindfulness to awaken.

A young woman became very ill and was told that she had a twenty-percent chance of surviving the illness for only several months. Devastated by the diagnosis, she went into a black depression, feeling the reality of annihilation. She fell asleep and dreamed:

> I am in a tunnel that is very dark, walking with a lit candle in my outstretched hands, trying to light my way in the great darkness. Then I realize that a serene feminine being has her arms stretched around me from behind. This feminine presence is larger than my own body and emanates deep caring. The presence holds her own large hands around and behind both my hands and the candle flame, in order to guard the flame from the wind in the dark tunnel. She says to me, "Whatever you do, don't let the candle flame go out!"

With these words, the woman awoke, still feeling the profoundly comforting arms of this feminine presence (or, as the Sufis would say, the arms of the angel; in Jungian terms, the embracing guidance of a manifestation of Self, or perhaps, an inner guide, or an ally from the psychoidal realm).[6]

Later that same week, the woman got out of bed for the first time since her diagnosis. The physical pain became so excruciating, she felt that she would pass out. She wanted to call out but did not have the energy. In her thoughts, she heard herself calling out to her husband, but the feminine presence responded, saying, *Don't call out to him. Call out to me!* With that, she indeed did call out to the feminine presence. A dynamic love poured over her and accompanied her throughout her illness; profound healing brought her back into life. At times, it seems as though the depth of suffering and blackness, the downgoing, penetrates the psyche and breaks the barrier between the human and the divine so that the grace of the divine may respond.

This is what we might think of as an activation of Mercurius, god of the *axis mundi*, traverser of realms. Mercurius brings to us guides capable of helping us in the darkness. Getting in sympathy with our angel or inner guide is vital in times of crisis. As the angst of this woman's darkness illustrates, our pain can penetrate the psyche, and a presence sympathetic to us may respond. In areas of darkness or difficult change, relationship with the unconscious can provide a *temenos*, a sacred holding place for that darkness, and provide a penetration of the over, under, and earth worlds, thereby bringing Mercurius to light. We might say the descent brings out Mercurius's light—a new light—a dark light, born from darkness, revealing a new way through.

Meditating on the realms of the downgoing brings us closer to the light of Mercurius and illuminates the terrifying but unifying darkness from which, for example, this dreamer's experience of the feminine presence emerged. Earlier I mentioned that we need not only consciousness but also the ability to become unconscious in order to drink from the deepest well of our inner being. Hermetical shamanic initiation, where healing occurs, depends on the ability to become unconscious in a way that is attended to, so that we receive the fruit of the journey. Amid the darkness, the unknown, the dissolving, through the release of antiquated ego elements, we may discover the forces that initiate, heal, and bring new vision.

The Philosopher's Stone and the Birth of the Black Light

As consciousness descends into the darkness, the ego's light becomes inferior to a deeper light that appears from the Philosopher's Stone, as the alchemists call it. The Stone is the *opus*, the work of our lives, and in psychological terms represents the Self (the center and totality of the psyche) as it comes to manifestation in our lives. This Stone is not fixed; it is a living dynamism continually flowing between and transmuting in all dimensions. There are references to the light within the center of the Stone as being a black light.[7] The black light emerges in the alchemical Stone in the foundation of our lives where consciousness seeks renewal.

Turn, and Kiss the Black Stone

The black stone image came my way via a woman who had led her life in a state of tremendous emotional denial. Her adaptation crashed when her husband of twenty-five years left her for a younger woman, without offering to communicate meaningfully about their relationship. The initial dream of her analysis stumped her. She wondered what it could possibly mean.

In the dream she was asleep, sitting in a meditative position, when she heard a helping voice say to her, "You must turn around and find the *black stone* behind you. Look behind, through the detritus. Hunt through the wreckage you've left. Allow your feet to follow the wake of your slumber. When you find the black stone, kiss it, and with all your heart. I will meet you there."

Locating the black stone in the detritus of her life, and then kissing it, was an incredible prescription from her inner guide. It called her to turn toward the hidden and dark and discarded, which her consciousness had devalued. Kissing intimates love. She is instructed to learn to love all she has discarded or avoided and to invest this work with her heart, with Eros. Turning toward the rejected with love will call forth the teacher, the light, out of the blackness. The dream also generates a kiss from psyche to her. "Follow the wake of your slumber" is a mythopoetic kiss from the psyche itself, with the promise of awakening, as in the fairy tale "Sleeping Beauty." There is irony in this dream element for she had lost the Eros connection with her husband and now has to dive inside, in the dark, to find a new source of Eros. She was an angry, pained, rigid woman; her typology was introverted-sensate-thinking. Thus, the image of the kiss of the stone could not have been more to the point. In turning toward the unconscious and investing it with Eros, she begins her part in the creation of the inner *lapis*, the Philosopher's Stone, that third thing, the mystic center now activated within her.

Jung tells us that the legendary alchemist Ostanes, speaking of the secret of the "philosophy," said to his student Cleopatra, "In you is hidden the whole terrible and marvelous secret. Make known to us how the highest descends to the lowest, and how the lowest ascends to the highest, and how the midmost draws near to the highest and is made one with it. This midmost is the stone, the mediator which unites the opposites."[8] The appearance of the stone in this dream parallels this alchemical wisdom.

This is what mystics have known for ages, and what life wants to find in us anew. If we go into the solitary reality of our own being and its interfacings with the infinite, with heart and eyes open, the energy of our focus, our intent, helps constellate the inner compass, the third thing, which is neither spirit nor matter alone. Here we may find our "guide." Sometimes this guide comes from grounding dialogue and contact with a numinous figure via active imagination, creativity, and dream work, such as the young woman dreamer did with the feminine presence in her dream. Sometimes the guide comes with a sense of peace we cannot explain. Sometimes it comes as a sense of wholeness experienced in the body, an inner quiet or sacred emptiness, a new inner compass, healing in relationship problems, harmony with nature. However it comes—dropping or ascending—into our lives, it originates from our contact with the "night world," the *mysterium* itself.

Loss of earlier constellations of power or control, even loss of many familiarities common to the world of the ego, may occur as the energy of life asks us to change. The journey may require us to release our ordinary coordinates that attempt to make the world smaller than it is. Then we must enter the cavern of darkness and unknowing, hoping to locate the *opus*, the Stone in the darkness, and wait on the powers that be who will guide us and help us develop the new inner light as we contact the numinous.

The Sufi knew the cave of the heart, the *himma*, to be the dwelling place of the imagination and rebirth.[9] Thus, like the message to the woman above, turning toward the darkness with the heart open also helps create the ground of being on which we will be able to receive our guides. Without an open human heart center, many snares may entangle us such as power problems, inflation, and so on. We can become lost in our own inner deserts without water or contact with the divine if we stray for long from the path with heart.

When All Other Lights Go Out

These transformational processes in the alchemical rounds of renewal have been depicted through the ages of humankind and in all cultures in some manner, and remain alive and available in the depths of psyche. The alchemists knew of this renewing light source and found ways to tend the flame of transformation that unites the hidden and the visible worlds.

Paracelsus, a physician, chemist, and alchemist who lived in the 1500s, worked with this light as it manifests in nature and started the traditions of homeopathy. He saw that the *lumen naturale*—that inhabits all living beings—is in the inner body of the inner person, as well as in animals, plants, and so on. People in nonordinary states of consciousness confirm this perception and experience. There are many layers of the psyche-body mysteries of which we are a part. At the core of every living being is a light body, a star body, which is the "astral spirit" in us. Healing traditions of numerous cultures tap this knowing, and myths abound regarding the truth that the core light of being that is the star body is what helps one heal. And dreams point to this truth again and again.

Sometimes the birth of the new way in life comes to us from a spiritual experience within the natural world. Something living in the natural world communicates with our soul and brings healing. An elderly single woman came to work with me after attending a lecture I gave about working with dreams of people who are dying. My talk that day was titled "The Soul Is a Midnight Blossom: Dreams of the Dying." This title became relevant to what was coming in her life, although neither of us knew the synchronicity and difficulty of what lay ahead. After one year of working with me on her dreams, she realized that she had a serious problem with her thirty-year-old son. In his depression and inability to find his way in life, he wanted to regress and, literally, return to his mother, live with her, use her car, her money, and so on. After trying that difficult road, she helped him get a new apartment with a friend and to work with a psychiatrist, who prescribed medications and saw him regularly. She communicated clear boundaries to him and carried on a loving connection with him from her separate home. Months later, he rejected life. He could not find his way out of his *nigredo* and committed suicide in *her* apartment. The shock, pain, rage, grief, and horror sent her into an understandably serious dark night of the soul. Over time, she had dreams of him that helped her family and her to heal. They were able to continue loving him and their memories of him, beyond his tragic and tormented way of leaving life.

What helped her in her darkest hours came through communion with the natural world. She had a night-blooming cereus in her city apartment. Communion with this plant at night brought her out of utter darkness. This cactus has a rare flower that forms only once a year. The white, translucent bloom (the size of open hands) begins quaking at around 10 P.M.—on its one spectacular night of the year—and opens by midnight. Biologists explain that this phenomenon evolved in order to attract a short-lived night moth for pollination purposes. By dawn, the exquisite, delicate bloom, with its woody orange-and-mimosa-like fragrance, is gone.

In the hours of despair and solitude in her apartment during the weeks following her son's suicide, this woman watched the plant forming its midnight blossom. One night, unable to sleep, she sat up in the darkness and watched for hours as the midnight blossom opened itself, petal by petal, in the hope of the night visitor who would pollinate its core. As it revealed its stamen, its deep center and aroma, she felt the depths of her own soul open as well. In a mystical oneness with the light of nature in the plant, she knew, in an instant, that this light was also inside her: She was like this plant. A soul flower within her was forming and blooming, quaking and opening, aching for pollination in her dark night. Her soul and the souls of her son and family had a way to go on. The soul was showing her its depths, its life, and its mysteries and that these mysteries live in the natural world *and* in the depths of her dark night. A peace overcame her as she experienced the subtle body realm within her mirrored by the midnight blooming.

Curiously, her plant bloomed again and again that winter. These plants usually bloom in late May and have only a few blossoms all year. That winter, her life came into remarkable synchronicity and inner harmony with the nature spirit. Before one of the blooms faded, she managed to bring it to my office by the sea, and we sat and drank in its presence and aroma together before dawn. She discovered from her dark night what Paracelsus knew—the intercorrespondences of the nature spirit in all forms of life communicate with us (and we with them) the way of the larger soul, of which we are but a part.

The Light That Cultivates

In tending to inner life, we learn to cultivate psyche, spirit, presence, and even culture in unique ways that may lead us to the birth of light beyond ordinary ego consciousness. The words *cultivate* and *culture* share roots with the word *cult*—roots that mean "to revolve, move around, sojourn, dwell." *Cultivate* also takes us archetypally into the field of the Greek god Eros, who, as the deity of earth, irrigation, water sources, and crops in ancient Boetia, was called upon for help in all matters of cultivating land. Indeed, the Eros cult of Boetia encouraged members to cultivate an active love of the land. This active love represents an inner attitude of tending the ground of the soul so that a nourishing harvest may result. In applying Jung's psychological discoveries in our own lives, we learn to cultivate the nonrational soil of *our own existence*, discovering organic frameworks for life's lessons and ways of passing on the means of cultivation to others. In this way, many sojourners feel reverence for the *cultivation* of psyche as they learn about it from Jung's writings and others. It is a "moving around," a furrowing of consciousness

Fig. 3. Alchemy is "celestial agriculture." D. Stolcius von Stolcenberg, Viridarium chymicum, *Frankfurt, 1624, in Roob,* Alchemy and Mysticicsm, p. 225.

into inner experience that mysteriously brings fruit. This cultivation includes a passing on of the light that cultivates the darkness. These images appear in the following dream of a woman who was in the grips of an eventually successful struggle with a deadly illness:

> I am standing in my back yard at the fire pit in the middle of the garden. A star comes out of the heavens and lands in the fire pit. I have a tiller in my hands. I am to work the light outward from the center of the pit into all the dark earth. I begin tilling the dark earth with this starlight that has landed. The rich earth, the dark loam, opens easily as I furrow the starlight in rays from the center out into the garden. I realize that the shape on the earth I am creating is like a star, too, the radiant center emanating in rays outward into the earth.[10]

In the case of this dreamer, she was in dire need of contact with divine help, or her life on Earth would end. A star of consciousness, larger than the ego and well beyond the rational mind, comes to earth. The star landing in the ground of being is capable of healing both body and psyche and brings a felt experience of the transcendent, of grace, into the mortal sphere. Literally, through her cultivation skills, the dreamer learned ways to till this healing light into her life, the "soil of her existence," her ground of being, and her physical body responded. The psyche's salvific and destructive potentialities found new relationship, and her life force was renewed. The illness reversed its death grip and, in time, she was healed, largely through the "irrational," through initiatory gifts present in the psyche and psychoid that came to Earth as she paid attention to the presences, messages, and transformations in dreamtime and active imagination.

The earthing of spirit and the spiritualization of earth—the mystery unfolding in the dreamer's life—illuminates what Jung calls the *hieros gamos*, the inner union of opposites whereby splits are healed. Mundane earth life and the profound spiritual dimensions of existence are brought into unity.[11]

A light that cultivates the darkness and seeks to be furrowed into all areas of life is a profound mystery. Experiencing the divine through intuition or thought alone is not enough. The divine wants to land in the ground of our time-and-space lives as an active agent available to us in the "down and dirty" of daily life. This light wants to be tilled into the corners of our lives where we need it most—be it relationship dynamics, energetics, destructive attitudes, addictive or obsessive patterns, financial difficulties, health or emotional problems, inner emptiness, etc.—and it is capable of illuminating the very ground of our existence.

The alchemists created images of this mystery. In figure 3, page 18, Gold (Sol) and Silver (Luna) are added to matter as fermenting agents to increase it. "If you throw the two pieces on our land, this living flame will give off its forces."[12] The heavenly energy is furrowed into the earth, fertilizing the ground of being with the light of the sun and moon, the numinous heavens.

Ruland says, "Imagination is the star in man, the celestial or supercelestial body." Jung says that the imaginal realm points to the psychic realm of subtle bodies—an intermediary realm that manifests in mental, as well as material, form. Subtle body energies are both corporeal and semispiritual in nature.[13] The symbolizing function alive in the imagination unites the opposites of spirit and body and brings us into experience with the third, the intermediary, realm, which is both corporeal and spiritual and also more than the sum of the parts. The star in humankind—the living imagination and its connection to the divine—mediates psyche/body dimensions and misalignments, as in the starlight cultivation dream.

The Fire of the Alchemists

Discovering this light that cultivates requires entering the processes of change in our lives and discovering inner attitudes and means to tend the fire of the imagination. To reach the star light energy—the multiple luminosities of the archetypal realms that fertilize human ground—the alchemists found that a fire has to be made that takes the earthy elements and cooks them, sending their purified forms into the heavens where the elements then mingle with the "seeds of the stars."[14] Then the transformed elements come back to earth renewed, for they have suffered the fires of change, risen in purified essence into the over-world, and joined with and been fertilized by their celestial, archetypal source.

The tending of this fire is at the heart of the alchemical art, and psychologically is in essence an inner attentiveness to the life of the soul, and learning how to live and work with this flame that burns within in ways that are life enhancing, rather than destructive. That takes time to learn, and is impossible unless we enter the *nigredo* and become aware of what lives beyond and informs the light of ego consciousness. It may bring to light a deeper connection with nature, people, desires, life issues, complexes, creativity, relationships, longing for and contact with the transcendent, including a new evolving relationship with the mysteries which bears fruit in real life.

Learning the art of regulation of the flame determines that line between life-enhancing, soul-renewing, and needlessly destructive. When life becomes rote or deadened, the fire of imagination is most likely out. Dreams of going through your yard and gathering firewood are a common call to bring to the fire of the imagination whatever in your life is no longer alive, and offer that to the fires of change. On the other hand, the heat, when it builds within, can bring out an activation of the psyche with drives and archetypal presences that can burn your life up in a destructive way. Then compulsive or addictive patterns usually occur. Eventually the process can lead to connection between human and divine so that the fire is born of the center, as the alchemists saw it. Jung points out that the fire to be used is a symbolic fire born of the infinite abyss of the mysteries. It originates from the indivisible center, that which is simple, indestruc-

Fig. 4. Alchemist and the spirit of the work. Miniature painting by Jehan Perréal, painter at the court of Margaretha of Austria, 1516. In Alexander Roob, Alchemy and Mysticism, *p. 504.*

tible, and eternal.[15] The life-long subtle art of discovering and tending this inner fire leads us into growing awareness and participation in new transmutations between heaven and earth, between human and divine. The alchemist learns the art of tending the fire of the imagination, and the guiding wisdom spirit of the work appears to him, as shown in figure 4.

In the heart of transformation—inner alchemical work with the fire of the imagination—we and the guiding spirit of wisdom grow in relationship to one another. The fruit of the *nigredo* comes into our lives if we discover the light that is born in the darkness, and how to tend that growing light and transformative heat source.

A woman who had dedicated several decades of life and work to the study and practice of shamanism and to Jung's psychology had a dream-vision of the light born in the darkness, the fire of the alchemists:

> I am standing in the dark with numerous people, all of us gathered around a pillar of fire. Each one is there of his or her own accord, standing in relationship with this mysterious fire. It is rather like gathering around a campfire at night, except that this fire is a huge, inexhaustible pillar whose breadth, depth, height are an unfathomable mystery. I look to the pillar of fire and notice that it goes on into the heavens above, into infinity. Beings of all sorts, not only humans, gather around this flame. All have their own relationship to it. I can see many types of different beings. . . . gathered at levels *ad infinitum*.
>
> Here, standing on earth, I see *the great human being*, the great woman-man, come up to the flame. Naked, vulnerable, and courageous, as well as primal and eternal, this human being curls up on the earth at the base of the fire and, in so doing, is warming her-himself and healing, too. In my heart, I feel compassion and appreciation. As part of the great human soul, I see we are capable of approaching this pillar of fire, and of warming and healing there. I see that my own calling, too, is to serve this fire with my life and work, by directing my human hands toward the flame and giving and receiving energy, back and forth, with the flame. I have graduated because I have found my human place with human hands, where I am able to tend the flame and not be burned up by the fire. Others are finding their own unique relationships with this flame, as well.

When we descend into the *nigredo*, the polarity of light—the inner flame—may appear. This flame, born between the opposites of darkness and light, is a medium that governs relationship between the opposites. The pillar image itself links earth and heaven, the human and the material to the invisible and spiritual. Jung points out that the alchemical fire reveals the "rearrangement of the heavenly spiritual powers in the lower chthonic world of matter."[16] Indeed, in this dream of the central fire the human being witnesses these interrelated dimensions.

As we work to gather our own dream bundles, our evidences of god in our lives, we discover this inner fire, and begin to help Self and ego,

Fig. 5. Hermes Trismegistus. Michael Maier, Symbola Aurea Mensae *(Frankfurt, 1617), p. 5. In de Jong,* Michael Maier's *Atalanta Fugiens, p. 452.*

divine and human come into life-enhancing relationship. That the dreamer finds ways to tend this fire and relate to it in her normal human form with her human hands signifies that the darkness and the fire, the source of light, are working out a *coniunctio*, a mysterious inner union or marriage, within her life, and that she is discovering ways to live in relationship with it. To unite with the mysteries requires the ground of our mortal lives; otherwise, we have not succeeded in bringing the presence of the Self into each moment of time. Living our mortal lives in connection with the Self's presence is very different from getting an intuitive hit or glimpse. We seek, through the *nigredo* and the tending of the new light source or secret fire, to build this center of consciousness into a *temenos* of such strength that our ordinary consciousness discovers increasing means to live close to it moment by moment.

The dream vision also speaks to the impersonal qualities of this pillar of fire: This alchemical flame could surely burn us up if we are not careful. Through discerning what would foster an optimal relationship with the fire, we can also heal. What Jung and von Franz called the divine *Anthropos* (the *Adam Kadmon*, primordial ancestral human), with all her or his resourcefulness and potentialities, comes alive within us as we relate with the alchemical flame. This theme is depicted by the great human being envisioned at the fire warming and healing in the glow of the flame. Jung described his version of the "more eternal man": "Its essence [that of ego consciousness] is limitation, even though it reach to the farthest nebulae among the stars. All consciousness separates; but in dreams we put on the likeness of that more universal, truer, more eternal man dwelling in the darkness of the primordial night. There he is still whole, and the whole is in him, indistinguishable from nature and bare of all egohood." [17]

Seeking connection with the original spirit present in all nature, the force of creation, we can be initiated into psyche's mysteries, which the alchemists also sought, discovered, and expressed in their emblematic depictions of the ways of transformation.

Figure 5 on page 23 provides a window into the original mysterious spirit of change, the fire that mediates and transforms. The Egyptian mystery god of alchemy, Hermes Trismegistus, who legend says brought to Earth great emerald tablets of alchemical wisdom is shown with this flame. The fire is containing a conjunction of opposites, the sun and moon, yang and yin. In Hermes' right hand is the *astrolabium*, signifying the universal wholeness sought by Hermes's son. Of the philosopher's son, the mystery god says, "His father is the sun wedded to his mother, the white moon. The fire comes as the third, as governor."[18]

When we open our hearts to experience the opposites in our lives, we open ourselves to the legitimate suffering inherent in life. Contact with the forces in the psyche and psychoid leads us to the alchemical fire, which also may show us the deity that suffers as it incarnates with us. The fire that unites heaven and Earth burns, unites, and contains the opposites, but does not consume the human being. We discover the incorruptible center of the personality growing from working with this flame.

Whenever something in life is more difficult than we can meet as human beings alone, we must find a way to open to the experience of it and turn to what is greater, to make a transcendent bridge. As the poet W. H. Auden saw it, this is the "cold impossible" that may bring us to the new way:

> Cold impossible ahead
> lifts the mountain's lovely head
> whose white waterfall could bless
> travelers in their last distress.

As we seek the wellspring of the soul and spirit world for participation and partnership in times of the "cold impossible," we open ourselves to the living waters and to the fire of Hermes. The containment and tending of this fire—that is, the transcendent function—grows in our lives as we learn to cultivate our connection with the numinous. Just as the alchemists saw into these ancient mysteries, our modern dreams bring them to life as we learn to tend the nature spirit and apply "nature to nature." Then guides and allies may come to companion us and create the mystical center between spirit and matter.

2

Beginning the Alchemical Process: Rooting in the Psyche and Psychoid

Yet no matter how deeply I go down into myself
my God is dark, and like a webbing made
of a hundred roots, that drink in silence
I know that my trunk rose from his warmth,
but that is all . . .
—Rainer Maria Rilke

Crisis and pain often catalyze a genuine, heart-felt attempt to reach toward the mysteries. In the grip of pain, we more readily reach through the veils of forgetfulness and wiles of the shadow attitudes that block the heart path. Suffering can add conscious fuel to the inner fire so that it burns through our deceits and self-deceptions as we find a life close to the mysteries. Then, our contact with the mysteries takes hold not because it is fashionable or interesting but because an individual inner imperative arises in the core of our life.

In one of his songs, Jackson Browne laments that, "There is a god-size hunger under the questions of the age."[1] The religious function in the psyche is fueled by this hunger, this longing. The ability to contain and embody this "god-size hunger"—rather than nullify it, fill it, put it to sleep, sterilize it, run from it (or have it run one's life unconsciously)—brings the longing into contact with the divine, the interface between humanity and divinity where redemption and grace occur.

The way we embody our "god-size hunger" is the unique signature of the religious function at work in our life. The road to embodying hunger for contact with the divine may be dominated initially by suffering and by explorations in woundedness—such as becoming lost in complexes, addictions, or other painful patterns that do not directly serve life. Yet, as C. G. Jung states, "The right way to wholeness is full of detours and supposed wrong turnings."[2] Indeed, the road to embodying this hunger and discovering remarkable wholeness can pass through difficult psychic territory. Finding a way to suffer more consciously and relate with emptiness and then finding forms that link us fruitfully with the transcendent is half the work. Devotedly cultivating the fruits of a life lived close to psyche's mysteries is the other half.

Regarding emptiness, Jung once commented, "Your inner emptiness conceals just as great a fullness, if only you will allow it to penetrate you."[3] This statement crystallizes the mystery of psyche and the religious function in human life. Being penetrated by emptiness is, itself, a *complexio oppositorum*. Emptiness, formlessness that is also full and has the power to penetrate, is a mystery indeed, both womb-like and phallic in the same moment, a yin/yang mystery.[4] The ego's role? Simply, profoundly, to allow the emptiness to penetrate us, to reflect on our suffering. The result? Discovery of how the ego has lost its way.

INSTINCT AND SPIRIT, EGO AND SELF

Part of the religious problem of our age involves a one-sided overvaluation of consciousness at the expense of soul. Christianity's shadow side, in part, is the "spiritualization" or disembodiment of religious life—a predominant ethos that tends to cut off the roots of instinctual life. The psyche's religious function heals this severance with its instinctual flow of energy, which helps us grow roots beyond ordinary consciousness that inform and can renew our lives.

As Jung saw it, the mystery of the divine Self within each of us forms in the flow of energy between polarities, or opposites, where conscious and unconscious meet. Spirit and instinct are a central pair of polarities between which psychic energy flows. Opposites define each other; they are dynamic polarities reflecting a mysterious oneness. There is not one without the other, unless the ego's experience within the polarity is split, or if the archetype itself, in the collective unconscious, is split.[5]

Instincts, from a Jungian mytho-poetic point of view, are roots of archetypal patterns that reside and thrive in the experiential soil of our existence. These underground (that is, unconscious) root patterns of the instinctual dimensions of archetypes autonomously emerge above ground as the life force present in the archetypes pushes to work itself out in our life. Importantly, the activity between Self and ego brings to consciousness and influences these archetypal patterns. The Self is the active force of the archetypal *imago Dei*, image of God. Jung saw the ego and Self as two distinct centers of personality that live in dynamic polarity, connected by an underlying unity.

Developmentally, phylogenetically, and ontologically, the development of ego is related to the Self. Both the reality of the primordial human being at one with all of nature *and* our own egohood are crucial elements in the development of the human psyche; one does not replace the other completely. During development of the ego complex, it acquires an autonomous functioning, as is possible with any other complex in the psyche. Thus, it can also become split off from the Self and from direct relationship with the primal roots of ancient human beingness.

This developmental reality of emerging egohood in humankind points to archetypal constellations in many world religions regarding our need to discover connection and alignment with a "higher power" or "higher will" in order to find our most harmonious place in relationship with life and the divine. This need for the ego to discover conscious relationship with what is larger than itself has always been at the basis of not only modern world religions but also the religions of primal human beings, although the language and means for connecting to that which is beyond ego consciousness differ.

Part of our modern delusion is that ego consciousness is now completely in charge of all life. This fantasy resides at the bedrock of all our modern problems, such as the worldwide ecological crisis, as the separatist ego greedily runs off with its plan for life, no matter that the planet may perish in the process. The devastating effects of the split between ego and Self mysteries, felt in every region on Earth, are wakeup calls to which we must attend.

Although ego consciousness is indispensable, it is not the supreme ruler of psychic life, or life on the planet. The religious function of the psyche addresses the ego when it is out of balance with a larger reality, and attempts to relate consciousness to the central organizing principles of higher consciousness. Learning to hear and value the religious function at work in your life helps reconnect ego consciousness in specific, unique ways with the mysteries of life. As you will see, the religious function that addresses modern consciousness is present in numberless forms; all it requires is learning to hear and see and becoming penetrated to the depths so that your innermost Self changes in the process, and thus actions and outward manifestations in life change as well.

RELIGIOUS INSTINCT AS ROOTS

An Athenian sort of rational woman—a psychologist in practice as a mediator of department conflicts at a renowned California university—dreamed:

> I am in my back yard, and someone whom I am told to listen to has pulled up my fruit trees and is giving me instruction. I am having to replant my fruit trees farther over to the left in my back yard. On the tree farthest to the left, I am instructed to apply root stimulator so that the tree will grow *new* roots beneath the ground and eventually produce *new* fruit.

This is a lovely image of turning toward the left (literally, "the sinister"), the unknown, the feminine, the dark and irrational zone, and getting rooted beneath the rational. The religious function of the psyche requires devotion to a larger reality than the ego's point of view. It requires devotion to a creative and corrective presence inside our very nature that seeks to realign us with a larger reality of being that is often just outside conscious apprehension.

The religious function can be seen in the above dream as instruction to the ego function to expand beyond its limited knowing. Specifically, it instructs the dream ego to get connected to the left, *to assist* in stimulating new roots. These roots seem to be the urge of the religious instinct itself to bring new fruit in the over-world, fruit that comes from rooting in the great below, the unconscious. The religious function appears as the dream ego finds its place in the mystery—learns its role in what it must tend in order to bring forth such fruit. Its role here appears to be more of the gardener taking directions than the actual executor of the overall plan for the garden, psyche, or life.

At the outset of the dreamer's situation, her perceptions of reality were heavily based on cognitive functioning and ego adaptation. This created a false sense of ego control, a one-sidedness that left her devoid of contact with the numinous in her life and work. Both her life and work became rote, and rather lifeless because she had missed seeing the shadow that this kind of ego consciousness was casting on life in and around her. After she suffered the dryness of her attitude, and the bold fact that her businesslike attitude of taking charge of life's problems did not bring much life energy to her or to her clients, she opened to the larger sources that inform life, addressed and healed many areas of her life.

In a nut shell, the dreamer successfully made a mid-life sea change toward yin, which was undeveloped and rather woundedly tucked beneath the yang adaptations in her psyche and life. We can generally think of yang as focused concentration with will and action, and yin as magnetic, receptive, diffuse awareness. Also, yang and Logos/knowledge correlate, while yin and Eros/all qualities of relatedness correlate. Yin brought up anger and vulnerability, and the corresponding archetypes informing these came to the fore of her experience. Eventually these experiences and new openness to the flow of life took hold in a more humanly integrated way. It is easy to get lost in such territory, but the religious instinct presented itself to her in dreams and in life, and helped her find her way with the world in and around her through a growing differentiating spirit of Eros. The new life path itself that formed amid the chaos became its own best reward. It led her to new ground of being, new means of living and loving, and new fruit in life.

Rooting for the Living Reality of Psyche

What else does this image of roots point to specifically? Roots suck up moisture, minerals, and nutrients in the darkness of the Earth's soil. They push and grow and reach into the darkness (the bedrock of our existence beyond ordinary ego function), downward, away from the sunlight of the over-world, to both anchor and gather nourishment. Indeed, like trees, the soul's life depends on the roots' underground counterforce to the equal and opposite reaction of consciousness and upward growth.

Following an instinctual longing, we root around in the psyche to find its living waters, where renewal of consciousness occurs. Jung and von Franz often worked with the color spectrum to show the range of human experience with archetypes between instinct and image. The red end of the color spectrum signifies the earthy, lusty, embodied urges of instinct, and the other end, the purple-violet end, signifies the image/

spirit dimension of the spectrum. Both ends of the continuum are vital for the soul's life, and contact with the numinous is found at both the instinctual and image ends of the continuum. For what are archetypal images in dreams or myths without connections to experience in instinctual life? And what are instinctual patterns without the images and myths that depict, personify, and mirror the meaning, presence, and nature of the patterns?

We could say that rooting around in the psyche via the religious instinct and then bringing consciousness to the development and refinement of the instinctual process can lead us to *the living root,* the living reality of psyche. Here, both red-instinct, and purple-image come together, *as instinct becomes aware of the source it seeks.* And arising images then link the human being to transformations of consciousness occurring in instinctual experience.

The following dream illustrates this mystery, using the root metaphor. A woman with a devastating illness that emerged amid a terribly repressed grief process began rooting around in her psyche to find the help to get well. She encountered many dream experiences that helped her locate the grief and the ways in which she was stuck. Then she dreamed this:

> I am walking along on a trail in the woods, and it leads me to an embankment looming before me, a sheer cliff. My path clearly continues on the top of the cliff. I am lost, not knowing how I will possibly go on. Then it becomes clear somehow that the only way to go on, to ascend, is to reach into the soil and try to find a live root. I reach into the soil and, rooting around, finally feel a root that is intensely alive. I grab hold of the root, and *it pulls me up* to the top of cliff. I see that I am on my path, which continues into the woods amid lovely deciduous trees. I do not recognize the type, but their leaves are gently flickering in the wind, beckoning. I continue onward.

We can think of the live root image as symbolizing a live connection to the autonomous psyche, located deep in the soil of existence. Rooting around internally via a deep analysis, this woman was searching for that live root. Finding that living root lifts her onto "higher ground"—higher consciousness—where both her body and psyche respond with remarkable spontaneous healing. The live root itself—psyche mystery—lifts her. The ego's role is to root around, recognize the living quality in this root, and then hold on to it, say "yes," get into relationship with it. The living psyche, with its symbolizing function, then uplifts, transforms, and leads to the new way, where before there was no clear path.

Rooting in the Psyche for the "Mother"

Looking further into the mystery of roots and instinct in personal and transpersonal dimensions of experience, we go in search of the goddess or god Rilke describes as the one who is "like a webbing made of a hundred roots that drink in silence."

Johannes Fabricius's *Alchemy* shows alchemical images of prenatal life that show the fetus lying on its back. From the umbilical cord grows an intricate web of roots that sustain and nourish the fetus. In another image, these roots are actually a tree, like the world tree growing from the belly of the fetus.[6]

There is a mythopoetic quality to developmental psychology's notion of the "rooting" reflex in infants. When you touch the cheek of a newborn, the infant turns toward the stimulus and its mouth roots around for the nipple, longing for the mother, the source of sustenance. Rooting is an instinctual expression of a singular life turning toward the source of life.

The religious instinct is similar. It requires turning toward what touches us, rooting around amid the experience of longing, searching, and reaching for nourishment in life. When this palate becomes differentiated, discerning what nourishes inner life most, the alchemical gold, the elixir of soul, is the boon.

"Rooting" for the "mother" leads imagination from the personal to the transpersonal. In a similar pattern, libido moves from the concrete to the symbolic and returns to infuse the ensouled world with awareness of the mysteries seeking embodiment, as archetypal patterns express themselves in our lives. Jung precisely addressed the flow of libido from the concrete and personal to the transpersonal mother, in his 1912 essay "The Dual Mother." He illustrates the hero's task of being born of *two mothers*, the embodied, biological mother and the spirit-instinct mother, the unconscious, which is the source of the second birth:

> The "mother" as the first incarnation of the anima archetype, personifies in fact the whole unconscious. Hence the regression leads back only apparently to the mother; in reality she is the gateway into the unconscious, into the "realm of the mothers."
>
> . . . For regression, if left undisturbed, does not stop short at the "mother" but goes back beyond her to the prenatal realm of the "Eternal Feminine," to the immemorial world of archetypal possibilities where "thronged round with images of all creation" slumbers the "divine child," patiently awaiting its conscious realization. This son is the germ of wholeness, and he is characterized as such by his specific symbols.

> . . . It is these inherent possibilities of "spiritual" or "symbolic" life and of progress which form the ultimate, though unconscious, goal of regression. By serving as a means of expression, as bridges and pointers, symbols help to prevent the libido from getting stuck in the material corporeality of the mother.[7]

Psychologically, the image of rooting for the mother carries with it the reality of rooting for the realm of the mothers, the prenatal "eternal feminine," the symbolic or spiritual life infusing existence. Jung continues in this essay to point out that the antidote to neurosis in adult life lies in connecting with the body and spirit of the mother in her countless forms of existence. This is also the heart of ancient Bhakti yogic wisdom: namely, the recognition of and devotion to the divine presently incarnating in all beings. The infusion from the "prenatal realm of the Eternal Feminine" eventually creates individual, autonomous human beings through the intricacies of the unfolding individuation processes.

Although it is important to relate consciously to the source, and to submit to regressions in life that are in service of the higher Self, it is equally important to remain true to the forces of individuation that move to develop a unique person, for to become lost for long in the "realm of the mothers" puts us at risk of being pulled back into the unconscious in a destructive way. One such destructive orientation occurs in addictive processes in which the ego hasn't the strength to assist the divine center within to incarnate, but instead opts out of individuation via regression in service of the infantile ego. On the other hand, healthy individuation includes the ego's devoted efforts to assisting the *latent* Self within to incarnate into its *actualized* presence in our life and personality, which means the ego also differentiates from the contents of the psyche, and emerges out of identifications with the anima/animus, or shadow, or Self, and so on.

Rooting, Divine Appetite, and Addiction

Desire for contact with the divine can lead to regressive wishes for contact highs such as excessive stimulation or consumption and reckless sexual behavior. Here, the ego can become lost and weakened, sidetracked in the individuation process, and destructively engaged with the archetypes, not truly assisting the Self to come from its latent state to its actualized state in the totality of our life.

Sometimes the addictive patterns express again and again the compulsive urges from the deep, and sometimes the addictive patterns reveal the crippling repression of these instincts. We eventually gain the middle ground by consciously wrestling with the instincts and tending to the individuation process.

Maeve and the Wild Pigs

A Celtic myth addresses the heart of the destructive forces present in the psyche and the work and grace required to hone divine appetite. Wild pigs that no one can tame run out of the Cave of Cruachan—the cave that holds the crack between the worlds.[8] Immediately, they begin rooting about in the open land, devouring and ravaging the fields. For seven years, their unabated appetite devastates the crops. Finally, the goddess Maeve, in her human form and in the company of her consort, goes out among the pigs and begins counting them. One wild pig jumps over Maeve's head and her chariot, threatening her. She grabs the pig in her hands and pins its snout. Its hind leg and skin come off in her hand, and she gains power over the whole herd. Their devouring, devastating ways change.

Psychologically, the wild pigs embody raw, ravenous, archetypal appetite. The attention and organizing principle present in counting the pigs begins the process of taming. Sylvia Perera points out in her book on Maeve that the pig who leaps over Maeve's head shows us that the rational, heady approach is not sufficient to control the devourers. They can jump right over rational thought.[9] The pinning of the beast's snout by the goddess/human energy brings grace. The pig sacrifices one leg and its skin to her—she has gained relationship with it—and it becomes more tamed in the process. The moment of pinning the snout of the presenting urges is pivotal in their transformation.

As an archetypal image, Maeve signifies the transformational moment with desire, with nature, when careful handling of instinct (that is, giving attention to the inner world and its symbols) initiates a new dynamic. The same goddess who brings desire, nature, and the roots of such psychic patterns is also the revered who assists in uprooting—tracking, extracting, and transforming—destructive archetypal desires that turn demonic or somehow run amok.

The archetypal pattern Maeve reflects contains both desire-nature itself *and* the transformation of libido, pointing to the mystery that the heat of desire and the transformer of libido are intricately and mysteriously interrelated.

Just as a lack of flow in instinctual energy constricts vitality in human life, its opposite (desire-nature that turns demonic or runs amok) can distort the inner life of our human soul relating with the divine. This precise constellation (regulating the "too-muchness/not-enoughness" of instinctual libidinal flow of the various drives) is often tremendously split in many of our family lines and cultural backgrounds. These patterns of repressive or distorted overenactment of drives reside at the core of most maladjustment and suffering.

Often, those who have suffered severe repression of their "pig nature" feel vexed when the alchemical changes of individuation bring all that repressed desire to the fore. When that *enantiodromia* occurs, they find their ego dominance over instinct now in the overwhelming custody of pig nature. This pattern is mythically paralleled in the fear that these instinctual uprisings will leave us possessed by pig nature. We are reminded of this in the image from Homer's *Odyssey* of the goddess Circe, who creates "possession by pig nature" when she transforms men into pigs.

Yet, Maeve's double nature—her life-giving, lusty dimension and her regulation of the destructive demonic appetite—is composed of a pair of vital opposites between which great consciousness can be gained. When individuals suffer through these opposites, this archetypal core duality is accessed in the psyche through dream life, and it penetrates consciousness. Something in the personality beyond the ego's fantasy of control can grab hold of the "pig snout" and assist in the changes. New patterns more in service of soul life—energies related to libidinal flow, regulation, and transformations of psychic-instinctual energy—become available.

Jung's statement that "it may even be assumed that just as the unconscious affects us, so the increase in our consciousness affects the unconscious"[10] points to the mystery of how reaching for healing our splits helps heal splits involved in the archetypes themselves. Those whose fate it is to wrestle with overindulgent addictive patterns or their opposite (that is, wounds that create ongoing repression and dominance of instincts) may, via the bridges built between the conscious and the unconscious, affect these archetypal constellations in their own transformations, thereby changing the constellation of the collective unconscious—the psychic inheritance in family lineages and in all culture.

The myth of Maeve comes from the Celtic tradition. When the ruling superego constellation present in Roman Catholicism landed on the shores of Ireland in the mythic form of St. Patrick, it drove out all the goddesses' snakes. We could think of this action as wrenching a fundamental split in the psyche between a dominant superego consciousness and instinctual life itself. However, looking more deeply into the archetypal pattern in the myth of Maeve, we discover an image of a feminine presence that represents the potential for instinctuality and its natural regulation and transformation to occur hand in hand; this makes unnecessary a collective, rule-based superego consciousness that bans the instinctual realm in the interest of preserving culture. This vast split in the Western psyche is evidenced by our ambivalence toward instinctuality. The healing of this split calls each of us to transform libido through development of spiritual and psychological connection with the archetypal forces that inform and shape our instinctual patterns.

Rooting for Religious Experience via Eros

Taking the image of the goddess Maeve and the rooting instinct one step further, we can see how images and experiences in the development of genital sexuality (stemming from the "root" chakra) carry this interwoven mystery. The goddess Maeve, for instance, was known to draw her initiates into her service through the force of desire. Sylvia Perera's exploration of the myth of Maeve discovered that during Maeve's sovereignty in ancient times, there were heroes who were "led by their loins" to follow goddess-fated paths.[11] Instinctual patterns in love and sexuality link us from the roots of our being into erotic mystery and fate. Sexuality, at its best, carries the longing for the divine, for the mystery. The *petit mort* (the French phrase for "orgasm," literally translated as "little death") that is the power of sexuality can launch us into the unknown, dissolving I-ness into the mystery and even into visionary states. Amid the "love" mysteries new, unpredictable "singularities" are formed, in a synchronistic dimension of reality, beyond causal reality. At this level, love births a unique creation of being—a field of participation where individuals experience synchronization with the great human soul.

Rooting in the unknown via love and passion potentially assists in birthing the third, the new, the forward, future star of being. With the release of consciousness into the unconsciousness of the *petit mort*, we may also encounter the demonic in the bedrock of the psyche. Consciousness amid these waters sorts through and relates with what is encountered and brings the boon back into living and loving. The boon entails not just the infusion from the ecstatic experience but also intricate differentiation of psyche and development of Eros along the way—all of which are telltale fruits of the religious function.

The Religious Instinct and the Erotic Leap into the Unknown

The differentiation of feeling, Eros, and the religious instinct cannot take place without contact with what is chaotic, mysterious, and beyond ego control. "Eros" here refers to all qualities and fields of relatedness, and when a refined spirit of Eros takes hold between people, or between people and animals or people and the gods, or people and land, the possibility of peace appears. This is because refined Eros makes the differences apparent and tolerates them without diluting them, thereby creating a bridge of connection, understanding, or acknowledgement across the opposites. When we are under the influence of this side of Eros we, too, can take leaps of love without knowing the outcome.

The risk-taking leap into the void is a theme common to many heroines who, through a whole lot of trouble, work, and grace participate in the creation of Eros bridges between the old and the new, transforming the cosmology. Legends and fairy tales weave these patterns of the maiden able to take the risk necessary to transform culture.

One such legend exemplifies this pattern. The Algonquian Sioux had been slaughtering the buffalo like the white man by driving them off cliffs, killing thousands in the process, and devastating herds. One maiden sees the trouble and with a trick, leaps into the rift between the buffalo and her father the chief. (She actually seduces the buffalo to *leap to her*, and promises to marry one—which is her leap to the buffalo spirit!) She subsequently marries one of the buffalo, one who is a shaman. Later in the story she has to transform her dead father with her own medicine, after he is killed by the shaman buffalo. She literally sings over her father's dismembered parts, as a new chief arises from under her ceremonial deer skin. In the end, she is the instrument that creates the Eros bridge between her people and their sacred animal, helping to bring about ritual and respect in hunting the sacred buffalo, and she resurrects her dead father into a new chief with new attitudes in the process. The animal kingdom and the ruling consciousness, the chief, are transformed by her erotic leap, and the buffalo's leap to her—as they both leap into the crack between her people and their devastated sacred animal. Without the maiden's daring erotic leap into the crack between these worlds, and her erotic invitation to the split-off animal world, redemption of the split was not possible.

On an individual level, earthed relationship of every sort has potential to become a vehicle of alchemical change. At a wedding, I witnessed a deeply actualized, mature, childless woman of the world take that leap of Eros into the unknown. She turned to her mate and spoke her vows of commitment to him, including her promise to open her heart to her mate's children, ex-wife, and extended family, and agreeing to become another parent to the children, in cooperation with all parents involved. The sincerity of her commitment, which she looked squarely in the eye, took my breath away. She was not innocent of the difficulty ahead, and yet she turned her open eyes and heart to the soup she was leaping into, and promised to give it her best. She knew it would also take grace and work and the outcomes could never be known ahead of time. Would the family open to her? Would she be able to discover her own relationships with the children, would they have the courage to bond with her? Would the other parents make room for her or secretly sabotage her efforts to the children? Who knew.

Over the following years she has lived that grounded commitment to the family. As is true of nearly all blended families, some of the struggles have been enormous, and the steady presence of intention and openness to reality at many levels have led to bridges being built by her with the children and the other set of parents. She has made a remarkable difference in all of their lives, and they in hers. Her presence has specifically added loving structure, conscientiousness, more risky and open communication, and artistic mediums and values into the family. Her cohesive self could see the leap and acknowledge the risks, face them squarely without knowing the outcome, and say "yes." And in so doing, then dive in and relate, love, fight, and change, while eros bridges formed. Love indeed found a new home among them.

Sometimes the erotic leap involves leaving a relationship. A woman in her fifties had the courage to leave her husband after 20 years of marriage, knowing she would have no money, given she had signed a stiff prenuptial agreement. She faced the inner poverty of her life and decided that life without money and the marriage and its façade in the community was going to support her more than the situation she was in. The erotic leap involved a financial, social, and marital sacrifice. She has lived alone for ten years since and has a life she finds much richer and truer to her soul.

This leaping, fresh spirit of Eros also finds its way into life through men as often as women. How many men we can think of who have stood up for the spirit of refined love at just the most risky and important moments in their lives and in the lives of those around them! If you think for a moment about the people in your life and in the world who have been instruments of refined Eros—those who have taught you, or revealed this guiding principal of love, *refined Eros as an active force in life*—then you can discover a circle of vital, significant men and woman who are truly culture changers.

Differentiated Eros and differentiated religious instinctuality develop together. Without a growing process of experience and differentiation, we risk lapsing into a dumb animalhood in which either the inner music of the soul may be so repressed that it seems nonexistent or a substitute may take its place in the form of regressive or sappy derivatives. It requires tremendous patience, honesty, and cultivating an ear to hear the complexity of what is constellating. There is a time to leap, and a time not to leap, and these are completely individual fates and responsibilities. There is also a way to take that leap in your life that may also completely change later in life. Perhaps life suddenly requires that you discover different arenas in which to leap with Eros. Such arenas include intrapsychic, interpersonal, intraspecies, intercultural, and so on.

These subtle changes and directives require an individually-honed connection to the religious instinct, and to the development of Eros within, in order to have the leap be connected with soul and the true development of individuality. Then the way in which the leap takes place, the arena, and the spirit of the leap also are instruments of Eros refining itself in your life. Eros does seem to require—even with refinement—a touch of the sacred fool who can leap into the unknown, into the cracks between the worlds, into the splits in human consciousness to discover healing, contact with the numinous, and new bridges.

As such, the differentiation of Eros and the religious instinct brings us closer to the divine inner music of soul life, which sustains and transforms. Conscious experience of Eros and the religious instinct leads us in the darkness and through the void to the source of the spring, from which being is created. It is the honing of the longing for the divine that reaches for the living water beneath the surface of our lives. It teaches us how to tend the living spring, to differentiate and live in such a way that sweet healing water arises from within. And when the water becomes muddy and troubled, the water also can become clear and healing again as we take the directive of the spirit of the spring. Often in individuation, tremendous refinement of love is required over the course of our lives. Then unconscious shadow attitudes are identified at the spring and with grace, compassion, and work these shadows transform, and find their appropriate place. As they do, then true humanity and individuality arise. Or, to use Yeats's metaphor, "the face one had before the world was made"[12] and the counterpart in others' faces begin to appear as well, when the differentiation of the shadow attitudes and the refinement of Eros take root in our lives.

The *Axis Mundi* as Bridge between Archaic and Modern Humankind

Connection with the transcendent dimensions of reality fosters new psychic life. It bridges the old and the new, between the *roots* of humanity and the far-reaching *branches* of growth in the over-world. As we move into the new millennium, it becomes clearer, ever pressing, that the roots of the human experiment be driven deeper into the psyche and psychoid. These roots counterbalance the weight and height of modern developments and realign human consciousness with that of the *anima mundi*, the world soul.

Musing on the image of the "world tree," or world soul, and the necessary roots that nourish and support it, a personal experience and an accompanying dream come to mind. The experience occurred while I was in France to see the 8,000-year-old cave drawings at Peche Merle in the Dordogne region. Entering these caves is a profoundly religious experience. Among the pristinely preserved cave drawings is the taproot of an old oak tree, a few thousand years old. The root winds its way down from the surface through the 30-foot-tall, open cavern space and then right on down beneath the bedrock of the cave, where you can see ancient human footprints perfectly preserved in the floor of the cave. The living taproot of the ancient tree rooting into the cavern and the remains of ancient man were a breathtaking sight. It felt as though an ancient human being had just walked by moments before.

After visiting the cave paintings and taking in the mystery of the oak tree's taproot, I dreamed:

> I am winding my way down a taproot that reaches throughout time and through the development of civilizations. This root is both a spiral stairway and a living taproot that grows throughout time; all dimensions of time are simultaneously present. These downward spiral steps

> lead into and through the bedrock of the psyche of archaic human beings, our ancient ancestors, *still alive* in the stratum of the psyche that exists below the modern world. The taproot draws nourishment from this bedrock and brings the flow and nourishment upward into the over-world, above ground. At the same time, the life above depends on the healthy, continued existence of this taproot into the archaic human psyche.

The religious instinct is like this taproot. It leads us, like the ancient shaman, to inner experience that assists our modern consciousness in linking back down the DNA ladder, the *axis mundi,* into ancestral memory and then bridging this knowledge with that of the new forms in the modern world.

The recent stretches of humankind—globalization, technology, probing of outer space, world powers located in big business, and so on—demand this connection down the ladder, for protection of the world soul, for the *anima mundi* to survive. The religious instinct, as this taproot, is of primary importance for all life forms. The human ego, without enough conscious living connection to the divine, collectively spins perilously toward destruction of itself and other life forms. In our archaic roots, we remember our living interdependence with the world soul, our place in the mysteries. Here, the relatively recent evolution of the human psyche, manifested in the autonomy of the ego portion of human consciousness, can come into check with the larger realities of creation and destruction.

More than ever, we need to look into our part of what we are creating within the *anima mundi*, and look deep enough to discover the *a priori* medium of creation, the living root dwelling in the autonomous psyche. In the alchemical text titled *The Rosarium Philosophorum*, which Jung deals with in depth in his essay, "The Psychology of the Transference"[13], the *prima materia* ("first matter," or source of all creation) is called *radix ipsius*, meaning "root of itself." It roots in itself, autonomous, dependent on nothing. It is uncreated, *increatum*. The unique *materia*, says Paracelsus, is a great secret having nothing in common with the elements, yet is the mother of the elements and of all created things. If we can delve in deep enough and locate this root, we have a better chance of restoring our attunement to, and balanced relationship with, the world soul.

Roots into the archaic layers of consciousness, the living waters from which mystical experiences arise, draw up the ancient mysteries and teach us our place in the cosmos through felt experiences in which these waters make themselves known. According to Sufi mystics such as Ibn al' Arabi, integrating our mystical experiences into our living philosophies is the gift we give back to the divine. Individual consciousness is a carrier of these living waters and the destructive forces present in the psyche. Relating through felt experience with what the alchemists termed the *humidum radicale*, or root moisture, present in the psyche, and heeding the mercurial spirit of the waters, we then transform and affect the inner and outer psychic collective inheritance.

3

Finding the Living Waters

. . . What hurts
The soul? To live
without tasting the water of its own essence. People
focus on death and this
material earth. They have doubts about soul water.
Those doubts can be
reduced! Use night to wake your clarity. Darkness
and living water are
lovers. Let them stay up together. . .
—Rumi

How do we discover the source of renewal and transformation alive in the soul? Rumi's poem intimates something about how the Sufis discover the source. They enter into the psychic darkness beyond the light of the ego, and discover inner clarity and soon, "living water." People throughout time have had ways to search for and discover a source of renewal, often depicted as living water, in the soul. The Yeome Native Americans (also known as the Yaqui), for example, say that in times of trouble the people seek contact with "the enchanted being" who lives deep in the mountain, along with the enchanted water, the living water capable of renewing life, healing, and other great works between the people and the many worlds. Their 5,000-year-old shamanic practices contact this renewing water as the people dance the deer dance and drum to the deer spirit who can walk between the worlds and find the enchanted being and the sacred water. Deer then brings the living water to the people, along with healing, creation of words, and new vision.

In alchemy, a similar mystery is pictured. There is a source that is called "living water" that heals, unifies, brings new visions, harmony between realms of being, and so on. It often is discovered with original human being, the Anthropos, nearby. In modern life and dreams we discover means to attain this renewing source.

In the early 1980s, while at the University of California San Diego Medical Center, I connected with Marie-Louise von Franz. I was conducting research by gathering the dreams of the dying and exploring von Franz's hypotheses. Years later, two nights after Dr. von Franz died, and before I had heard of her passing, I had a dream:

> I am standing with Marie-Louise von Franz in a kitchen that exists on the other side of life. I can feel that she has just died and I am not to interact too much with her since she is between the worlds. She has a task to do before her life is complete, and I am watching her fulfill it. On the kitchen floor is a large compost pile of decaying organic matter that is somehow the "Jungian world." She says, "It is time to sort genuine from fake." With this, she reaches deep into the pile of decaying matter and unearths a vessel made of plastic. She examines it and throws it to the side. Then she plunges in deeper and, rummaging around, pulls out a beautiful glass vessel. Drawing it up above her head, with long arms, she examines it. It contains the water of life. She takes it to her lips and drinks some of the living water from the vessel. The sweet feeling of completion, of fulfillment of her task, lingers in the kitchen.

If we think of this dream as possibly speaking to von Franz's own life, the ability to locate and then pour the living waters and to drink them in seems an appropriate living symbol for the culmination of her life's alchemical work with the psyche and psychoid.

The figure of von Franz also can be seen as a personification of the feminine mediatrix connected with the divine, as the feminine alchemist. This alchemist dives into what is decomposing, into what the alchemists called a *putreficatio.* What is decaying is the "Jungian world," the compost heap of psychology, thought forms, knowledge fixed in dogma. This alchemist's instinct also knows that if she reaches deep enough, she will recognize and identify what is inauthentic, pass it by, locate the living mysteries, and drink them.

This dream is also a gift of direction for those of us who follow in time. On this level, Marie-Louise von Franz represents a needed activity in the alchemical kitchen of the human psyche: to engage in a vital, differentiating labor that leads to discovering the vessel containing the living water of life. This labor and the vessel point toward contact with the mysterious human soul.

Also, this dream seems to hold a promise to extend an invitation to plunge deeply into the compost heap of the "Jungian world," to sort genuine from artificial within and around us, and to reach for the living waters that beckon us all. With instincts toward the mysteries, which von Franz represents, the sorting, the reaching, the discovery, the pouring, and the drinking become possible.

These images also point to the myth of our times, as do the life and work of von Franz. As we move now into the new 2,000-year cycle, from Pisces (the sign of the fishes) to Aquarius (the water bearer), this image is also particularly meaningful to us collectively. Pisces represents the psychic reality of swimming in the unconscious, in the mysteries. The precession of the equinox takes us to the Age of Aquarius, the alchemist. Our new 2000-year era is imaged as the alchemist who, in pouring the living waters of the paradoxical *mysterium*, creates a bridge from heaven to earth. The uniting of heaven and earth refers psychologically to the interplay and marriage of the archetypal and psychoidal realms with the mortal human dimensions of existence.

The Living Water and Its Vessel: An Inner Attitude

In a remarkably poignant passage, Jung muses over the mystery of moisture, the vessel, and the soul as these three elements emerge together in alchemical texts. "Prima materia as radical moisture has to do with the soul," states Jung. The soul, he goes on, "moist by nature, is sometimes symbolized by dew. The symbol of the vessel then gets transferred to the soul." Jung then refers to the words of the alchemist Caesarius of Heisterbach: "The soul is a spiritual substance of spherical nature, like the globe of the moon, or like a glass vessel that is furnished before and behind with eyes. . ." According to Jung, this soul vessel is created in our lives by a psychic operation, "the creation of an inner readiness to accept the archetype of the Self in whatever subjective form it appears."[1]

This prescription may sound simple, but it requires tremendous humility, honesty, and willingness. The subtleties of the dialogue between consciousness and the unconscious leave room for the trickery of complexes and ego drives. Without a heart dedicated to the dialogue, to the unveiling of Self as it exists and appears in our lives, we can become hopelessly stuck or off track. Receptivity to the manifestations and processes of Self, to "God," the numinous, requires a willingness to see the unconscious point of view about ourselves in any given aspect or situation. This kind of receptivity means fateful encounters with the dark-light and terrible-marvelous *numinosum* arising from our own life experiences. As Jung said about these encounters with Self, the "experience of the opposites has nothing whatever to do with intellectual insight or with empathy. It is more what we would call fate."[2]

However, the religious instinct rises up from the soul, so when relationship with this instinct is refined, assistance from the transpersonal dimensions of the psyche and psychoid arrives amid these encounters. Here we confront the paradoxes within our nature—and the divine's nature as well—where "good and evil are indeed closer than identical twins."[3] The religious instinct, when embodied, refines our connection with the divine and assists us in *becoming* soulful, becoming a worthy vessel for the heights and depths of soul. We learn not only to descend into the introverted, incubating womb-space of the imagination but also to become vessels that can contain the experiences of the paradoxical nature of existence. We become, as the Sufis put it, "capable of god." God is the transforming, paradoxical, changing Tao itself, full of transmutations for us to serve, partner, and emanate. For Western humankind, this partnership is an enormous stretch. Jung addressed this: "Western man is held in thrall by the 'ten thousand things'; he sees only particulars, he is ego-bound and thing-bound, and unaware of the deep root of all being."[4]

The psyche incarnating during our era essentially asks that Westerners learn a new relationship to it, one that confronts the enormity of the psyche and psychoid, tolerates the paradoxes as they appear in our life experiences, and then helps us discover new unions and transmutations. What the alchemists called *aqua permanens* ("permanent water") is a psychic operation we can learn. It hones inner receptivity and attentiveness to image, vision, presence, and instincts of the larger psyche when they appear. From contact with the psyche (Jung's definition of psychology is "contact with the psyche") we can learn this new relationship. We can learn to discard certain thought forms and ego desires and then receive fresh images, vision, direction, input, instinct, from the larger psyche and psychoid.

My von Franz dream portrays this psychic operation, *aqua permanens,* for it accepts and sorts what it discovers in the decay. The religious instinct embodied in the dream reaches for the goal, for the simple, clear vessel and the divine waters it holds. Von Franz devoted her life's work to explicating the reality of how the divine is transforming in the human soul even when we are unaware of it. The dream vessel shows this mystery, for in the alchemical kitchen, the soul vessel carries the living waters that nourish us in the ultimate hour between the worlds, as our life is concluded. In a way, the dream is speaking the truths von Franz expressed in her writing. The divine is transforming in the vessel of the soul, and the religious instinct brings her to the vessel to drink those satisfying waters where the divine and human have discovered relationship.

The dream differentiation between what is plastic and what is glass is interesting. You could think of the plastic vessel as the kind of consciousness you create out of artificial attitudes. Such attitudes not open to the Self as it appears and are therefore not capable of locating, containing, pouring, and drinking the living waters of life. Glass is made from a common substance, sand, and is heated in fire. Now that is quite important, for as the religious instinct gains strength within us, it creates a contained fire that burns through many false attitudes and constellations of instinctual or psychic energy that must change in order for the religious instinct to make the relationship between the human being and the divine, between the ego and the Self. This fire burns off what is inessential, if we participate with it, and make the necessary sacrifices and choices. Then this glass vessel is discovered—a simple, clear vessel in us that is uncontaminated with falsities, but instead is simply capable of containing, in our own life processes, the mysterious presence of the soul's living waters.

Glass and ash were often synonymous in alchemical texts. On account of both being purified by fire (*calcinatio*, as the alchemists called these operations of fire transforming the *prima materia*), what is left is "incorruptible" and transparent. Jung thought that glass and ash both resemble the glorified body.[5] Von Franz, at the end of life in this dream, locating this simple purified transparent vessel capable of carrying the living water of life is deeply moving in light of these alchemical insights. Her life work was deeply devoted to the religious instinct, and her work and life fed that flame that burns its way through to the goal, the ash, the glass vessel capable of god. A signpost for us as well, following in time, who seek to serve this alchemical fire and these waters to the goal of the ash and the glass.

The story of Isis having a dialogue with the angel in order to learn the mysteries of alchemy contains a remarkably poignant mythic parallel to my dream of von Franz locating the clear vessel and drinking the living water. I came upon this story months after the dream, in my attempt to research the meaning of the images of von Franz on her "way out of life." In the ancient Egyptian text titled *Isis to Horus, or The Prophetess Isis to Her Son*—to which both Jung and von Franz refer in their work[6]—Isis, imaged in one of her forms as an adept alchemist, meets with the angel who knows the alchemical art. Before this meeting occurs, however, a different angel comes. This angel wants to have intercourse with her, but Isis wants to know the secrets of the art, so she puts off his sexual advances. When she demands the knowledge from him, he tells her that he is not permitted to speak about the mysteries because of their supreme importance. He leaves, telling her that the next day an angel would arrive with the solution to the problem. Isis says he also spoke of the sign of this angel—"He bore it on his head and would show me a small, unpitched vessel filled with a translucent water. He would tell me the truth."[7]

The next day, an angel greater than the first, Amnael, appears before her with the vessel, and he, too, is full of desire for Isis. Again, Isis begins inquiring into the matter. The angel reveals the secret—the vessel and the water and recipes—which she can pass on to her son, Horus.

Jung tells us that the water in Egypt has a special significance. As the Nile, it is "Osiris, the dismembered god *par excellence*."[8] A text from Edfu reads, "I bring you the vessels with the god's limbs [that is, the Nile] that you may drink of them; I refresh your heart so that you may be satisfied."[9] The god's limbs are the fourteen parts into which Osiris was divided. Osiris is the Egyptian god of renewal; his mythic cycle of death, dismemberment, and rebirth infused the core of ancient Egyptian mythology. The waters referred to in Isis's dialogue with the angel were the mysterious waters of resuscitation, of rebirth.

Ancient Egyptian cosmology reveals intricate relationship with many realms of being, and highly differentiated interpenetration between realms. In our modern times, we can discover the death and rebirth mysteries they depicted. All processes of change on our way through life give us opportunity for the dialogue between what is mortal and immortal, permanent and impermanent. The work of creating the dialogue with the unconscious lies at the heart of the death and rebirth mysteries.

On the Composition of the Alchemical Waters at Work in Our Lives

> It is the water that kills, the water that vivifies.[10]

The alchemists speak of the mystery of the living waters and of the "composition of the alchemical waters." To what are they referring? A synchronistic event happened while I worked on this chapter. This story shows the images of alchemy enacted quite exactly and plays with the notion of the "composition of the waters."

My father visited me at my cabin, where I was working on this book (of which he knew nothing). He had just come from a long soak in a hot spring in Thermopolis, Wyoming, once tended by the Shoshoni Indians. As he walked in the door, he said to me, holding out his hands, "Look! It's incredible. After all these years of that terrible, incurable, cracking rash, my hand is fine! It must have been the composition of the waters."

Struck by the synchronicity, I awaited the rest of the story. Being an extroverted, sensation-feeling type, he told, in great detail, how the Shoshoni gave the U.S. government rights to their ancestral spring and land to thank the white people for treating them well. Not long after, the government turned on them, taking more of their land and slaughtering many of them. The government authorities neither understood the sacred gift of the spring, nor did they then entrust the spring to anyone who would tend it in a manner befitting the gift. My father then told me how the healing properties of the spring live on, in spite of the white man. He described the sacred healing he experienced at these springs—the healing of an affliction he had suffered for many years—and the healing of his relationship with his half-brother.

The rash (an open wound, really) had developed twelve years prior, covering my father's right palm. It appeared during an incredible crisis in his life, which eventually led to a divorce, and much later, new discoveries in life. The rash made woodworking, his primary love, nearly impossible. He tried everything dermatologists recommended, various potions, and diet changes. Nothing worked. Family members kidded him that, because it was on his palm, perhaps it was stigmata of sorts (something he did not find particularly funny).

My father and his younger half-brother, Lynn, met at the springs to spend time together after a lifetime of emotional disconnection. For days, the two of them sat, side by side, in the springs. They found themselves disarmed, able to speak naturally and honestly to each other unlike any other time in their lives. As my father continued to talk about this, it became clear that much healing, at many levels, did indeed cook up in those waters. The central emotional and psychological wound of my father's life is his father wound. His birth father, Claude, divorced my grandmother right after my father was born. During my father's entire childhood, Claude lived just down the street but never introduced himself to my father. My father even went to school with cousins who lived in the same house with Claude, but Claude never spoke to him, never owned him.

After 70 years of carrying this primal rejection, my father finally expressed out loud to himself and his half-brother what it was like to have his stepfather, Harry (Lynn's birth father), *also* ignore him all those years while openly loving my father's half-brothers. Somehow Lynn never registered my father's reality, and my father had never spoken of his emotional pain. Instead, he carried a huge silent hole inside over the course of his life. Sitting in the hot springs, he told Lynn how this chasm had separated them as well. With that secret pain boiling up into conscious view, the two of them bonded, as my father said, for the first time.

When he left the springs, his hand also was healed, and it remains healed. Perhaps this was his fate, his "stigmata," of sorts, that had finally come into consciousness and healing in the hot spring waters.

In the alchemical process of soaking (*solutio*), cooking (*calcinatio*), honoring their separateness (*separatio*), experiencing and then divulging secret pain with honesty (*nigredo* and *sublimatio*), the two brothers discovered a new bond, as well as new inner harmony within themselves (*coniunctio*). My father's emotional and physical wounds healed, as did his brother's emotional being (*coagulatio*—by uniting the new spirit with the body, the "lapis" becomes a changed, living body and an agent of change). This is a wonderful mirror of the processes of the soul captured by alchemical imagery and embodied and active in nature.

As he said when he burst in my cabin door, "It must have been the composition of the waters!" My father, being an engineer, meant the actual chemical composition. He told me that he looked at the composition board and saw nothing specific in the substrates that warranted such a change. Nonetheless, he was sure that there was something in the composition—and certainly there was, at several levels, literal and metaphoric.

Sometimes the transformations happen in a potently dynamic way in the flow of synchronicity with the natural world and sometimes the transformations happen more subtly. The motif of the composition of the waters reflects the reality of looking into the particulars of the processes of change and the elements or forces of activation that drive the changes in these transmutations between heaven and earth, human and divine, inner and outer, and so on. For the alchemists, the mysterious idea of the composition of the waters of change led them to study the many components and elements that have different properties and wonder-working effects. For example, sulphur, salt, arsenic, and numerous other elements were imagined into and studied extensively, which eventually became the root of the natural sciences as we know them; when taken psychologically, their works also became the root of depth psychology. In the initiatory waters of change in the psyche appears the mercurial line of what operates as medicinal, homeopathic, or toxic, mirroring the paradoxical nature of the Self as it incarnates.

Embodying the Vessel via the Wound

Tremendously difficult life experiences can throw us into an unexpected encounter with the waters of the unconscious. The following dream and life story comes from a half-Hopi woman who was raised among her tribe and suddenly lost her mother and daughter in a car accident. Her grief was so great that she was unable to speak. She showed no affect, had no dreams. When she came to see me, she would often be quiet the entire time. I would talk very soothingly to her and read myths or stories with strong feminine characters. I thought of how the alchemists say that there is a way to create the water—an alchemical operation called *benedictio fontis*. If we do our part, the divine elements of the imagination may come. My best sense of how to do this was simply to attempt to create a loving, warm environment that was open to the psyche, and wait.

Eventually, as she began to connect with me, her voice came back, and her feelings began to thaw. Then she had the following dream:

> I go to the spring at the river, to the pool I have always known since I was a girl. It is the spring of my mother's people. In the pool, you are with me and another, older woman, mother's old friend from the pueblo. You two hold your hands underneath my body, and I float. Closing my eyes . . . I feel peace. Then my body, as I know it, is on one wing of a giant butterfly on top of the water. This butterfly gently flaps its wings together, apart, together, apart, together, apart. . . . I seem to be chanting this while the wings so gently open and close. My mother's friend tells you not to take your hands away but to leave them under the butterfly that sits in the water between you and her. You flinched a

> little as my body became one with the wing of the butterfly, and you and she were upholding the butterfly in the water, instead of just me. I think she was trying to be sure you didn't let go.
>
> Now my body on the left wing, where you stand, is experiencing something new as the wings open and close. The right wing has someone forming in it. Just like my body is in the left wing, this new being is forming in the right wing. As it takes shape, it is evident it is a new kachina I have never seen. The wings open and close some more. I keep chanting with the rhythm, "Together, apart, together, apart." Each time the wings close, my body is pressed up to and touching this kachina. Then, finally, it is all different.
>
> I am standing outside the pool and am completely in my body. The butterfly is now small and comes toward me. It lands just above my belly. I have a hole there that is very deep. It sits there and drinks in some water and then beats its wings. I feel sad and empty. But I am back in my body and am comforted by this incredible butterfly sitting on the entrance to this hole in me. I am feeling clear-minded and large of presence gazing at the pool from which I have emerged and gazing then on down the river as it shimmers into the valley. I feel sober and peaceful, made new. I have been reborn. I wonder that maybe my mother and daughter experienced the same thing I just did, somehow, since we all come from this pool.

To further understand this dream, it is important to visit something of the mystery of the kachina. For the Hopi Indians, when the inner and outer worlds are going through great change or stress, one of their visionary people sees, with her or his inner eye, the new kachina that embodies these new healing qualities. Then the kachina is created in a physical form. The new kachina then carries forward the vision and the fresh energy of the new dimensions of the divine, or changing god image, among them.

Her dream used her own imaginal tribal medicine to move and comfort her. The inner water of life, the inner spirit, and the new vision came with great clarity. Her assimilation of and participation in the processes this dream heralded took a long time to unfold.

The winged messenger being who transforms with her is from the insect kingdom and has a hermetical, feminine shape-shifting quality. The dreamer calls it "Butterfly Woman," which reminds her of a kachina among the Hopi. The underworld experience brought on by such terrible loss and trauma in her life sent her down to that midnight hour, and the insect stratum of the psyche (supposedly the furthest stratum from ego consciousness) responds. Like the humming of bees accompanying the Egyptian sun god on his way through the underworld, the insect kingdom appears along the descent, symbolizing the deep regenerative forces in nature. Her need to merge with this Self presence was clear. She would not have made it through the trauma without the grace of psyche absorbing her for a while, carrying her on its wings, *in* its wings. Merging with the archetypal dimensions is, of course, dangerous, and her dream's comment on the need for me to keep my hands steady under her, supporting this experience, is completely clear. The joining and separating of the conscious and unconscious takes hold. The dream supports the patterns of immersion in and emerging from these waters. She emerges from the pool, able to embody the great pain and loss in the deep hole in her solar plexus area. Then, as she makes the mythic "return," an amazing thing happens: The butterfly comes to drink from the well of her wound! Such poetic medicine of the soul!

The Sufis tell us that the divine angel feeds on the essence of our beingness. Here we witness this mystery. From the immersion, she is reborn as a woman, embodying the pain, the experience, the transformation. The transfusion of the archetypal experience in the soul brings her to exactly this embodiment. After immersing in the alchemical waters, we become a carrier of these waters. The water drawn up through our wound, as it is healing, becomes healing to the world around us. The wound and the gift are intricately intertwined, and the healing extends past the personal self to the divine itself. The dream portrays the living psyche itself being nourished by the nectar of her essence that this healing and wounding bring about.

And what waters are these? The feminine in her family line knows these waters, as does the internal feminine. These are the ancestral living waters at the heart of creation, available to us all. They initiate and bring about a unique trans-sensory theophany of healing.

The Dew of the Living Spirit of the Imagination

The Sufis tell us that we must court the soul or it will leave us. The following life story and dream portray a woman's path to cultivating a soul/spirit relationship. A tomboy and "Daddy's girl" in her youth, she sided against her mother's suffering and mental illness, as she also painfully sided against her own emotions and core feminine qualities and instincts. One memory in her childhood portrays the acquisition of her "thick skin" and tomboyish rough-and-tough attitude. When she was 10, she instigated a game with two friends in the neighborhood. The game evolved as an invitation to all the children in the neighborhood to gather around and see whether any of them could pinch her arms hard enough to make her flinch or grimace. No matter how much pain they inflicted, she proudly maintained a stone-like appearance. The game eventually died out. This window into the formation of her early character parallels remarkably what her dreams depicted as "armadillo" nature. This stubborn, defensive, armadillo skin *does* work, and little penetrates to the vulnerable flesh. The problem felt at the core, then, is that very little dialogue occurs between the self and the world.

At fundamental levels within her personality, she turned toward and chose independence, power, separateness, and achievement. Yet, her path led her into service to others when she decided to take vows and become a nun. This choice, she stated, seemed to be the "higher road" compared with the other option she saw, which did not interest her—namely, marriage, children, and family. Her adaptations to the world clearly served her for a time; she achieved a medical degree in the convent and became a renowned medical researcher after leaving the convent.

As the dream world worked to bring her into relationship with the psyche, the truths dawned. Cracks in the old layers of defensive structures led her into the healing mysteries of Self beneath all these adaptations, via profound dream experiences and then fresh contact with others. The dissolution of the old self brought an invitation to freedom but also anxiety as psyche called her into her instinctual nature. She had been trapped outside her own core. In discovery of this truth, she had to suffer not only the humanity of coming into her instincts but also the shock of seeing how far she had wandered from her feminine nature.

When insight began to dawn upon her, she asked for a vision to help her. Here is the dream vision that spoke to her amid these changes:

> A divine feminine presence appears at night from a dark hole in the earth under a bridge. I sit in the grass watching, amazed at the appearance of this feminine presence of light, which somehow is the divine queen fairy, though the light is so bright, her form is not visible. Her presence, inside these sparks of emanating light, shines in all directions, revealing her as the queen of fairies. Other fairies gather around this queen; each fairy sits in this circle atop her own drop of dew on individual blades of grass, all facing the queen. The dew-drop seats for each fairy become *crowns* of dew. The fairies themselves seem, then, like divine emanations coming from the *dew-crowns* on each blade of grass. As the diaphanous wings of the fairies flicker in the central light of the queen's divine presence, the voice of the divine fairy queen speaks: "I am

> the Divine-Crown-of-Beingness. I crown all those beings in nature who have the courage to inhabit themselves."

The dream world's portrayal of the source of divine light as a fairy goes straight to the mark for this dreamer's healing. Mythically, fairies are nature spirits, connected to the mysteries of the light *inside* nature, the autonomous, mysterious presence uniquely inhabiting sacred sites such as springs, rivers, and mountain glens. Instead of seeing the divine only as disembodied masculine spirit, she *felt the experience* of the divine incarnating into matter. The earth spirit's appearance generated healing in the split between spirit and instinct from which the dreamer was suffering (under the Zeitgeist of this same split in Christianity). The dream changed her points of reference and brought her the "crowning dew," the felt occurrence of her *being* as a light in nature as well, blessed by (and part of) the forces of creation itself. Contact with this feminine presence from the darkness opened experiential inner doorways into her emotional, instinctual, and physical dimensions and pointed to a path of redemption composed of the courage to inhabit her own nature.

As she was finding herself anew, she fell in love. She sensed a new presence in love that was unlike anything she had ever experienced. The essence of the love shared contained a calling toward deeper intimacy and honesty with her core feminine self as well as her lover. As individuation would have it, her lover was a man whose feeling world was deeply intact and available in the relational field with her. There was no way for her to remain in the armored, "armadillo" adaptation and make love with this man, because his love penetrated her thick defenses to her core, and the mystery of love brought these falsities to light as love itself sought out her essence. The feminine presence in the dream, she stated, also seemed to use the feeling in the love relationship to call her into the authentic mystery of her core being.

This mystery takes us so profoundly into the core of the psyche that it illuminates the four main problems addressed by alchemical mythology. First, both this dream and alchemy, as von Franz points out, "heighten the value of the feminine principle or Eros (in both men and women)."[11]

The central mystery of the dream brings the feminine erotic mystery of embodiment to light and brings the feminine divinity's voice and principles to a more valued place. Dew gathers at night on the tips of each blade of grass. Against the pull of gravity, it gathers upward, holding its shape in a droplet, and catches the morning light, which glitters in each drop. The other side of our diurnal consciousness has its own feminine laws. Nighttime has a voice born from a hole in the dark earth, which is speaking its mystery.

Second, the dream and its parallels in alchemical imagery illustrate von Franz's sense that alchemical mythology seeks to "elevate the status of the individual in relation to the uniformity of the mass."[12] The dream instruction points to the fact that every single blade of grass has its own distinct fairy spirit and that each being in nature, including the human being, has individuality and access to its own divine crown of being. This crown is brought to the human soul by the *lumina naturale*—in this example, by nature's dew.

Third, the dream and alchemical mythology address the "the problem of evil."[13] For this woman dreamer, who was deeply ensconced in Roman Catholicism, inhabiting the instincts meant conflict for her. Her ego perspective, influenced by the collective teachings by which she was raised, saw the life of the body as evil and denial of instincts as "holy." This ideology led to a one-sided "spirit"-based religiosity, in contrast to a balanced spirit-instinct dynamism informing a truly religious life spent in contact with the numen.

The dream turns this one-sided attitude around, saying that, to achieve the crown of divinity (our rightful spiritual nature), we must have the courage to inhabit ourselves. It would be sinful, "evil," not to do so, for we would be refusing to welcome the divinity, the numen, into our full instinctual constitution. Regarding the nature of evil, Jung said that "deviation from the Numen seems to be universally understood as being the worst and the most original sin."[14] Jung points out Paracelsus' remark, which also sheds light on this dreamer's plight of the need to integrate the divine with the nature spirit: "And as little as aught can exist in man without the divine numen, so little can aught exist in man without the natural lumen. A man is made perfect by numen and lumen and these two alone. Everything springs from these two, and these two are in man, but without them man is nothing, though they can be without man."[15]

Thus, the reality of "evil," as the dreamer had known it, was perfectly addressed by the alchemical psyche, bringing both the numen and lumen into a new relationship that invalidates her old experiences of evil.

Last, this dream and alchemy address "reconciling opposites in the fundamental psychic structure of the human being."[16] The dream leads the way for her toward reconciling the opposites within, by bringing her splits between spirit and matter into a new experiential unity in her psyche.

To discover our instinctual roots in connection with the center of personality is to rediscover the wholeness of "the eternal man dwelling in the darkness of the primordial night,"[17] as Jung states, and to reach for reality beyond separatist egohood, beyond *specifically* the leftover Christian split in collective consciousness involving maniacal "dominion over nature." This inner healing, in turn, affects all relationships between the individual and others within the *anima mundi*, as evidenced in this dream. Alchemists such as Gerhard Dorn, in his work "The Speculative Philosophy," referred to this next alchemical stage as *Unus Mundus*, where splits are healed, duality ceases, and the individual, the *vir unus*, unites with the world soul.[18]

Such experiences naturally place our ego consciousness in service to, and partnership with, the mysterious center. Although the psyche is clearly polytheistic, it also has organizing principles and centralizing forces of unity, revealed in dreams such as this dream of the fairy light. Polytheism and the unifying, uniting, centralizing forces of the unconscious are not mutually exclusive but mysteriously coexist.

The central light source was not a light that assimilated the dreamer's consciousness. Instead, it placed her ego consciousness into nature, into relationship with the light and the divine moisture present in each embodiment of nature. Part of the terrible imbalance in the West is this split between ego consciousness and "God." The ego and the *imago Dei*, as a divine force of transformation, have grown so far apart that the dynamic energy linking the two is often nearly unavailable to the ego. This dream is a bridge connecting the dreamer's separate consciousness with the numen and all of nature. Unlike the tendency in traditions of the East, in which the personal Atman is reabsorbed into the source, here the consciousness of the ego has its autonomy *and* a relationship with divinity.[19] Jung said that the secret and goal of alchemy are, in fact, the transcendent function and that, from the series of continuous transformations, a new center of the personality between conscious and unconscious is created, ensuring a new, more solid foundation for the personality.[20] The mystery of all incarnate beings, crowned in individual divinity and yet related to the central divine light, is the fruit of this transcendent function and brings with it the possibilities for the new, dynamic center of personality, with newly found experience in relationship with nature and the world soul.

It seems tremendously meaningful, also, that the crown is of dew. In alchemy, dew is known as both divine water and sulfur water. This double nature links dew to Mercurius, that dynamism of the unconscious that lives in all individuation processes. This quality points to the fact that this state, represented by the crown of dew, is not some fixed place for the dreamer to "hang her hat," so to speak, to identify with in some fixed manner, thereby halting the inherent fluidity of the new transformation process. Instead, the *relationship with* the moist dew of transformation, with the spirit of Mercurius, becomes her crown! Jung points out that this water is also the *ros-marinus,* or sea-dew, dew of grace, *aqua vitae,* or simply, sea. He tells us that it is "the great sea over which the alchemist sailed in his mystic peregrination, guided by the 'heart' of Mercurius in the heavenly North Pole, to which nature herself points with the magnetic compass." It is also, as he points out, the "bath of regeneration," the "spring rain which brings forth the vegetation," and the "*aqua doctrinae.*"[21]

All these allusions present the dew as the substance manifesting via the alchemical work of the dreamer, as a mercurial water that teaches. Our spiritual experience and philosophy must develop together. Only then does integration occur between the archaic levels of psyche and those of consciousness and the mystical dimensions. This is the boon of the religious function, and a gift that individuals give back to the collective unconscious.

The teaching regarding the need to inhabit oneself also seems to come from, and be somehow contained in, the mercurial water of the alchemical processes itself. Thus, it encourages the dreamer to remain close to the psyche in its mysterious, dynamic processes and to inhabit the alchemical changes of personality, body, and soul along the way.

The regeneration of the personality—the rebirth or renewal—is contained in the dynamic water of the dew-crown, in the moisture of divine being—an experience emerging in the processes of change that the totality of the psyche is undergoing.

The dream shows us what Jung meant when he pointed to the alchemical mystery of the light within nature as the *humidum radicale*, the "radical moisture," (*radical* meaning literally "of the root"; interestingly, *humidum* shares its root word with *human*). The dream reveals the light within nature as a mysterious moisture living in the roots of beingness and drawn upward by the feminine mysteries as the "crown of being" for all incarnating creatures. A crown signifies the highest value upheld and honored, so for us human beings, this "highest value," this crown, is our "radical humanity." At the root of our humanity lives this mysterious, radical moisture, the living

Fig. 6. The crown and the philosophical tree. S. Trismosin, Splendor Solis, *London, 16th century. In Alexander Roob,* Alchemy and Mysticism, *p. 309.*

water of renewal that instructs and inspires and is the crown of being. As Jung says, this moisture works like balm—a shining inner light dwelling in the heart of humankind.[22]

The crown at the root base of the philosophical tree appears in the alchemical emblem in figure 6.

The crown represents the divinity arising from the root source in existence that grows into the living wisdom where the worlds of heaven and earth interrelate and unite. Here the soul-nourishing field of synchronicity resides. This is the coming crown of creation, an invitation to an evolving partnership between the human and the divine, between consciousness and the mysteries of creation.

THE STINKING WATERS OF THE DESCENT

Locating the living waters in our lives often requires a descent into darkness and unknowing, into the *prima materia* of what is rotten, what the alchemists called the *putreficatio.* Sometimes the psyche finds what we create in the way we live to be "all rotten." When this is so, we must submit to the fact and allow the reality of the decaying inner situation to penetrate our consciousness.

Alchemists speak of the stinking waters as containing everything necessary for transformation. This is where imagination is "caught," suffers, has a stuck, non-life-giving repetitive fantasy, illness, and so on. The alchemical imagination demands attention and here the gold of soul may emerge. Chances for regressions (fruitful and otherwise) abound when we are in contact with the waters of stagnation. Sometimes contact with these waters also brings panic and fear. In a panic seizure, there is no room for new communications and new experiences (unless, of course, the panic leads to a fruitful break in constricted consciousness). If possible, entering the dire experience consciously while breathing deeply and looking for a window to open in the imagination is usually more desirable.

The inner readiness to meet the larger facets of the psyche in the ways it manifests in our lives is known as the *descent.* Submitting to and even suffering through what is constellated often requires a learned lowering of the threshold of consciousness to attend to and receive the realities of other foci. Ultimately, this lowering leads to a stilling of the mind and the emergence of differentiating faculties, where renewal can find a birthplace.

Facing the soul's inner situation when we are "stuck" can require incredible courage. A successful businessman in his mid-forties, with a 10-year marriage and three children, sought Jungian analysis because he was interested in Jung's ideas and felt "flat" and out of sorts in his life. His initial dream appeared repeatedly—alarmingly enough to eventually penetrate his numb conscious attitude: *I can see a pool of water, like a big pond. The water is stagnant, and I see that I am stuck on the bottom of the pond, lifeless. The dream ends there.*

Fig. 7. The drowning king. "He who saves me will get a tremendous reward."[24] *Michael Maier,* Atalanta Fugiens, *Emblem XXXI, in de Jong,* Michael Maier's *Atalanta Fugiens, p. 407.*

He needed help with a latent depressive condition that left him feeling disconnected and lifeless. He felt as though the spark in him had gone out, that nothing for him was real any longer, not his job, his marriage, or even parenting. His voice was flat, his expression lifeless. The emotional reality and pain of his inner condition had not hit him. He could not see how cut off he was, nor could he "rationalize" why anything should be wrong, because he "had everything." He continued through his demanding routine as an automaton. His face was pale, his demeanor rather ghost- or zombie-like. He "had everything" except what is most essential—himself, his soul, his ability to experience life within himself.

As a blocked feeling type who had learned to distrust his core function of relating with the world inside and around him, learning now to face his deadly predicament meant getting into the experience of the stagnant waters, the *putreficatio* of his inner situation. Who wants to take that as a prescription for getting better? It is difficult to tell someone uninitiated into the ways of the psyche that to get well, he must join with this dream reality—with the person left for dead, voiceless, motionless in stagnant waters.

He did accept and learn to work with the spontaneous reality of the Self as it was appearing in his life. A part of his essence, once alive in childhood and still present somewhere in the core of the divine buried within him, helped him pick up the task. This part, in fact, rejoiced at his newfound courage. As he turned toward his dreams and his inner death, his feelings began to thaw, and the depths of the psyche sent helpers and erotic presences. He dreamed that he and I were sitting facing each other in a deep, green nest. My heart secretly rejoiced, for here the psyche brought the reality of the emerging Eros field to the fore.

The Self was also in these early dreams, crying out for help. Alchemical texts show the drowning king (see figure 7 on page 63) crying out for help: ". . . out of the depths have I cried, and from the abyss of the earth. . . . Attend and see me if any shall find one like unto me, I will give into his hand the morning star."[23]

The morning star, Venus, symbolizes the guiding feminine principle that rises before the light of day to guide the way from darkness to light. The star of love began to rise within his consciousness as he turned toward his hurting soul and the love from the soul turned toward him as well.

The dream world supported him and brought him through the stagnation to a renewed and spirited place in life. The divine in him also revived. He did turn to the drowning king, and instead of drowning, both survived. He eventually changed his work commitments, divorced, and settled into parenthood and his passion for writing music and lyrics. Waters that were stagnant changed as he faced the reality of his depression. The spontaneous imagination took shape amid his suffering and honest, persistent effort with the psyche. The psychopomp (inner guide) arrived in his dreams as he and the life force in him found renewal. The slimy, stagnant waters of the inner world let him emerge from the old shape of his life that was dead, and his descent became an ascent. On the shore of the deadened affect and inner turmoil he learned to face, the ecstatic guide awaited.

Figure 8 on page 65, from *Splendor Solis*, depicts this moment in the transformation. The author, "Trismosin, tells of an angel (a code name for the mercurial components of the *Materia* that can be sublimated) which helps 'a man, black as a Moor,' out of an 'unclean slime' (the putrefied sediment in the retort [the vessel in which the alchemical changes are performed]), clads him in crimson and leads him to heaven. This is an image which shows that spirit and soul 'are freed from the body by being gently boiled' and later guided back to it, whereby the body becomes stable in the 'power of the spirit.'"[25]

Fig. 8. An angel (a code name for the mercurial components of the prima materia*) helps a man out of an 'unclean slime.' From Salomon Trismosin,* Splendor Solis, *London, 16th century. In Roob,* Alchemy and Mysticism, *p. 199.*

In the round of sublimation, which portrays the core of transformation in our lives, the alchemists cooked the old form with the heat from the flame of change, released the spirit from that old form, and joined the freed spirit with the great spirit source. Then they reintroduced renewed essence, renewed consciousness, back into form—a round depicting our renewal processes.

When the dreamer emerged from the stagnant waters, he was taken into relationship with his own unencumbered essence. As he joined in the *sublimatio* with connection to his inner guide source, his experiences grew, like the morning star living in the imagination. This grounded in his daily life, as the *sublimatio* moved into the *rubedo*. His own personality took on depth, wisdom, compassion, and humor, bringing out the personal soul through the healing of early childhood wounds in which he had learned to shut down his feelings, impressions, and inner musings and promptings. After his divorce, he began to help his anima develop in the world of relationship. This inaugurated another difficult part of his journey, for he had to encounter the anima's trying aspects and eventually pull it off of women and own it within. His relationship with this inner guiding spirit was essential to this work.

ON LOVE AND THE WATERS THAT UNITE

The initiatory living waters of the psyche kill, separate, vivify, and reunite. The mysteries of reunification present in the psyche can be profound. The experience of love between two people engaged in the work may accompany such a journey as the spirit of the waters arrives. I would most definitely say that this love is a grace imparted in the work if the bedrock of the opposites is discovered and a new union found. Neither of these are work for the faint-hearted.

A new unity means that love and attraction abound. Hate and repellence also have their vital places in life, of course. I do not see love and hate as opposites; rather, love and apathy are the opposites. Indeed, love's medicine often appears when there is tremendous apathy toward the soul and the opposites are at war.

It is important that love is part of the composition of the waters. If love is *not* part of the process, we might need to start over and go in search of love/Eros and its mysteries. Among the Dogon people of Africa is a creation story that sheds light on the psychological function of the element of water as the unifying force of Eros.

The Dogon have a unique culture with remarkably differentiated Eros at its center. Amma, their creation spirit, unfolds slowly into all of nature and is still incarnating now into his many forms. Amma began to create the world but made a mistake and had to start over. He had created the elements before the world was made but had forgotten to create unity, so water ran off and got lost. Amma had to go in search of water and start creation over again. This time, Amma remembered to create unity. Amma became water itself, living water. For the Dogon, this is the easiest way to find God: Go to the water. Amma also created twins, Nommo the redeemer and Fox the rebel, who are intricately involved in his unfolding creation in the world. One holds light, the other darkness. It is crucial that the two stay related, for if they do not—if they oppose rather than complement each other—the world will fall apart.[26]

Water as unity is like the poetic idea of "love's inclusive sea," which holds all the elements, the opposites (like Nommo and Fox), the warring metals, and all the alchemical unions and incarnating mysteries in which we participate. Although the waters divide, kill, initiate, and revivify, they also bring the new unity of being.

The Dogon creation myth is marvelous alchemical language. The agility and humility of the Dogon creator, who is willing to start creation again in search of water, with an increased intentionality about the necessity of a unity containing all the elements, is a stunning symbol of the ideal role of ego in relation to the Self. *Unity* in this mythology is not a regressive merger or latent ouroboric state, or a static state that one "achieves." It is ongoing, evolving, eternally transformative, creating itself again and again. Perhaps this African myth contains a sacred prescription for renewal of self and relationships today: To participate consciously in these processes, with humility and agility, to start over again, continually and whenever necessary, in search of unity and the lost elements when our life, relationships, or consciousness become one-sided.

It also may point to one of our better active definitions of *love*. It sheds light on the erotic presence of the living waters residing in the bedrock of the human soul. When we run dry, we can rediscover these again and again, like Amma did. Last, it reminds us that, as Jung saw it, the final consummation of the work that binds the opposites is the mystery of love.[27]

4

Tending the Living Waters

If attention is directed to the unconscious, the unconscious will yield up its contents, and these in turn will fructify the conscious like a fountain of living water. For consciousness is just as arid as the unconscious if the two halves of our psychic life are separated. The bath of renewal, the ever-flowing fountain expresses a continual flow of interest toward the unconscious, a kind of constant attention or "religio" which might also be called devotion.
—*C. G. Jung*

Dwelling in the wilderness along a pristine river flowing with the headwaters from the high country snowmelt, there is abundant wildlife: deer, bear, eagles, heron, elk, fox, coyote, badger, antelope. Their nesting, mating, and migratory patterns pivot around wild river-water running through the heart of the wilderness. Without the water source, there is no life; with it, there is abounding life. This is true, as well, for the inner world of soul. An inner flowing source of nourishing "living water" resides here. Like von Franz in the dream described in chapter 3, we can take a nourishing, soul-satisfying drink where, as the alchemists pointed out, there is a "making of the water." This making of the water is the heart of the religious attitude and the fruit of a life lived with the spirit of the imagination. As our devotion to the depths of existence grows, our connection to the flowing source strengthens,

Fig. 9. Alchemical font of changes. Rosarium Philosophorum, *Frankfurt, 1550. In Roob,* Alchemy and Mysticism, *p. 515.*

and our experiences with the "wildlife" gathering in the great human soul increase. Our human place in the family of all beings becomes apparent. When we discover the inner spring of the imagination, we also discover the prospect of becoming a steward of the spring.

The "divine water" of the alchemists wants to flow into each area of our lives. Looking at the mercurial fountain image in figure 9 (above), you can see the four elements, and the star born above the fountain from the circulation process is this fifth, this emanation of wholeness coming from the waters coursing through all the elements. The alchemists depicted this with the circulation processes of the transformative substance making its way through the four elements, the four corners of the Earth. Then, as we are touched by the transforming substance in this circulation process, the quintessence (the unified fifth element), emanates from the wholeness created by the living waters.

The Lovers Appearing at the Font

Earlier I pointed out that Jung found that the final consummation of the work to unite the opposites occurs in the mystery of love. Often the opposites must strengthen in themselves before a true marriage can occur. As we become aware in a relationship of any kind, opposites can attract, war, or polarize; they can dismiss, discount, or diminish each other; or they can differentiate, strengthen, and cohabitate, and of course genuinely marry. Differentiation, development, and strengthening of the elements involved must happen for new unions to take place. The image of the alchemical fountain also shows the moon and sun in relationship with the flowing waters. As we seek these living waters, we see dynamisms between polarities seeking differentiation and renewing unity with each other. Dreams and various constellations in our lives mirror these dynamisms, revealing a map for the passage from one stage of life to the next. The images of yin and yang in our lives and dreams track the making of the divine water within the human personality, for they depict the flow of the Tao, and the differentiation of the opposites and the relationship our consciousness is working out with the opposites in the Tao.

In Jung's work with the *Rosarium Philosophorum* pictures, he discovered that the spirit of the alchemical fountain is the truer, nobler spirit of Mercurius. Mercurius can unite opposites, for he is a "spirit of truth," a *sapientia dei.* Most importantly, as Jung tells us, Mercurius is a spirit who ". . . presses downward into the depths of matter, and whose acquisition is a *donum Spiritus Sancti* [a gift of the Holy Spirit]. He is the spirit who knows the secrets of matter, and to possess him brings illumination."[1]

Mercurius is depicted by the alchemists as being a *duplex spirit,* consisting of both yin and yang, and being a self-fertilizing spirit, as well. When the opposites in our lives find a way to come home to our own inner center and discover new unity, we too discover this self-fertilizing power the alchemists knew. Something new in the Self is born at these times. Alchemy depicts the lovers appearing at the fountain, and in making love, they conceive and birth the *filius*, the child of the new union. This is the new consciousness born in us when the opposites find the lovemaking mystery of unity within us. The ego plays its role of awareness and tolerating and relating to the opposites, and turning to the transcendent for help, for there is where the resolution, the new, continually evolving higher consciousness can be born.

EVOLUTION OF CONSCIOUSNESS REQUIRES CONTACT WITH SPIRIT MERCURIUS

Learning how to live close to the inner spring, the font of the muses, so that we discover a path of unfolding individuation and wholeness, involves for some, learning how to tend to the spirit of the imagination. This means dancing with its presence, with its messages, so that our inner attitudes can change in response, and hence our qualities of relatedness to each area of life. Then the relationship between our self and the divine center becomes alive, and the *coniunctio* can evolve.

This spirit of the imagination ("Mercurius") in alchemy transforms in the hermetic vessel of our lives. The spirit of the imagination takes both baser and nobler forms. When the work is refined, relationship with the nobler spirit strengthens.

The wisdom spirit of Mercurius knows the secrets of matter and can penetrate our "stuck" life situations, renewing our consciousness as it incarnates in us. Curiously, Mercurius is mutable but so strong that it penetrates even the most stuck matter. This is the tremendous mystery that alchemy offers to the human soul.

Mercurius is a spirit of paradox, capable of relating stark opposites and developing an undifferentiated side of consciousness. The bottom line is that in the great experiment of nature, modern human consciousness was bought with a price, and that price is awareness of duality, of opposites. The Adam and Eve myth and other creation stories depict the awakening of human kind from the garden of participation mystique—undifferentiated oneness with creation—to awareness of dualities that differentiate, such as good and bad, self and other, heaven and earth. The "crack between the worlds" we have been speaking of is that liminal space between the opposites. Humankind's evolution of consciousness doesn't stop with fundamentalist thinking and perception of the good and evil as unrelated opposites. Both the Eastern and Western fundamentalist religions, with the concretization of opposites into dogma about how the world is, how God is and so on, have lost the liminal space between the dualities where the mysteries inform life anew.

Renewal of consciousness, connection to the divine, to the transforming nature spirit who works to discover the new levels of consciousness beyond duality, resides in a psychic energy interplay in which we participate. Westerners are moving from participation mystique, the undifferentiated consciousness, to awakening to the opposites and the role of human choice that comes with that awareness.[2] And following that comes illumined consciousness, where the human being experiences relationship with the spirit that lives in the liminal space and helps our consciousness to discover awareness beyond duality.

In the evolution of consciousness, Mercurius's importance is key. The alchemists discovered in Mercurius a presence who embodies the opposites, the dualities, and who is capable, when we work with this presence, of helping us discover new unities, new solutions, new experiences of the marriage between heaven and earth, mortal and immortal, consciousness and nature, and so on. By being in touch with this phenomenon, we can discover new windows to illumined consciousness, and hence a new sense of harmony and peace which we then carry in the world.

In our most difficult dilemmas—mid-life changes, relationship crisis, family troubles, paradigm clashes, faith crises, and so on—the opposites are often warring, polarizing, or discounting and diminishing each other. These times require us to turn to the psyche and psychoid for help in order for the transcendent function to arrive and help us find a new way that is beyond the powers of the ego alone to even envision. Before the new way arrives, the ego's fantasies often have to be killed off, which usually means tremendous pain, dissapointment, sorrow, and detachment. The alchemists depicted this as the time of the ash, when what is "corruptible" or changing is cooked down to dry ash, and the water, the psychic energy, and the feeling goes out of the old way of going. The living waters will lead us to the necessary sacrifices and to the experience of ash in order to bring about the new way. So surrender and the death of ego attitudes or attachments is often individually required in unique ways in the lives of those who live near the inner spring and seek the new way.

The new way will produce the new center of consciousness, the new midpoint between the opposites that contains them so that they may even learn to discover attraction and the mystery of the *coniunctio*, joining. *Coniunctio* is a central mystery of the transcendent function, where the splits between opposites learn to join, and literally create a new center of consciousness that is indestructible and no longer thrown between the opposites. This work is a kind of *yoga*, which shares the same root as "yoke." Yoga in this sense resides at the foundation of the evolution of consciousness that reaches for illumined consciousness where human and divine connect in immediate experience and in ever-renewing unions. And opposites find new relationship, and harmony. A tall claim, yes, but also a reality we discover.

Watching life's constellations, creative endeavors, and dream images depicting yin and yang figures reveals to us the essence of these principles developing within the personality, and coming into the manifest Self. The duplex quality of spirit Mercurius, the spirit of the imagination, brings into view the lovers, the yin/yang principles, and their processes within bring about the eventual yoking, joining of the dualities, so that this illumined consciousness gains ground within our awareness.

When are we making this water that reveals the yin/yang mysteries of the flow of the Tao in our lives? Any time we tend to the nature spirit, the dream spirit, the imagination, and allow it to penetrate us. When we recognize that the dream spirit also inhabits all matter and allow the psyche's flow to reveal itself in all things, we are learning to make this water. Jung said that "psyche is a quality of matter."[3] He also made the powerful observation that "psyche creates reality every day."[4] Each of us on a dream-path can learn to discover daily how to awaken to the inner music inside all creation and to change fluidly in response to the depths that speak to us.

When we become aware of our deep soul-thirst, our inner deserts, our psychic dryness, our flatness of mood, we can cry out and arouse the spirit of the imagination amid our troubles, our stuckness. By creating bridges between conscious and unconscious, we can find sustenance at our unique inner springs, and means for expression or exploration of the discoveries.

Our relationship with these waters brings us the fruit of the yang/yin principles as they (and we) transform. Literally new masculine and feminine presences and principles arise within the soul, bringing conscious life with them.

W. B. Yeats, in his poem "The Song of Wandering Aengus," relates a story an old Irishman told him about a visitation by a young girl, an apparition, leading to these alchemical mysteries of the fruit of the sun and the moon.

> Though I am old with wandering
> Through hollow lands and hilly lands,

I will find out where she has gone,
And kiss her lips and take her hands;
And walk among long dappled grass,
And pluck till time and times are done
The silver apples of the moon,
The golden apples of the sun.[5]

The new principles and presences of being, represented by "the silver apples of the moon" and "the golden apples of the sun," incarnate into our human lives. However, these fruits of yin and yang do not flourish if we remain passive and unconscious. They need our partnering. In Yeats's poem, the speaker holds this union with the soul, or anima presence, as the highest value and places all his longing where eternity unfolds in the mortal sphere—namely, where the fruit of the sun and moon mysteries reside within reach—at the fingertips of the lovers. Union is not projected onto the afterlife. The longing for unity with her and with these fruits drives the old man's consciousness *in this life.* The alchemists, too, were driven by the desire for this union and discovered means toward it. Jung did as well. So, too, can we, through our own committed explorations.

When the divine lovers appear at the inner font, their presence enhances the quality of life, leading to a blossoming and harvesting of soul and spirit in us and around us. Sometimes, in our dreams, the *coniunctio* appears as flowering trees. A friend of mine dreamed, after completing eleven years of arduous and rich analytic training:

> I am in a bed with my lover in the open air of the country, in a meadow off some dirt road. I am writing down some feeling inspiration and snuzzling my lover. We have just made love and are in the afterglow together. I look up to find there are two animals in the bed with us, standing at the foot of the bed, accompanying us. The two unique animals (their species unidentifiable) have dormant fruit tree branches emanating out of their bodies. These branches are now beginning to bud and flower.

Her dream and experience in finishing analytic training mirror the *coniunctio*, yin/yang mysteries the alchemists valued so highly. Here, the fructifying interest in the psyche and soul bring about an eventual maturation of the lovers, a fresh union, and mysterious flowering of new life. A new kind of animal is born in the process, a new singularity particular to the individual.

Fig. 10. Alchemist eating the fruit of the work in arbor of wisdom. Michael Maier, Atalanta Fugiens, *Emblem IX (Oppenheim, 1618). In de Jong,* Michael Maier's *Atalanta Fugiens, p. 385.*

The alchemists had images of these fruits of the coniunctio. As the alchemists depicted it, this fruit comes gradually, entering our lives as we work and live with the spirit of the font, with these changing yang and yin presences manifesting in us and in our relationship with the world around us. Sometimes the alchemists depict the fruit of the moon tree and of the solar tree, and there are also images of eating of the tree of wisdom, the fruit of the *coniunctio*, grown from the work of the alchemist.

WHOLENESS, NOT PERFECTION

The mercurial fountain image in figure 9, page 70, depicts the emanation of wholeness coming from the waters coursing through all the elements.

That is a mystery the waters seek to do with our lives as well over time, and not just in flash moments of insight or breakthrough. No realm, no issue, no element is left out in this kind of wholeness, so clearly an entire life lived with the spirit of the waters supports this process. However, this kind of circulation process of the living waters of the psyche through each area of our lives takes us toward wholeness, not perfection. Living close to the heart of the divine is not about becoming holy or perfect or elevated; it is a process of becoming more fully and deeply human, a growing interrelationship with what the Sufis called the "friend," "guest," or the "inner companion."

Living with this spirit and its journey to wholeness, in fact, is completely different from the ego's fantasies of perfection. Perfection can be a devilish spirit that blocks us and our relationship with these waters. As Jung points out:

> The unconscious is always the fly in the ointment, the skeleton in the cupboard of perfection, the painful lie given to all idealistic pronouncements, the earthliness that clings to our human nature and sadly clouds the crystal clarity we long for. . . . there is no light without shadow, and no psychic wholeness without imperfection. To round itself out, life calls not for perfection but for completeness; and for this the "thorn in the flesh" is needed, the suffering of defects without which there is no progress and no ascent.[6]

Tracking a Few Devils at the Spring

When we deal with Mercurius duplex, in addition to discovering the yin/yang pairings, we deal with the truth spirit and discover what is devilish. The process can teach us to discern subtle, devilish attitudes and stances that must be named and to some degree separated from in order to discover richer contact with Self and the accompanying wholeness.

One of these devils is the ego's fantasy or ideals that it can place on a relationship with the imagination. We looked at the devil of perfection versus the goal of wholeness. Active imaginations (or meditations) that mostly consist of images of people making supplications and confessions are obviously caught in fruitless dynamics. Or the active imaginations can consist of fantastical and wish-fulfillment images of ego heroics or other tones of narcissism or grandiosity. In each of these relationships with the imagination, there is no deep, truly life-sustaining current to keep it active for long. These stand in contrast to the presence of the spirit of truth who penetrates into our fields with experiences and images that lead to freedom of being and fructifying contact with the numinous.

Another devil arises when we try to escape our humanity and disappear into the unconscious, into the spiritual or archetypal realms. Some people get identified with the unconscious before they have become differentiated from these realms. The key word here is *before*, for that identification is usually a stage for people along the way. The yoga or union between the human and divine can happen only if we retain our very human ground, including our foibles and shadow. If we swing between opposites, then we either become possessed by the archetypes or afraid of the psyche's powers, and then keep them locked up, while the ego lives in fear. Neither of these polarities are ultimately life sustaining. But a midpoint can be discovered in which our humanity flourishes and contact with the numinous brings fruit and change to both human and divine. This requires working with the imagination, honing a relationship with the inner companion, and discovering this nobler Mercurius the alchemists knew, while discovering our devils as well.

When we understand, as the alchemists did, that Mercurius is a duplex spirit, numerous windows may open for us. For here we can see that anywhere the opposites are constellating, something of the psyche and of Mercurius is upon us. Development over a lifetime shows a course through the opposites. Perhaps you spend your career with numbers or intricately detailed systems such as computer programming, or data organization, and discover that, as you retire, you want to break free and create, paint, play, or dance in your free time. Mid-life crises are full of tidal shifts between the opposites. Career or partner changes, explored in depth, show the opposites seeking a new unity in the psyche. The goal is to reclaim for the soul the externalized drama of opposites and turn to the transcendent for help. Then the midpoint is discovered that is not either/or, but some solution of both/and present in a singularity inside our self and our life.

Parents often struggle with the different bonds they share with different children. The degree to which positive and negative projections remain unconscious and simply lived out upon the children is the degree to which parents set up painfully destructive patterns with their children. There are innumerable variations on these patterns, but here are a few examples. The child who carries the ego ideal or an anima or animus quality for a parent can either be the favored one or the shunned one. The child who carries a parent's shadow may be avoided by that parent, clashed with continually, or, in some cases, idealized in a soul projection, depending upon the temperament, sex of the child, and other dynamics.

Falling out of love with someone and falling in love with someone else nearly always reveals a tidal shift of the opposites that is externalized. Let's say you are an introverted intuitive type and you are struggling with your mate who is an extraverted sensation type. After the "honey moon" or the dominance of the Eden-like side of the merger experiences are over, opposites will often clash, and you and/or your mate will fall into judging the other's differences. The opposites may war to such a degree that both of you may become quite exhausted. The fruit of the relationship depends often upon both parties discovering the opposite within themselves and working with it there, so as to take the heat of the clash out of the external relationship. Sometimes new love relationships crop up when the heat is at its peak, for triangles will dissipate the clash of the opposites at first. Usually, both people will find another more similar in typology, unconsciously drawn to an island of relief from the clash of these opposites.

Then the degree to which the psychic clash becomes internalized over time is the degree to which the real shift in the Self takes place. Mercurius in the individual has found the other half within, and opposites begin to integrate. From here, the outer partners can best find their ways to go, lovingly. The same is true of the earlier example regarding parents' projections upon their children. The degree to which a parent can face the projection he or she has externalized upon a child (of the shadow or idealized self and so on) is the degree to which Mercurius can help the parent discover his or her other half and come to free the parent-child relationship. This brings integration within the parent and psychic freedom to the child. There are myriad examples, but if you begin to look around, you see the duplex spirit in operation. The other half of issues, ideas, and perspective is carried in all kinds of ways in our lives all day long. And if you look for how the psyche is constellating dualities in life, Mercurius has a better chance of bringing the opposites into a state of eventual peace within the Self. So unconscious splitting of the opposites is one devil that can assume numerous forms.

The alchemists tell us that all kinds of other psychic dangers also accompany tending this spring. Contaminants in our attitude toward the spring and how we handle our relationship to the divine reflect what the alchemists call the "devils in the work." Jung says that the devils are the psychic dangers that get us lost or off track.[7] They block the meaningful flow between our conscious selves and the mysteries in the unconscious, thwarting the religious function. Tracking these devils and *their* transformations is part of the work inherent in tending the spring.

One problem identified by the alchemists is achieving the optimal degree of "fixity" necessary to work with spirit and form, so that contact with spirit is alive and fresh, and the form serves this contact or inspiration of spirit. Think for example of any painting that moved your soul when you first stood in front of the painting. The fact that it could communicate a felt experience to you of some sort reflects that the form and the inspiration married in such a way that the spirit of the piece is alive in the work.

Working with fixity and its dynamics is like learning to walk a razor's edge, for it is ever-changing, and ever-specific to each situation. Wisdom gained with the nuances of fixity applies to all our endeavors in life. Like the duplex nature of Mercurius, we must be mindful of both too much and too little fixity. On the one hand, too much of the wrong kind of fixity, and the spirit is killed. For example, when a mystical religion turns into dogma, the spirit of the inspiration that brings fresh experience and revelation become caught in the wrong kind of fixity, and the immediacy of contact with the numen is killed.

On the other hand, too little fixity, and the spirit may run off, rather than marry into the new constellation of spirit and matter, where the Philosopher's Stone (that union between the *mysterium* and consciousness) is created and brought into the mortal sphere. When there is not enough "fixity" we may fall into escapist behavior, attempting to dissipate the tension of the opposites, thereby not taking enough fixity or form in our lives so as to avoid working out some issue crucial to the success of our individuation. Dissipating, avoiding, repetitive overstimulation, and escaping are key behaviors linked with the alchemical notion of the spirit running off due to a lack of fixity.

Individuation can often entail dealing with some devilish fixity or lack thereof in ourselves or our lives, in order to bring about the birth of the Philosopher's Stone into the human realm. Sometimes the trouble is blatantly visible. Other times it is so subtle that we are unconscious of it in our attitudes and actions, though others may be able to see it.

The Devilish Spell of Concretization

An example of the mythic tension regarding the value of the spring and the danger (or devil) of fixity is dramatized in the classic French movie *Jean de Florette* and its sequel, *Manon of the Spring*. A spring is discovered on a dry hillside in France. Its value to the quality of life there is immeasurable. Without water, nothing can grow, no animals can graze, and no human life can be supported. In a jealous fight over the *ownership* of the spring, one of the men pours concrete into the mouth of the spring. If he could not own it, he would keep it from everyone else. Later, after the devastation of drought, another man digs out the concrete, and the spring flows again, nourishing life.

The character who blocks the spring reflects inner attitudes that dismiss the spring's living autonomy *or* take its presence, communications, inspirations, and images blindly, literally, without dialogue, consideration, and responsibility. Either of these attitudes "pours concrete" over the living water, the life of the imagination.

Our Own Psychic Devilish Fixity and the Dream Spirit's Penetrating Arrows

In honing religious instincts, we cut through the nonessential to the most essential in life. We all know that time, like a "devil in the clock," is a great awakener. When we live in awareness of our mortality, we distinguish where and when to eliminate the nonessential and thus live a more meaningful life.

Being aware of the devil in the clock, we may find that turning toward our own stuck situations is better than expending life energy in unnecessarily crippling patterns. Certain dreams are nature's attempt to bring these stuck areas of our lives to the fore. These dreams often show us the way it will be if we do not discover and stay the course of individuation.

Such dreams may scare us into awakening. By playing out the stuck drama on the inner stage, psyche gets the message past our blind spot or one-sided consciousness.

One example is from a woman who at mid-life had to find a different relationship to the spirit of youth:

> I had taken a left-hand turn at an intersection, whizzing through it pretty quickly, and once I was out the other side, bells went off. So I stopped my car, went back to the intersection and realized my grandmother was in trouble. Sitting in the back of a moving vehicle that had no driver, my grandmother was headed the opposite way I had been going. So in the crossroad, I went to my grandmother, assessed the danger that might occur, and then jumped into the driver's seat of the runaway car, and found a way to stop it just in time. There was talk of how my grandmother's body and last rights ceremony needed to be kept in mind for the future, though she was alive and well now. Some priest-like man

> appeared at the scene and was very happy with me and my awareness of time, death, and the sacred last rites.

This woman found she needed to keep the reality of death and the accompanying awareness of the shortness of time in the fore of her consciousness, and that she would actually live her life differently by doing so. She also had to look into her lack of integration of the "grandmother"—that nurturing inner feminine authority—and how her child-like attitude kept projecting feminine authority outside herself. When she found new ways to stop both of these vehicles—her runaway unconscious child-like attitude, and the projection of feminine authority outside herself—her life began to change. Interestingly here, she learned to take on more fixity of self. For runaway *puella* (girl) or *puer* (boy) dynamics lend themselves to a fear or lack of appropriate fixity, firmness, singularity, and simplicity of the personality. With this integration she became more able to live a unique life in touch with death, time, and the need for more conscious choices. The right kind of fixity arrived and helped her become grounded in her mortality in a soul-enriching manner.

A different example regarding fixity issues comes from a man in his mid-seventies who was painfully stuck in his development in relationships. He found that he was tragically repeating the same old story, now with his fourth wife, of giving over his center by merging and then enacting primitive ways of declaring his separateness. He realized that he was in trouble and wanted to find a new way for the marriage. He hoped to live out his last few decades with his current partner in a marriage that felt good, unlike what he was currently experiencing.

In his stuckness, he was having minimal conversations with his wife, pulling out of decisions about their mutual concerns, and having an affair. Hopeless and completely unimaginative about his situation, he dreamed this:

> The end of the world had come. Alone in a room waiting for the disaster, I found I had a bag of toys that belonged to someone. I put the toys out around the room but didn't play with them. Then I hid under a table. The couple who had the toys came in and put them back in the bag. I hid under the table waiting for the end of the world.

This is one of those shocking dreams that mirrors the dreamer's situation and plays it out on the dream stage so that he can see himself and the direction his current attitude will take him. Hopeless and hiding, he is waiting passively for the "end of the world." The toys in the dream could represent the intermediary space of imagination where he could play and imagine into the situation, getting a sense of his psychic constellation or story. However, the dreamer's passivity and hopelessness leave him hiding, unable to play or imagine. He is clearly stuck in trouble. In this helpless attitude, fear of the "end of the world" gains strength.

The dream also shows that the dream ego experiences the couple as owning the imagination, the toys, the intermediary space. The ego doesn't have enough ownership of the parts involved in the coupling to take responsibility and make changes. Like a frightened child, the ego is powerless and hides in fear. This dream not only portrays his early life drama of being overwhelmed and powerless but also shows how he is playing out that story in the now. The oedipal triangle of childhood continues between the all-powerful couple and the child, and the adult dream ego is the child. The drastic crisis this stuck dynamic precipitates is magnified in the dream. If the dreamer allows his conscious awareness to be penetrated by the unconscious—a most energetically economical proposition, because any other road will lead back to this stuck dynamic—he might, with objectivity gained, discover grace and the road to freedom. Otherwise, his scared, passive, childish, unimaginative, and powerless attitude will bring on the devastation, which will then "change the world" (most likely, another divorce, another primitive means to change his painful situation utterly but temporarily).

The dreamer, in time, did discover that when he fell into hopelessness about his situation with his wife, he was falling into a frightened-child side of himself, a stubborn, rather autistic side with no ability to imagine, play, or discover his part of what was going on. He discovered a piece of himself that needed real watching or it could send off the bombs that would end a marriage he hoped to redeem.

At times, psyche's messages hit the mark like an expert archer's arrows. When we become stuck in a life-robbing pattern because our conscious attitude is off the mark, the unconscious helps us, through the penetrating spirit of Mercurius, to discover ourselves and find freedom again, to avert the dynamics that can literally diminish or even ruin parts of our lives. Then dreams may come to startle us out of our complacency or blindness. With the help of these dreams, we gain insight into our own nature and learn to separate and individuate from contents of the unconscious that may fuel destructive patterns. These patterns may change as well.

Another woman, in her fifties, experienced a painful dynamic with her loved ones in which they would elicit her involvement yet not respond as she had hoped they would. She was continually shown, by psyche, what her life would be like if she continued to allow this painful dynamic to assume the throne of control over her consciousness. The dream spirit illustrated where the destructive energy would lead, namely, to a decimation of all she held most valuable in life. Through the shock and pain of these images, she awakened.

Her journey also brought her a dream indicating the right "arena" for this flow of energy, imaging a male horse teacher and a riding arena! She was a horse lover who had not ridden for ten years. The dream "arena" did not refer only to literal horse riding, however. It was a call back to herself and her creativity. She had many creative impulses and instincts to ride, and this arena was the place for her to engage with her essence.

She had the courage to release several social commitments that had become churning arenas for anxiety and demonic compulsivity. She re-engaged with her literary and photographic essays of Native American cultures and became closer to her own inner *hieros gamos*, inner love affair and unity. She took that great managerial energy into a medium where it had room to run and she could follow her interests and passions. Wonderfully, it also freed up her relationship fields. At one point, she dreamed the following:

> I left a crowd of people, to whom I had social obligations, at a church. Instead, I went with my husband to Paris. Roaming the streets lit up in the dark, we found a tree and carved our initials in it. Later, when we returned to the church, we found the gathering had done okay without us.

The *coniunctio* of her inner masculine lover and herself—their ability to leave the collective and discover their "tree"—is like the image of the shaman who discovers her or his own shamanic world tree. In shamanic traditions, the tree represents the life force's connection with the mysteries, and through it the shaman travels up to the heavens and down into the regions beneath the earth to communicate with the gods individually. The *coniunctio* of the male and female initials on their tree in a "city of romance and the arts," as she put it, shows her hard work in separating from the inner and outer collective. Her conscious participation with the dream spirit is what made all the difference. She took in its outlook on her old life and opened to its guidance into her new life, channeling the energy into creativity. This willingness brought her into the center of her creative flow, where the life force's individuality is alive, where dynamic receptive dimensions of being find a new unity.

Having served in active ways in her church for her entire life, this woman discovered the next step in the dream's last image. She had gone her own way to discover the *hieros gamos*, and then returned to the collective (the church) with this new unity. How the collective (inside and out) will receive her newly found creative union is the next mystery.

For a time her journey in the dream world literally frightened her awake with images of destruction. In response to these shocking dreams and visions, we must avoid dropping into a concretistic fixity. When we give away power to such images, we may fall into thinking that there is nothing we can do. We render ourselves useless, and darkness takes hold.

Disturbing dreams and visions are to be respected, for they are a shocking form of grace from the nature spirit. Their value can be immeasurable. Most importantly, our response to these dreams—when the inner heart awakens to a deeper truth—is important to the nature spirit. By our staying the course with the call of individuation, the nature spirit also finds fulfillment.

Devils of Calcified Ideas

Whenever we think that we know something, we risk limiting our contact with the numinous. Calcified ideas, which we all risk creating about the mysteries, keep us from fresh contact with psyche and those very mysteries. The dream spirit addresses this attitude of all-knowingness, if we pay attention. One woman, a psychologist, entered an analysis and was fighting the depths of the process with her intellectualizations. In the night, she awoke in awe. She reports this:

> I heard the dream voice echoing the dream as I awoke. The presence of a feminine elvin being with immense feminine authority, like nothing I have ever known, spoke in a low command, or more like a growl, "Old man, OLD MAN! Lay that tired theory to rest. Get it out of your hands. Let it go. Let it go!! For with it you attempt to choke out all the dimensions of reality you actually seek."

This feminine being addressed the stodgy masculine presence in her consciousness, the part of her that thinks it knows the ways things are and agrees with collectively accepted realities about the nature of life. Suddenly, she felt free in the experience of this autonomous feminine being. In active imagination, she learned to live in relationship with this inner being, her

Fig. 11. Saturn cooking in the alchemical waters, and dove appearing. S. Trismosin, Splendor Solis, *London, 16th century. In Roob,* Alchemy and Mysticism, *p. 198.*

guide. The feminine authority far surpassed the old man's strength. There was no question that this old man was history. The numinous within her formed the transcendent bridge that enabled the dreamer to pass over the domination of the old ruling spirit.

Regarding the release of the known, the Saturn-based collective teachings, we may discover again and again that not everything occurring in the psyche and psychoid is in compensatory relationship to our personal wound, personality pathology, or interpersonal healing. Sometimes spirits choose us to witness them. They gather, and we are part of these constellations in less personal or less involved ways.

Any masculine spirit in us that thinks it "knows how it is" can become the fixed, dominating thought form that kills experiential connection with the *numinosum*. Unaddressed, these introjected, autonomous, collective opinions and attitudes of dominant culture kill the most precious gift Jung pointed to—a felt, instinctual living relationship with the spirit of the imagination. The value of this pearl of great price is incalculable. It is the discovery of the highest value itself, for it is reverence for the Tao, the mysteries. It opens the way of discovering and rediscovering our true unfolding place in the family of the universe.

Let's identify the old fart where we can. Let him soak. Free a spirit! When the dry, deadened, leaden consciousness reigns, the inner divine lovers do not stand a chance of finding each other. If they do, they tend to polarize or war, not unite. The alchemists knew this imperative well. The classic image in figure 11 (page 86) shows the old man, the old king—the desiccated, outworn, old consciousness in each of us—soaking in the alchemical hot bath. A new spirit emerges out of his cracked-open head.

The dream voice of the feminine authority who can "stick it" to old Saturn is profound. Who is this presence? Interestingly, the dream voice is an elvin feminine being of immense authority. The elvin quality points us to a nature spirit dwelling in the heart of the forest, the heart of the wilderness, connected to magic. The elvin folk are said to have refused to choose good over evil when the Christian era began. They do not live in the split fields of consciousness but reside where nature and spirit remain dynamically related. The arrival of elvin consciousness heralds these strata of the psyche. Here, in the dream, nature's feminine authority is speaking. Here yin has awakened in the dreamer's psyche with ancient authority, a life-assisting presence of the feminine principle has awakened the dreamer's consciousness. This yin presence is stronger and more ancient than the old man, the saturnine influences in the dreamer's consciousness and in the collective consciousness.

The power of the dream spirit to address modern consciousness so that it can evolve in relationship with the mysteries opens the dreamer's psyche to presences beyond fixed thought forms. "Let it go, let it go!" the feminine presence commands. This authority is the *nature* of the psyche's core. Experience of this numinous spirit brings reverence and freedom of being.

When the Waters of the Inner Spring "Fix" or Freeze

Saturn's leaden shadow is also known to be psychically *cold.* He is known as Old Man Winter, the Grim Reaper with his scythe, the "devil in the clock," Mr. Reality, or the Tax Man. This Saturn archetype is Mercury's polarity, and they can be seen as two halves of each other as well, which also points to the important interchange between fixity and mutability in our alchemical endeavors and processes of change.

In his positive aspects, Saturn is the great differentiator, the wise man, lead that turns to gold. Life, however, is full of trouble and difficulty and provides many opportunities to experience the backside of this archetype. Life sometimes requires that we face something impossible. Confronted with the "impossible cold" (the death of a child, complete loss of meaningful work, loss of a lover, and so on), our hearts may shut down to the flow of life, sometimes even freeze, and our courage in love and life recedes. We may become stilted, guarded, and suspicious. Then the inner lovers connected to the source do not reach out for each other, and their psychic and physical lives become endangered. In this state, outer love relationships often have no chance either. The space that love and compassion are meant to occupy is taken instead by a critical spirit of one-sided judgment, negativity, and unconscious fear. The following poem looks into the coldness of Saturn's effects on love relationship. And with human warmth the poet calls to the spirit of movement and renewed love.

If I Could Wake the Dead

If I could wake the dead
I would wander down beside our home
along the riverbed
and there among the wintry heads
of the wild rose and pine
raise the bruised birds
up from beneath the ice
those birds of surprise

who once sang so gaily from our hearth
we gathered our lives
a nest around their song
of wild abandon to love, to life.

I would call up Spring Herself
who'd melt the tomb of winter's way—
cold ghosts upon the young lovers' brows
whose cursed visitations froze
the daring music and the courage.
And so
awaken the kernel from the sheath,
a rousing and greening dream. . .

The birds of love
would return with their own song.
And musing through the heart
and veins of our ripe age
the throaty trills
of the their hatching young
would warm
and fill this house.[8]

The courage to face the "cold impossible" (as W. H. Auden called it)—experiences that are so horrendous, we are not sure that we will survive or that we even want to survive—takes us to the door of the psyche and psychoid for renewal and recovery. We regain soul by seeing the painful place in life where we stand. This helps the human element to recover, for it brings objectivity and compassion to a humanity that suffers so.

Here the poet's voice inhabits both the terrible tragedy of frozen love and the seemingly impossible wish for recovery. Curiously, something of a spark thus begins to recover. The inspired *human* feeling function revives! All is not lost, for consciousness can look into, feel, and express the coldness and pain and regain a hint of warmth. Here, the human heart helps the Saturn archetype (the tomb of winter's way) to loosen its tragic grip on love.

In the dream of the elvin woman, there is no comparison of power, and that is the whole point. The elvin presence is more primal, more powerful. She dissipates the old man's authority with her very presence. "He" is put into context. We humans, however, often experience Saturn's chilly shadow as deadly. When we do not come in contact with this living numinous core of the psyche, which can move the situation, life can become dangerously stuck or frozen.

In this poem, we find another means of dealing with old man Saturn and his accompanying cold and calcified consciousness. The human heart, living within its limitations, brings the hints of transformation to his chilly spirit. The power of the simple human gesture shows itself. In the face of the impossible, speaking from human experience, *within* human limits, moves the heart of a stuck, frozen, life-denying situation, through sheer honest feeling. The poet discovers the human authority that can honestly say how bad it is at a human level. In turn, from these limitations, the poet longs to call up "Spring Herself," who could melt this spell. The poet calls up the archetypal field of spring, and by the end of the poem, the rousing and greening dream of spring seems possible, without denying the human suffering of the frozen state of love.

This is a fine line to walk—being present with the human point of view and the archetypal fields as we tend the life of the spring. Only when our human point of view is strong and honest can we penetrate the barrier between the divine and ourselves. Thus does the energetic pattern change, the transcendent function of the psyche activate, and grace enter the mortal sphere. The psychic waters may thaw, flow, enliven and nourish once again, away from Saturn's cold, fearful, critical shadow.

MERCURIUS AS THE INVALUABLE INNER JACKASS

> From the land of the dispossessed,
> bring me a donkey with Byzantine eyes.
> —Lisel Mueller, "Spell for a Traveler"

In the wilderness of the psyche, many presences, in their spirit and animal forms, are drawn to and live near the flowing spring of image, vision, energetics, and voice that resides in the alchemical imagination. The psyche brings the specific light in nature, the specific constellating presences, into our field of awareness, sometimes in flesh-and-blood form.

While traveling through Ireland once, I spent time at a holy well. While the local people were making their offerings and praying, the voice of a jackass came braying across the fields. Welling up with laughter, I had to take the long way around the shrine so as not to disturb others, for the voice of the well's water seemed to be that of the jackass, relentlessly demanding attention. I went over to the fence and communed with the animal a while, fed him some banana bread, and had a laugh. Here was Mercurius in his jackass form! Ah ha! Here, too, I thought, is the voice of the fountain. When I returned to the States, I

Fig. 12. Mercurius in the flesh. Ass looking over a rock wall in Ireland, photograph by Liam Blake, copyright © 2002.

put a photograph of the jackass on my office wall, to keep the light of nature in this animal form close at hand. I thought, "You never know when you're going to need to see and honor the inner jackass while tending the inner spring." Musing on Mercurius in this form got me to thinking, which led to reading and more laughter. Here are some of my discoveries of mythic images revealing the psychic patterns surrounding the invaluable jackass side of Mercurius, including material from historical religious communal life, and from individual lives related to these patterns as well.

TRICKSTER NATURE AND RELIGIOUS FORM IN COMMUNITY

Each archetype has its shadow, which can be balanced by an archetype that sits in polarity to it. For example, the Saturn archetype, which creates forms in our lives and can lead to wisdom, is also known as the god of lead, and lead has its shadow manifestations, its own attitudinal toxicities. "Lead poisoning" occurs in us when Saturn takes over our individual inner climate. Depression, despair, or rigid old attitudes or leaden qualities that forbid the flow of love, vision and movement are key signatures that this archetype has a foothold. One antidote to Saturn's lead poisoning is the arrival of the god's polar opposite, Mercurius, specifically through Mercurius's medicine of humor, his trickster and jackass role. This nature is often called up when Saturn's seriousness is overtaking our attitude toward life. There are also ritual mythic images that reveal how the trickster Mercurius lightens Saturn's lead poisoning.

The images of the Heyoka dancers of the Pueblo Indians of New Mexico, as well as those of the ancient Roman "Saturnalia," invoke this Mercurial antidote. The Heyokas fulfill a dual role of tending the form of the ceremonial dances and simultaneously making fun of the form. The bodies of the Heyoka dancers are painted in black and white stripes, and they carry two horn shapes on their heads (reminiscent of mythic renditions of the devil). They tend the shape of the dance, keeping the dancers "in line," and they tease, mirror, and make fun of both participants and spectators.

Likewise, the express purpose of the ancient Roman Saturnalia festivals was to make fun of the sacred forms and provide relief from the predominating religious solemnity. The people enacted mock Masses, with priests often dressed as women and riding donkeys into the churches. Rather than chant "amen" during the mock services, the congregation members would all sing "Heeehaaaw," like jackasses! The slaves would go free, and the masters would serve them. A child would sit where the priest usually convened the Mass, and instead of communion hosts, they ate a frosting mixture of sugar and fat. One could say that the god Dionysus got his foot in the door in this ritual.

Both of these examples show a healing communal context for this archetypal pattern. Where are our Heyoka dancers, our Saturnalias? What would it look like if we were to imagine ceremony based on making fun of our forms and foibles? Perhaps by playing with images of the path ascending, descending, appearing, and disappearing, or by cavorting with (or denying the existence of) the phantoms, demons, and daemons, or playing with, making fun of, our "sins"—the ways in which we all can be (somewhere along the way) real one-sided jackasses. There is some fun and play to be had, a freeing of spirit and potential gain in our human ground of being via trickster humor.

Whenever we become leaden, the spirit of the imagination, say the alchemists, is of supreme importance in uncovering an antidote. As in the myth of Gnosticism, spirit trapped in matter needs help. It needs to be freed through alchemical processes (that is, our attention to the imaginal realms) and its natural fluidity in the dance between matter/form and spirit restored. Mercurius is this god of change, tricks, and surprises, of imagination itself, and the wily god of humor. He keeps us close to the primitive, the chthonic, the animal realm (which remains a part of us all), and reminds us that, without humor and ownership of these sides of self, we can become possessed by the primitive shadow.

This alchemical trickster god appears in the fabric of our lives spontaneously, sometimes with shocking humor, and may often leave no stone unturned in order to reveal the paradoxical nature of the life force flowing through us. If we block the libido of our lives, we block this god's very essence. He doesn't seem to like it much, and as the spirit in nature, he may respond in kind. He may manifest in his jackass nature and may even enjoy making a jackass out of us! It's all in fun and a larger spirit of truth and freedom, *if* we learn to find a place for his shifty, sometimes raw or bawdy, jackass nature. When we learn to live in relationship with the wholeness present in paradoxical nature, including the ways in which we can be real jackasses, a "pain in the ass" to others, we keep the jackass nature—our raw, primitive, or unpleasing sides—upfront, near to, even integrated with, the persona.

The Ass: the Ordinary and Lowly Nature as Carrier of the God

Sometimes the ass is representative of sacred, lowly energy necessary to carry the god. In the Christian myth, Jesus appears on Palm Sunday riding a donkey, and Mary rides on a donkey to the stable where she gives birth to Jesus among the animals. The donkey, one of the lowliest of animals, is also, paradoxically, the perfect carrier for birth of the divine. The sensual, lowly instincts in the soul are necessary for birth amid the truly human domains of life, as lowly as the manger scene itself.

Genuine spirit of the ordinary is seen in the ass. The ass brings alive the mediating between human and divine precisely because it brings the ordinary or modest into view. When the modest or ordinary is present, then by contrast the opposite, the divine, constellates. You cannot have one without the other, and if the ordinary is abandoned, then inflation results, and no true union between human and divine can occur. In fact, the presence of the ass also plays with the manifestations of the ordinary and of the divine *not* as opposites. This leads us to the flame of the Greek goddess of modesty, Hestia, whose sacred animal was the ass.

Hestia—virgin goddess of the hearth, the keeper of the flame—loved the ass above all animals, and it was one of her helper spirits. For example, in the mythic pattern the braying ass lets Hestia know the lusty god Priapus, who plans to assault her, has broken into the temple.

Psychologically Hestia represents the value of the inner flame of awareness, the warmth of inner being, and the virginal qualities required for individuation—remaining true to oneself. She also lights the hearth flame in home life, and is the warmth that gathers people together, an eros flame of community life.[9] Her presence in relationships helps bring *humanity* alive, and stands in great contrast to the false self constellations which can keep people from experiencing their humanity and true exchanges in a spirit of love.

Hestia tends the sacred flame also present in the ordinary, and penetration of her spirit that resides in sympathy with the ass occurs when we encounter the divinity of modesty, the beauty of measuredness and simplicity. The religious function in the psyche can initiate us via experience with her presence and the ass, and usually it involves a shedding of the layers of false self that stand in the way of genuine being.

Looking further into the pattern of the ass in association with Hestia, or Vesta as she was called among the Romans, the vestal virgins carried on the work of Vesta/Hestia at the sacred temples, and celebrated the ass on their feast day. On this day, they would relieve the local miller's asses from work, and deck these asses with garlands and bread and lead them to the goddess Vesta/Hestia at the temple.[10] The elevating to divine status of the humble and at times devalued beast of burden who is all too easy to take for granted is part of the magic of this archetypal pattern. This beast of burden represents all the ordinary, important, humble instincts and properties of daily life that carry us along. The vestal virgins elevate these qualities to their proper divinity. Psychologically this changes the split of opposites between ordinary and divine, soul and spirit, lower and upper, and so on.

When this is happening in our lives, what we dismiss as ordinary suddenly reveals its miraculousness. That anything exists at all is the great miracle; that the many realms of existence, the many worlds, hold together and inform each other is a miracle operating continually in infinite ways. And when we see again with these eyes into the "ordinary," we are like the vestal virgins bringing along the sacred ass on the way to honor the goddess.

The miracles of life could be found in the unexpected presence of depth in a child's eyes, or in the beauty of your lover's skin in the firelight. Or it can be found in raptures with creatures in the natural world, such as when snorkeling you experience the miracle of a school of fish swimming in such tight unison that each is like a flick or a word teeming in god's thought stream.

Kabir, the 12th-century mystic poet from India, speaks to this mystery.

> Are you looking for me? I am in the next seat.
> My shoulder is against yours.
> You will not find me in stupas, not in Indian shrine rooms, nor in synagogue, nor in cathedrals:
> not in masses, nor kirtans, not in legs winding around your own neck, nor in eating nothing but vegetables.
> When you really look for me, you will see me instantly—
> you will find me in the tiniest house of time. . . ."[11]

This kind of perspective shift, the recognition of the divine in the "tiniest house of time," is related to the pattern of Hestia and the sacred jackass.

The Ass God in Dream

When the ass appears in dreams, looking into the particular essence of the appearance of the ass helps reveal the message and meaning. Is the lowly ass drawing you toward genuine modest ground of being where the divine is born, through its Byzantine eyes? Is the bawdy jackass revealing the backside of things by ushering in contact with shadow and a freeing of energy? Is the god Mercurius revealing his royal tricky presence? The nature of the ass is complex, and so the specific details and felt experience of the manifestation is of utmost importance to understand what side of the ass is communicating to you.

Here is a dream image of the ass god from a woman, who after a deep, 10-year analysis was getting ready to complete her work with her female analyst. I heard this dream ten years ago, and it stuck in my imagination with remarkable clarity, for the ass god here visits in uncanny form:

> I see I am at a huge intersection and there is a large quilt of mine that I made with my grandmothers that is covering the intersection. I am surprised by the quilt, and yet it is also mine, it feels like me, and has all my work and attention in it. I am instructed to gather the quilt together and get ready to leave. In picking up the ends of the quilt I cross over one corner of the intersection and see that my analyst is there seated on a throne and she is a donkey or jackass sitting upright on the chair. This donkey/jackass is somehow also a god! He has really interesting, long donkey fur with a curious, riveting texture, and it gets my attention. He is incredibly intelligent and tricky, to be respected. He is also sitting there upright, looking at me. He has his back ass-legs crossed, and his front legs touching the arms of the chair like a person. I acknowledge him and go to finish gathering up this quilt.

The ass appearing on the throne suggests this is a god, and the dreamer's experience felt him to be a god as well. The crossroad of the dreamer's life in completing an analysis entails both needing to gather what had been created—this quilt—and entails seeing into the divinity that had been present with the two of them in the work, the god embodied in the dream by the analyst.

First of all, gathering the grandmothers' quilt is a rich reflection of the soul of the feminine work, the stitching and creating aspect that generates something four-cornered that was made with the elder feminine ones. This imagery points to the co-creation of the Self with assistance of the ancestors, the wise counsel of the feminine, who obviously visited this work. Outerwardly, this woman has quilts her great grandmother hand made out of leftover fabrics that tell the stories of all the kinds of clothes patterns the family wore at the time she made them—in the 1930's. She cherishes these quilts as part of her feminine heritage. So, in a way, the psyche seems to be encouraging her, that she has been engaging in the equivalent in her own lifetime via her soul work and has generated experience of the divine feminine. The size of the quilt and the four directions being touched by the four corners of the quilt suggest this is the latent Self being made manifest.

Now, why does the ass god appear as the analyst also? On one level, the image of the analyst/ass god could be seen as the dreamer's own inner analyst who emanates this god, Mercurius. And on another level, it may herald some changes occurring for her psychically and in the relationship with her analyst. For the image in part points to the divinity discovered in the transference, and the discovery of the god of the work, a divinity this analyst has carried. We must consider that the analyst herself does embody and reflect this god to some degree. And this kind of work does also call up this god—Mercurius—when we follow the way of the dream.

Since Mercurius is in his ass nature in this dream, it may indicate the tricky shift the dreamer had yet to work out in herself at this difficult crossroad. When the Self and a god are discovered in the relational field that occurs in analysis, the road ahead is not an easy one. Crossroads are notoriously liminal places. In mythology, shamanism, and dreams, the god is often encountered at crossroads. In Roman and Greek mythology, Hermes/Mercurius is the god of the crossroads (as is Hecate the goddess of crossroads). Hermes is also called the lord of roads. And when you think about your life of individuation as a path, it is easy to see how this god is also the god of individuation. For he is present at all times of change, where choices and decisions are made, where a new path appears for you to walk, and the old, beloved path with certain adventures and experiences must be left behind.

In a way, this intersection can be thought of as a mirror of her life intersecting with this analyst and this work, and the god behind the work. Psychologically, with presence of the four directions and the quilt with four corners spread across the four ways, the intersection is a tremendous symbol of wholeness. In shamanic work, one always prays to the four directions to orient oneself with the four-fold path. The crossroad, according to Black Elk, a visionary medicine man, tells us that in the Native American Oglala tradition, the road from south to north is the enlightenment road, and the road from east to west is the human road of life experience, full of trials and tribulations.[12] The intersection of these roads is the making of a human being in touch with the spirit, the intersection itself mirrors the location of the incarnating and individuating personality.

Crossroads also entail changes, decisions, new direction. Here in the dream the intersection is a meeting with the god, and an integration of the work; the quilt is being taken up from the crossroad, separated from the intersection. Owning the quilt, stooping down to the ground and gathering it together corner by corner, picking it up off the crossroads and encountering the god of the crossroad, is an interesting image. We could think of it as both an acknowledgement of the god and analyst and separating from the constellation of the analyst and god as one. Life's timely crossroads bring her along in her individuation to another stage, one of separating and integrating.

Sometimes, in such deep work, the analyst's role includes tolerating the carrying of the projection of the Self, the divine, until the person can take it inside and carry it him- or herself. Sometimes the encounter also requires both people tolerating the fate of the Self *not* being carried by the analyst, because the frustration of that experience can also lead to new discoveries in human relationships and new integration of the Self. Both experiences are often crucial in individuation. When consciously engaged, both kinds of tolerance are equal acts of love on the part of the analyst. Both experiences are challenging to the analysand, who—if she or he goes fully through the cycle of integration—will discover equal gratitude for both experiences, and equal appreciation of those who meet her or him in both sides of this work.

So, watching for Mercurius, the god of change, in the work helps us meet these key moments of change. Here Mercurius, with his shocking appearance as the ass god analyst, is an awakener, and marks the moment, the constellation as it has been and as it begins to change.

King Midas's Fatal Flaw: An Inability to Own the Inner Jackass

A Greek myth illuminates the archetype of the jackass image, shedding light on the medicine of humor and the inner jackass.[13] When we joke that folks made jackasses out of themselves, we are, in effect, referring to the fact that their "backside" was showing. That is, their shadow, their ridiculous, stupid nature appeared somehow and made itself known. Now, when this jackass side can be received and welcomed home, nothing is lost by letting some of it show. In fact, something is often gained as a person opens to its appearance and works to integrate the energy and meaning of what constellates.

The Greek myth about King Midas shows us a poor mortal who fell into desperate trouble because he could *not* allow his jackass nature to express itself. His plight reminds us to invite the spirit Mercurius in as jackass when we need a raw, spontaneous reminder of the largeness of life and our funny humanity, which can be along the way also one-sided and ridiculous. When the jackass is allowed to show up, we regain our humor and balance, along with a greater humanity.

One day, the satyr Silenius, who taught the god Dionysus the art of ecstasy and rebirth, got a little too drunk and found himself tangled up in King Midas's favorite rose bush. The king helped untangle him and brought him inside. After five days of listening to Silenius talk about his travels to lands where tall, happy, long-lived mortals inhabited wonderful cities, King Midas let Silenius go his way. Dionysus was so grateful to the mortal King Midas for helping his teacher that Dionysus ordered Silenius to grant the king a wish. The king asked to be able to transform whatever he touched into gold. The gift backfired when King Midas accidentally turned his daughter into a statue, and because food and drink turned to gold as well, he nearly died of hunger and thirst. Dionysus, looking in on this ridiculous plight laughed loudly at the king, and then gestured for him to go to the river Pactolus and wash off the "gift." Dionysus then returned Midas' daughter to human life.

Later on in King Midas's life, a mortal, Marsyas, had challenged the god Apollo to a musical contest, and Apollo ordered the nine Muses and King Midas to act as judges. All the Muses voted for Apollo, but King Midas challenged the god, telling him that playing his instrument while upside down was unfair to Marsyas. Apollo then sent an arrow through Marsyas's heart for even challenging the god to the contest in the first place. Apollo gave the poor mortal's skin to the satyrs for making drums. Then he called King Midas an ass, and touched his ears, which sprouted up, long and hairy like a donkey's. King Midas was so upset about having jackass ears, he begged the Muses not to talk about it.

King Midas covered his ears with a cap, but he had to show his barber the secret. The barber promised not to tell, but he couldn't keep the secret to himself, so he went out into the woods and whispered into a hole, "King Midas has jackass ears." He then filled the hole, but the reeds heard, and they told the birds. Now, Melampus, a man who understood bird language, heard what had befallen Midas. He told his friends, and soon the secret was out about King Midas's ears. The king, refusing to remove his cap and show his jackass ears to his people, killed Melampus and then himself.

Poor King Midas. He gets called in the dance with hubris a number of times and survives the first encounter, but loses his sense of humor and humility in the second, and thus becomes possessed by destruction, and is destroyed by his own hand. The satyr, the teacher in the art of ecstasy, getting tangled up in his rose bush is a marvelous image of the fate of the encounter, for Midas's rose bush, an image of Midas's divine core, brings him into contact with this teacher. Midas's fate is to free this teacher, and to find right relationship with the arts of ecstasy and rebirth, which, with Dionysus's help, he begins to accomplish. The laughter and grace granted him helps redeem him. When he encounters Apollo, however, in this round with hubris another pattern emerges. Judgment and having to deal with his jackass nature ensues. Losing his sense of humor and his ability to tolerate being part jackass for a while, he loses his way toward redemption, and loses his life as well.

Midas's story, an enlightening mythologem, reveals a few archetypal patterns of hubris. For the trick is hubris is also human, so we humans may well have to explore the border between what is good for the gods and what is good for the human being. In fact, maybe this exploration of what is good for the gods and what is good for the human being is something even noble about human beings, as Edward Edinger once stated.[14] King Midas's story can help us in the exploration of hubris, for his story contacts both sides, both redemption and a vision of what it means to deny life its humorous mirroring of our jackass nature. With this denial, we also deny the spirit of life itself; like King Midas, we can kill off our own redemption and essence.

If the ego, like King Midas, is overly seduced by stories (from the "satyr," the trainer in the art of ecstasy and rebirth) of a land far away where everything is "better," the worlds of the ordinary and the ecstatic may split. This split is a sign that we have a journey to take and work to do with the spirit of the imagination in order to return to life with more integration between the human and divine, ordinary and nonordinary states of reality, and our daily lives and the divine core where renewal abounds. King Midas's story shows us how the ego fantasy can get caught up in a wrong-footed connection to inner alchemy. The ego's fantasy of what "gold" is—what the ego thinks is valuable because it offers an escape from life as it is—can actually ruin life. The false value of what "matters" (materialism) can render everything completely untouchable.

A common, classic, or mundane example of valuing the wrong thing, of materialism's shadow enacted in life, appears in people who think that money (literal gold) is the key to happiness and who set off after financial success, only to create a lifestyle that enslaves them in the pursuit, protection, and management of money. Meanwhile, their marriage dies, their children become strangers, and their inner spirit gains nothing. For most of us, there are countless examples of the ego's fantasy trying to run off with the show of our life, run off with our relationship to the mysteries, thus spoiling the life it boasts that it can improve. This can be incredibly subtle, too, in all the "supposed to" thoughts that run through our minds like TV commericials of perfectly happy consumers. These prevent us from being soulfully present to *what is*.

Our resistance to accepting life and love, and self and others *as they are* and working with *these* manifestations in conjunction with the spiritual dimensions of life, lead us into denial of the life force, the spirit in nature, as we incarnate. If we put these fantasies on the world around us, like King Midas, we "freeze-frame" everything. The lovely, young spirit of the feminine—the core essence of existence uniquely trying to come to life in each person—is then "statuefied" by the ego's projections of the good life, the fair life, the powerful life, and so on. The true dream of life comes from a deeper source. The ego, with all its presuppositions, needs to remain in contact with whichever aspect of the nature spirit is dreaming us and seeking to fulfill itself in our lives.

The myth mirrors to us that this active force, this god of rebirth alive in the psyche, allows the hero in us who has gone awry on this path to "rinse off" this trouble in the river of life.

King Midas finds his way out of the problem of living in a world of ego fantasy that leaves him starving to death and unable to touch anything. He is released by the god of ecstasy and rebirth, *who laughs at him*. Dionysius's laughter at the human king who takes the wish for power and ecstasy into his own ego fantasy is marvelous. We, too, gain human ground if we tune in to the laughter in the depths, where this god/archetype of ecstasy sees our folly and sends us on down to the river of life for a wash.

Rinsing there, we also gain perspective on how we have been handling things with the wrong "hands," the wrong attitude—taking life issues into our hands in a way that does not serve life. Perhaps the valuing function has been asleep, and we are unconscious of our deepest value and how that value is affecting the shape and spirit, the mood, of our life. Until we get into trouble by freezing life with a vision of no worth and we become bereft, we may not awaken to the deeper value and discover alchemical gold.

Life is full of trouble, and Midas, a truly *human* character, ends up in even more trouble after he finds his way out of the trouble with gold. Caught in hubris again, this time with temperamental Apollo, Midas supports the human who challenges the god of the Muses. This in itself is interesting, because we humans, via contact with the muses—inspiration and creativity—come in close contact with the god of the muses.

So, Midas's fate yet again brings him into an exploration of the relationship between the mortal and divine spheres. Apollo, in a rather nasty mood, turns Midas's ears into those of a jackass, to punish him for the hubris of challenging a god.

At this point in the story, it is not that Midas's relationship to the god or even his standing up for the human being who challenged the god was wrong or fatal to him. He still could have found redemption by accepting the fate of his jackass ears. If he could have taken on the humor and humility of his jackass side—owning that he had a fate of learning to discern the music of the spheres (distinguishing the divine from the mortals, and discovering relationship there as well)—then perhaps forgiveness, transformation, and renewed relationship with the gods would have come again. His inability to laugh at himself, to own his jackass nature, drives him to reject life, in homicide and suicide. His inability to *own* his process of complicated relationship between the human and divine brings him down in the end.

Killing the messenger (Melampus), who could hear the spirit of nature and understand its language, is a telling part of the mythologem. In the image of Melampus, who had *ears* to hear the spirit of nature and the truth that the king was part jackass, we see the possibility of a new union, a transformation. The proud King cannot let in this wisdom, though. And like King Midas, if we reject the spirit of nature telling us the truth—that we are part jackass somehow—then we are apt to go awry.

The spirit in nature knows, and it informs us. Dreams, active imaginations, felt experiences of our "off-ness," all are intimations of the nature spirit trying to tell us when we have fallen into the trap of an ego fantasy that "looks like gold" but is killing off the nourishment from relationship with life as it actually is. When we identify with the soul's inner music so much that we forget our human place in relationship with the gods, the nature spirit will tell us. Life loses its ability to touch us, and we it. The vulnerability of our humanity is the key to relationship with the mysteries. Losing our mortal status also means losing dialogue with the divine.

To befriend the inner jackass nature is to enjoy the freedom of the fool—the inner fool who can discover fresh means to make *foolish gestures*, which the gods seem to love and honor. These foolish gestures help to free the life force and even redirect the energies of the divine and human into a dancing connection (sometimes by honoring the complete disconnection and making fun of it).

If we cannot let in the message of the spirit of nature, we may become rigid and then painfully, hopelessly stuck. When Saturn's leaden spirit takes over, our spirits deaden—not a pretty picture, and hell to live. When Saturn's shadow takes us to the place of no imagination, no play, no humor, and no movement, the jackass brings us humor. Immediately our perspective changes, stirring new movement in our inner lives. Without humor about our own shadow aspects, we encounter difficulties that affect our connection with and participation in the mysteries of life. For example, Saturn can get a foothold in us when we cling to values of power, reputation, and status—values that the modern ego may be seduced into worshiping. As a result, we drop anchor in a static identity. Saturn's seductions also often involve a rigidity of character and disbelief in our ability to change or become more flexible and human. When a person has constructed a rigid protection of self around his or her wound, it often indicates the presence of Saturn's shadow and the need for Mercurius to come with his tricks and eventual penetration of truth. The other side of the coin happens when Hermes-ruled individuals hide out in identification with Hermes-Mercurius and refuse Saturn his due. A loss of soul then results from living without Saturn and human limitation.

Learning how to refine the religious attitude requires developing the ears to hear what psyche is telling us. Being brave enough, courageous enough, open enough to take in psyche's message, no matter how scathing, keeps us from getting stuck for too long in Saturn's molten lead. Observing the ego's wiles as it attempts to push away psyche's message, distort it, deflect it, helps us appreciate our own humanity and detach from the ego defenses that could block dialogue with the divine. From the tale of King Midas it becomes clear that owning the ways in which we can sport the ears of a jackass and laugh in the honesty of it would be more redemptive than refusing to bear the reflection of our state.

Religious Conscience and the IBD

Developing a live connection to the religious function requires honing our inner responses, instincts, and movements to reflect receptivity toward the invisible realms, toward the stirring of the Self. In part, it requires the ability to notice and respond to the deep and subtle feeling related to the nuances of the inner world, which in turn requires growing an attitude of inner devotion and a "religious conscience" infused with the spirit of humor. As we have seen with King Midas, without humor, we are dead in the water, so to speak!

Religious conscience is an IBD—an inner bullshit detector—that we turn toward our own foibles and odd shadow nature, not just toward the outer world. It is the ego's ability to humble itself before realities, both light and dark, that are larger than it and to discover a role for itself in relationship with the psyche and psychoid that is neither inflated nor deflated but that assists in the inner marriage. An IBD is like a refined wolf instinct that can sniff out what is off in us. This instinct is linked to the constellations of the wild feminine, like Artemis, perhaps, whose throne of silver has a wolf skin on it. Fresh instinct connected to the spirit of the font helps us discover the IBD. As we listen at the inner font, it awakens our instincts, our conscience, our inner bullshit detector. In such contact with the spirit of the font, we discover that keeping a nose truly on our own *prima materia* (on our own shit, to be quite graphic), leads in fact to the soul-filled life, to the true gold of the alchemists. The religious conscience that unfolds from the work is a deep part of the alchemical Stone's nature, and awakens instincts and subtle perceptions to the way of shadow and soul that were not previously linked to conscious life.

Once we detect the scent of the raw state of the matter, of the *prima materia* as it may be manifesting in our lives, we can then own up to and detach from the ego's infantile wishes and perceptions, self-aggrandizement, laziness, or whatever our ego tricks are, whatever our shadow machinations may be, or whatever our complexes may be up to. Energy between the divine center and ordinary consciousness is freed in this way, and more vitality, connection, and life force abound.

This process is mirrored in a horse I have whose name is Shan. He is a black Arabian with a wily personality. He has earned his Irish name, Shenanigans, for all the many tricky maneuvers he used in his youth to outpower and intimidate his rider. He was amazingly energetic about all his outfoxing, outhorsing. The first time I rode him, twenty years ago, he tried to roll in a river with me on his back, knock me off with low tree branches, and so on. His former wiliness is like the unbridled shadow and unworked complexes that just want to "do their own thing." As we know, these wiles are often autonomous and can be surprisingly enduring. To develop a "religious conscience," however, is to experience the incredible energy gained by submitting to a more differentiated center of consciousness. We naturally convert to the new way over time, for differentiated consciousness is energy-economical and the old way is not. When we get in sync with the Self (that is, the horse and rider and horse trainer!) and work to ride the energy of the personality, we find that the "horse" learns to direct all that great energy, all the impulses and instincts, into a flowing gait. Reaching this harmonious point takes incredible time and patience and no end of honesty. As with training a horse and rider, what would this work be if *love* were not at the core?

When our IBD is activated, (that is, the red light is bleeping and the alarm wailing), it is helpful to see into the way in which we are suffering and to discern which element of nature is having difficulty incarnating.

(*Suffer* means to "carry from below.") Keeping an eye on what of the divine is struggling to incarnate assists us in taking our foibles and troubles less personally. Then the larger spiritual frame around the things we carry from below is honored. After all, two parties are involved: humanity and divinity. They are attempting a marriage amid the ways we suffer. If the ego can see where it is off track and how it can help, the unbridled beast has a chance to become a riding partner on the path of life.

An amusing parallel notion in Sufism states that all the work with the *Nafs*, the personality or lower soul, is undertaken so that "one can ride one's horse more swiftly to the divine."[15] Dialogue with the unconscious, and living life close to the divine, leads to discoveries of the dynamic relationship between spirit and form, between love and transformation in our lives. An alchemical union is the higher aim of this dialogue. Spiritual practice in which we court these dimensions of the heart leads us to the inner marriage, the *hieros gamos*, where ego and Self come into relationship and the archetypes find a new harmonious unity, a new coherence, around the center. Keeping an eye on this goal prevents us from unconsciously accepting false gods for too long. The false gods brought to us via the prolonged, unbridled, and unconscious wiles of our shadow, self-deception, and ego-centeredness are no substitute for the union with the divine that is possible.

The Sufis write that "god epiphanizes himself to each of us in the forms of what we love."[16] What we love and attend to brings the epiphanizing god into our view and increases the potential for the union. Invitations to open to the renewing forces of the unconscious abound in our lives and inhabit everything we truly love. The following is an example of this love and union, offered as advice from a trainer to a horsewoman. The rider was striving for unity with a new, sensitive horse who was highly refined, trained much beyond the expertise of the rider, and who had a powerful spirit. The trainer precisely targets the uniting of presence/essence and focus/attention during a lesson:

> You cannot shut your horse down when you are scared. That imprisoning way sets her up to think you are the predator, whom she must escape to survive. You must stay present and have the courage to use *whatever energy comes up* and work with it. Give form to the energy she puts forth very specifically at those times. Make it a dance. Get back in contact with her via your seat and legs. Inhabit yourself. Breathe! Then you will tell her in a language she can understand that you are there for her. Send that wild energy she gives to you up to your supple hands, not a fearful prison. The bit she will then respect, and she will give, relax, and dance.

> Only then will she create a union with you. It is this union, this dance, you are after.[17]

Devotion to what we love and appreciation of the union we seek opens our eyes and hearts to the the infinite in our lives. The humbling or submitting of our will, wiles, designs, or perceptions to the larger dance, the union with the Self and all the psychic direction it offers, is the cornerstone of an inner religious life. Without a honed religious conscience and without a religious attitude about the value of what is transforming amid our suffering, there is no possibility of creating a conscious, relational, and *sustainable* bridge toward the infinite, into the mysteries. This union, the *hieros gamos* mystery, brings the unification of opposites and the incarnation of Self into our lives.

Relationships of all kinds are remarkable mirrors for our work with the inner bullshit detector. The degree to which we can keep our nose in our own *prima materia* when the "shit hits the fan" in our relationships is, in my mind, the degree to which union with the Self in the individual personality is taking place. If we achieve union with the Self in solitude but cannot find or hold that in relationship with all life, we are not yet sufficiently connected to the flow of the universe. Furthermore, the degree to which we unconsciously dump our personal issues onto others and hold them responsible for our unworked stuff, is the degree to which we are asleep, choosing infantilism and the backdoor to the unconscious. Untangling our devils from those of our loved ones produces incredible differentiation of Self and is often required in life. Allowing relationship dynamics to be part of the force that compels our attention and startles us back to the truth of who we are serves individuation and the formation of an individually honed IBD.

Conscious sacrifice of the old way, out of devotion to the forces of renewal, creates a place, a crèche, for the birth of the new life even when we cannot see the way ahead. True humility, reverence for the mystery, acknowledgment of the wiles of shadow, acceptance that the ego will always require reining in and realignment with the center in new ways, and an abiding love of the soul, all are fruits of a life lived close to the unconscious. The development and refinement of our IBD, a religious conscience active at the core of our life that our ego learns to help build, trust, and even enjoy is the gold developed from the *prima materia*. *Prima materia*, the shit, the alchemists say, is available everywhere. The alchemists' gold is neither a lofty nor unattainable gold. The possibilities for the creation of gold are everywhere—in daily life and in our dreams, the unfolding work offers itself to us.

The dream spirit is unfailingly honest. It continually brings in images of our changing states of being and helps us see the *unconscious* qualities of where we stand. How loving the dream/nature spirit is to give us the help each night to recenter ourselves in our humanity, in sync with the universe.

During a lecture in Holland on this topic, I brought out the idea of the IBD, and the group had a good laugh. That night at a special dinner, the trickster god arrived. We all began making jokes about the IBD. As we stepped outside under the starry sky, a "new" couple—who had just taken a great risk in their lives by revealing to everyone present that they had fallen in love—stepped together into a huge pile of shit which was unusual in those immaculate streets. The dear, shy analyst who had just stepped into the shit raised his finger in the air and, with wonderful humanity, said, "Ah, a bit of synchronicity." Terrific laughter ensued. The compassion among the group grew immensely from this analyst's agile "stepping" in Mercurius's tricky dance. For the entire plane ride home, I laughed with them and with Mercurius about the *prima materia* we *all* land in, and how love too seems to go in step with this alchemical work.

Looking for the Invaluable Inner Jackass and Decoding Saturn's Lead

If we lapse into patterns or repression in our relationships, old Saturn trudges into our midst and threatens to take over the house. Mercury, on the other hand, brings us fluidity, the spirit of spontaneity, the way of imagination. When we become stuck in lifeless patterns, we need the spirit of the imagination to free the energy and restore movement so that the life force can flow again. On the other hand, if we have a connection to imagination but no ability to give form to it or ground it in healthy, life-giving ways in our daily lives, we need Saturn.

The alchemists described the antidote to each of these imbalances: On one hand, they sought to free spirit trapped in form, unite it with the Source, and return it, renewed, back into form, reinfusing matter with new life. On the other hand, they sought to take something imaginal and fix it (imaged in alchemy as arrows penetrating into something) so that it could be worked with and fully incarnated, transforming in the process.

A couple seeking marriage counseling came in with the following dream:

> The three of us are meeting in your office, and we each placed our own egg into the center. A Celtic knot appears, and it is the spirit of the raven and a bottle of wine at the same time. The lead is pulled off the top of the bottle. The cork is pulled out. It is clear that we now have to look into the lead and decode it. There are glyphs appearing in the lead. This is the way to a new wine.

This seemed difficult, yet hopeful, and "decoding lead" sounded like a good prescription for the work. The image of the lead seal as carrying images to be decoded is profound. It is the old alchemical prescription—the hermetic seal of the contained vessel has caught a spirit in the vessel (the relationship and its dynamics) that needs to be transformed. The imprints in the hermetic seal that need to be decoded suggest that the archetypal imprints, images, and dynamics present in what is leaden or stuck need to be explored and understood. What patterns, archetypes, images appear in the suffering each person experiences in the relational field? This work with what has become fixed, rote, or unconscious in the relationship could lead to awareness of the shadow and the creation of a new spirit, a new wine, a new relational inspiration, renewed love. The decoding for this couple was no simple task (and only a beginning), but nonetheless a *nigredo* with a promise, for the images of imagination emerged. The medicinal levity of humor was not long in following.

Musing on this valuable, Mercurial "spirit of the well," I was reminded of when a friend of mine divorced her husband and the "old jackass," Mercurius, came to visit. She left her marriage when a tidal wave of change hit her life. Emotionally, she was in a nasty snare, feeling mortally wounded and utterly victimized upon learning that her husband had begun a relationship with her best friend. Understandably, it took her quite a while before she could feel anything but rage and pain. She found the boundary stone, Saturn, to be of incredible help in her recovery, and she avoided communication with her ex for some time. One morning, on their anniversary, while her inner eye was focused on healing herself and recovering memories of her love for and experiences with this man, she dreamed: *I was talking to my ex-husband on the phone and looking at the ass of a horse. I surprisingly said to him, "Oh, I see. I finally see now what an ass I, also, have been," and we laughed.* When she awoke, she decided to call him and tell him this. The humorous image of the ass broke the cold war with shared laughter and great relief on both their parts—a little help from Mercurius in his inner jackass form.

Nowhere is this medicine more immediate, vitally necessary, and real than in our relational lives, for relationships continually mirror our inner states, with their effects on the spirit of the connection. Common and true wisdom tells us that the one key in relationship is to be able to own when we are off, when we are caught in something or bringing in difficulty that is altering the climate of love. Happily, nothing clears the climate for love like owning the inner jackass upfront, authentically. The spirit of nature, in all its spontaneity, provides humorous, sudden, even shocking insight into the ridiculousness of our shadow, which alchemically releases our sticky, leaden qualities into the flow of life. God knows the tending of the spring of the imagination is tricky territory, and there is no way to learn to tend this spring without getting to know the backside of archetypes and ourselves.

Hail, Melampus, whose ears hear the spirit in nature and who lets us know when the old jackass form of Mercurius is trying to give us back our humanity and humor!

The alchemical journey is about living a full human life close to the heart of the divine. That is no easy task, and no completely peaceful place to dwell. As the inner alchemical Stone gets built, though, we do find the place in us that is peaceful, beyond the "corruptible" changing emotions or feeling states, the opposites at work in our lives, and all the rest in life that is in constant flux. The alchemical rounds in our lives that go through the darkening, the whitening, the reddening lead to this new inner union, where our capacity for resolving the opposites increases as we daily seek fresh experience with the numinous. Here we can discover the partnership between human and divine.

In the following dream example, that partnership is discovered. This dream is from a man in his fifties with a deep, long history of inner work. At one point in the journey he was working out his relationship with the divine and discovering differentiation between his human role, and the role for the divine. It is natural to confuse those along the way, and dreams often will help bring in the new differentiation. Here is the dream:

> I am walking along the sea with a few friends on a trail. The trail comes to a large stone, and the path just stops. I wonder, what am I supposed to do? I put my foot up alongside the stone, wondering about stepping up around the right side of the stone, and going then further down the coast line I have been traveling. But as I do, I look down and see the sea to my right and realize that is too high and I don't want to tempt the fates and fall into the sea. So I ask my friends for help, and they help me step to the bottom of the stone. Once there, my feet move on ground that is shifting. There are different centuries in time that are opening up in the ground beneath my feet. It astonishes me. The cracks in the ground reveal the soul of the sixth century, the sixteenth, and so on. I

> reach across the stone upward and cry out! A hand of an angel comes from the top of the stone and reaches back to me. Our right arms clasp around each other's wrists in a solid embrace, our left arms and hands reach out across the stone. We are both layed out across the stone now, me from below, and the angel from above. The feel of the stone against my whole body, and the feel of the angel's grip on me, and me on the angel feels unprecedented in my life, a solidity I cannot describe.
>
> I wake up from the dream and hear my inner voice exclaiming "angel of god" in awe and recognition of who it is that grabbed my hand from above across the stone.

The alchemical work leads to a discovery of the joint process, the two who engage in the creation of the alchemical Stone, the creation of the manifest Self. The immediacy of the feel of the stone and the hand of the angel are exquisitely brought to life in this dream. And the discovery of this solidity comes to the dreamer as he nearly explores the danger of inflation, and finds instead his human ground of being numinously fluid and connected to the soul of humankind through the ages. He stands on the work of many people through the ages who have contributed to the discovery of the alchemical work that leads to this partnership with the angel of god.

Without discovery of the partner from the celestial realms who would assist him in life, he would have charged ahead willfully and risked inflation and falling from inflation into the chaos once again. With this partnership discovered, his true path is discovered. This is reminiscent of the alchemical wisdom that sees Sophia, the guide of souls, as the spirit of the Stone, here appearing to guide this dreamer to his true path, and that is connection in the partnership with the inner companion, the ally.

The full-out body sprawl across the stone to reach for the celestial companion's hand that is his next step is quite moving. Now *that* is contact, full-bodied, dependent contact. He could not go another step along his life path in any other direction but into partnership with the celestial companion who is the partner in the creation of the Philosopher's Stone. It is delightfully clear. The dream announces he needs this immediate, real, honest and full-bodied contact to find his way. And the dream brings experience to the dreamer of that contact. The active imagination world opened for him with the inner companion, the ally, and his creative work served to ground the contact with joy and discovery

And just so—it is possible.

5

Alchemical Patterns of Initiation: Sun-Moon Mysteries

Close the language door,
and open the love-window
The moon won't use the door,
only the window.
—Rumi

The moon uses the "love-window," not the language door, and can breathe into us with passion and mystery. This mysterious inner moon announces to us the presence of a plane of consciousness distinct from rational processes—a plane where image, felt presence, and symbol are ciphers of the mystery.

The alchemists tell us that the "creature of rebirth processes" is a lunar creature. Without the appearance of the lunar mysteries, the solar rebirth—the renewal of consciousness—cannot take place. The term "*lunar consciousness*" comes from alchemical texts in which the moon is related to the soul, to the "radical moisture" of the *prima materia*. "Radical moisture" refers to the very essence of the root of being as it lives in all things. It is used here to specify the connection with Yin, the feminine mysterious consciousness that rules the dark half of our diurnal consciousness, beyond the ego. Importantly, the terms "yin" and "feminine" are not gender specifications. All men and women live with yin and yang principles in all areas of their lives and personalities.

THE HUMAN HAND AMID THE MYSTERIES

Standing at the ancient well beneath Chartres Cathedral, on the old Druidic holy site, you will discover the image in figure 13 (page 113). If you look up at the ceiling as you step from the well through the passage way toward the crypt where the oak-leaf crowned Madonna-and-Child statue is housed, you will discover this image of the sun, moon, stars, and the human hand painted in the rounded limestone arch. A numinous feeling accompanies this image. The human hand reaches into the vast night sky, has its place among the sun and moon and stars. Alchemical initiatory patterns alive in the human soul today reveal to us these sun-moon mysteries and their accompanying development of illumined consciousness.

The relationship between yang and yin, the masculine and feminine principles within us, is transformed as we tend the inner spring, just as the flux of yin and yang is in constant flow in all of creation. Like the alchemical image of the font, the opposites, represented in the sun and moon, appear as we approach the inner spring. We discover warring opposites, or dissociation, or eventual new union, and sometimes each of these. The opposites, or polarities, require relationship with each other in human fields of awareness. Our conscious participation at the spring makes all the difference. We must lend our own hand, so to speak, to usher in the discoveries and new union.

The human hand amid the marvels of the vast psyche, seen mirrored in the night sky, makes all the difference. But discovering the human hand, the right attitude and handling that can touch and create with the sun and moon mysteries is half of the alchemical undertaking. This handling, this attitude of relating and holding the mysteries of life refines infinitely over our lifetimes. This chapter will explore the development of human contact with the sun-moon mysteries, and development of the human hand and attitude.

Jung found the *abaisement niveau*—the lowering of the threshold of consciousness—to be both dangerous and central to the process of contacting mysteries that exist beyond the ego.[1] Many of us would agree that Jung made the monumental discoveries he did because he had the courage to live close to the chaotic and to grope in his own darkness. The ego will often have to work to grow, to stretch, to find contact with the source, and to grow wiser in order to go into the dark and learn to individuate. We then begin to create a center of consciousness that is not the light of the ego alone, nor of the raw *mysterium* alone, but a new meeting point between the two, encompassing more than either alone. The new center is continually born

Fig. 13. Sun, moon, stars, and human hand, from the crypt ceiling at Chartres Cathedral, France. Photograph courtesy of Melina Leodas-Whelan, copyright 2002.

from the dialogue between the ego and the *mysterium* of the unconscious. This dialogue feeds the new center; without the dialogue, this vital center recedes from contact with consciousness.

The heart of the religious function, the crowning point of the alchemical imagination, aims at the creation and sustenance of a new center, between human and divine, within the individual. This work begins to discover the midpoint between sun and moon, between solar and lunar consciousness, and therefore links us with the primordial night and the mysteries of the inner moon. Regarding solar and lunar consciousness, Jung points out:

> Luna is really the mother of the sun, which means, psychologically, that the unconscious is pregnant with consciousness and gives birth to it. It is the night, which is older than the day:
>
> > Part of the darkness which gave birth to light
> > that proud light which is struggling to usurp
> > the rank and realm of Mother night. (Goethe, *Faust*, trans. by
> > MacNeice, p. 48)
>
> [Moonlight] does not show up objects in all their pitiless discreteness and separateness, like the harsh glaring light of day, but blends in a deceptive shimmer the near and the far, magically transforming little things into big, high into low, softening all color into a bluish haze and blending nocturnal landscape into an unsuspected unity.[2]

In the *Rosarium* pictures (at the beginning of chapter 4), the sun and moon appear above the flowing waters of the font. Later in that series, the sun and moon are personified and go through their stages toward unity. There is no incarnating *hieros gamos* without the sun and moon and the polarities they represent coming into the human psyche. One-sided consciousness is so deadly because it prevents the formation and unification of the polarities within the personality from giving way to the *hieros gamos*, the high note in the life of the human soul.

APOLLO AND ARTEMIS BEFORE THE UNION

The opposites need to form first, and they frequently struggle or even war before uniting. They often have to strengthen in their own right before uniting with their opposite. One important pairing of the sun and moon at the font, depicted by the alchemists, expresses this sparring tension and the yin and yang learning to strengthen in their own right. The sibling deities, Artemis the moon goddess and Apollo the sun god, reveal archetypal patterns of yin and yang that exist *a priori*—before and underneath the divine lovers who join in the deeper *coniunctio*. These instinctual patterns often lay the foundation for the incarnating *coniunctio* mysteries, individually and collectively. We look specifically to the brother-sister pair, Apollo and Artemis, to witness the sun and moon mysteries in their dynamic *pre-coupling* state.

The archetypal constellations represented in Apollo and Artemis bring out the vitality of the masculine and feminine coming into their own, in relationship but not as lovers. Instead, the incest taboo and the explorations around it in the myth of this archetypal brother-sister/sun-moon pair bring alive the creative pre-*hieros gamos* union of the masculine and feminine principles. Their mythic plights shed light on our own progress toward the sacred union. Their core vitality and dangerous pitfalls reveal signposts for our journeys toward the divine union at the spring. Importantly, certain experiences in dreamtime bring in guides who promote the inner development, restoration, and refortification of solar and lunar vitality within the soul and personality.

Many love relationships, same-sex and heterosexual couplings, and friendships have a few informing roots in the Artemis/Apollo archetypes. The process of coming into distinct individuality can be served by becoming *conscious* of the brother-sister patterns of teasing, competing, supporting, denying, and mirroring each other but also pushing off each other psychologically to explore the radical individuality that has nothing to do with the other. These relationship patterns reveal the sun and moon in us, calling to the individual for inner recognition and rebirth. Often these dynamics constellate where Self is still forming. Here, the manifest Self that is unique within—the "orphan stone" of the alchemists—is not fortified enough to take us out of the sibling patterns in outer relationships. The ability to tolerate and enjoy differences between self and other is the fruit of these dynamics brought to consciousness and can lead to rich, meaningful connections.

Solid presence and identity are present in this archetypal pattern between Apollo and Artemis as they learn to push off into their own distinct soul and spirit landscapes. Separating out from sibling dynamics in relationships, we help the outer love relationships to mature, making deeper unities possible.

On a collective level, modern humankind appears to be encapsulated in this pre-*coniunctio* consciousness. The solar ego is still trying to discover its autonomy in relationship to the rest of the mysteries while also integrating the shadow that consciousness casts on the world soul. The lunar power of the feminine is still emerging in her own totality, yet to be respected. These dimensions of being remain unaccepted manifestations, awaiting integration in the fields of modern consciousness.

The Sun God's Shadow at the Font

The Greek myth of the Pythian priestesses and their plight with Apollo sheds light on a few archetypal patterns in the development of consciousness and where we stand now as a collective with the changing god image. During the pre-Hellenic and Hellenic periods, the Pythian priestesses served the spirit of the oracle at the spring in Delphi. Sitting on the tripod at the edge of a great crevice, they would achieve ecstatic trance states and receive images, smells, and messages from the spring and the great python snake living in the crevice. Then they would deliver their images, experiences, and messages to those who sought their help.

Greek mythology tells us that Apollo and his priests took over the site, killed the great snake, and co-opted the crevice, the spring, and the oracle. Apollo declared himself lord of the oracle and began the Pythian games at Delphi. Legend has it that as Apollo slew the python guardian of the oracle, the oracular power died, and ultimately, so did its use. During the time Apollo's priests seized control of the oracle, they took the messages and delivered their own interpretations. The priests changed the puzzling "pythia" messages into enigmatic verses that suited their socio-political aims.

Eventually, Apollo became lord of several oracles in Greece and Rome. With the collective cultural overtaking of the sites, the oracular images and messages were appropriated for political purposes, obscuring the original spirit and visions.

Apollo's domination of the oracle is a myth of our time. Modern ego consciousness is split off from the natural world and the psychic realms. Like Apollo, the sun god of rationality, our collective consciousness kills the spirit—the oracular source living in the human soul, which also connects us with the psychoid—that would assist us in healing our world.

Looking further into this parallel, certain helpful mythologems appear. Apollo represents a complex archetypal pattern of spirit and instinct. As a god, he not only rules the sciences but is also the lord of music and resides among the muses. His adolescent pattern is alluded to in that he never wholeheartedly couples with a goddess, although he pursues many. Some run, some turn into trees to get away from him, and so on. However, he is successful at tricking nymphs and others to his bed.

Apollo has a curious side in mythology, depicted also as an adept of the occult arts crossing the ocean on a tripod. He is not thought of as a god of ecstasy, as is Dionysus, but his music and love of the muses reflect his attraction to realms of creativity, soul, and the ecstatic. His attempts to establish life-giving relationship with these realms seem to abound in stories of Apollo, as in his relationship with the Pythian priestesses at the Delphic oracle. The *shadow side* of this god (and the corresponding psychological equivalent, that similar shadow of modern ego consciousness) exerts domination over nature and the psyche that leads to a costly, destructive end when unmediated. When we fall into this attitude—Apollo's shadow side—we are left with a deadened world, devoid of the numen. The actual spirit lives on, of course, but we can split off from creation and the nature spirit that brings visions and helps us connect with the objective psyche and the celestial counterpart. In effect, then, "God is dead." When the numinous and other layers of reality beyond the ego are repressed, they may reappear in dark manifestations in life, such as warring, illness, and depression.

This pattern and its trouble are also present in the collective development of consciousness. The emergence of the ego is new, evolutionarily speaking. Alienation from the healing, informing, original presence in the soul is the shadowy cost of modern collective consciousness. The mythic pattern of Apollo shows how obliterating the ego's autonomy can be in its assertions of I-ness. Our task is to *remember* our intimate interconnection with creation at all levels—the seen and unseen. Perhaps Apollo's slaying of the python reflects a step in the development of the ego. The heroic attitude discovers that it can slay the "primal monster" in order to act out of distinct and separate volition.[3] However, this precise mythology is seeking its next developmental step in human consciousness, individually and collectively. Can we learn to partner with this spirit of transformation and imagination rather than slay it or co-opt its messages and images?

Because the nature spirit represented in the python guides each soul uniquely from within and requires that we attend to its life, as well as our own as it evolves in the manifest world with our development, it is dependent upon us, and we upon it. Without Snake, the world becomes lifeless, and we can become hopelessly stuck, collectively and individually. Living with Snake, we have the chance to find new marriages, new interminglings, ever-new unities among us, human and divine.

The myth of the sun god Apollo mirrors psychologically how difficult it is for modern consciousness to discover a union with the nature spirit, because humankind's consciousness has evolved over the centuries in a direction of separation and differentiation. The problem is that living too separately from this spirit causes further splitting of the worlds, which in turn causes more pain and alienation for modern consciousness, as it does for the nature spirit living in the world soul.

We know that opposites attract. However, when opposites get close, they can also destroy each other. Approaching the *coniunctio* can be dangerous. For example, in a psychosis, when the moon destroys the sun, or in the launching of a tremendous ego defense against the unconscious, when the sun discounts the moon. If the solar and lunar principles find a way through the destructive potentialities with each other, they may discover a *coniunctio*. When the *coniunctio* happens, something of the divine Self is born and made manifest. In dreams, this new unity is often depicted as a special child being born, a golden child, or green child, and so on. Sometimes a new being is born who embodies both opposites, where before the opposites were unrelated.

Sun-Moon Rebirth Pattern in Myth, Dream, and Waking Life

What do alchemy and mythology tell us about the renewal of Apollo, the sun god, our consciousness? The sun god's submission to the processes of change, dissolution, and renewal is depicted in the alchemical imagery in figure 14 (page 118). Apollo bathes in a deeper renewal when his sister, Artemis, gets ahold of him. Artemis, the moon goddess who dwells in the heart of the forest, aims her arrow at the sun god's neck to assist him in his alchemical death and rebirth.

Fig. 14. The moon goddess aims an arrow into the sun god Apollo. In Fabricius, Alchemy, *p. 179.*

Artemis (Diana in Roman mythology) is a prototype for the emissaries of the lunar terrain who assist consciousness in the processes of renewal. As an archetypal mythic pattern, Artemis reveals many mythologems about lunar landscape within the soul.

Artemis's lunar arrow takes hold of consciousness when new instincts try to emerge in our lives. This emergence requires an initial death of the ego. When energy that has been fixed in consciousness needs to descend, dissolve, and detach, these arrows appear in life. The arrow in the neck is an interesting image. Linking mind to body, the neck represents the flow between consciousness and instinct. A death arrow is aimed specifically at the connection between spirit and matter. The lunar reality of yin, with her dark and light phases, her "corruptibility," her changeability, delivers new energy that kills off the old adaptation no longer serving the flow of life. The old way of living, loving, or relating gives way to a new constellation, a new midpoint between spirit and matter.

Suffering the arrow and integrating the emerging instinct are vital and remarkably *individual* tasks. Can we recognize our diurnal nature *and* the presence in the darkness that is asking us to change? Recognition of what has penetrated our old way of life in the descent can allow the mysterious renewal to reveal itself.

Certainly this terrain is not easy to negotiate. Sometimes crises are born of the dark primitive feminine—illness, physical pain, depression, marriage or work problems. Consider the following ancient hymn to the moon goddess:

> I sing of burning Artemis of the golden arrows, the adored Virgin, the Archeress who with one shot strikes the stag, the true sister of Apollo of the golden sceptre, she who, on the shadowy mountains and the wind-swept peaks, draws her bow of pure gold and shoots death-dealing arrows in the joy of the chase. The summits of the high mountains tremble, and the shady forest holds the frightened cries of the beasts of the woods; the earth trembles, as well as the sea, filled with fish. The goddess of the valiant heart springs forth on all sides and sows death among the race of wild humans.[4]

To tangle with the moon means, potentially, to be initiated by yin, and as the hymn above expresses it, initiated by she "of the valiant heart who springs forth on all sides." This is *not* a romantic idea, but a matter of life or death. It is certainly a matter of either psychological vibrancy to life or psychic deadness. Experience in the lunar terrain can entail discovering new organization to our life and personality. However, new organization takes time, as encounters with the larger psyche are integrated into daily life in the form of meaningful wisdom. The emissaries of the psyche and psychoid play a major part in healing.

The alchemists depicted this process in emblems. Step-by-step, it involves:

1. The sun becoming darkened. (The light of consciousness no longer possesses the vitality, the vision, the answer, the way. See figure 13, page 113.)
2. The sun submitting to the vast night sky. (Consciousness goes into quiescence, emptying and waiting on movement in the unconscious.)

Fig. 15. Zodiacal archetypes organize around the menstruating yin, while yang, the sun is darkened. Aurora Consurgens, *late 14th century. In Roob,* Alchemy and Mysticism, *p. 80.*

3. The lunar field of the archetypes gaining energy. (The unconscious is activated.)

4. The religious instinct awakening; a path forming. (The archetypes and instincts infuse and organize around a unique center as yin mysteries light the way. Connection to the divine source within the depths occurs and constellates a new organization and infusion of life energy. Yet the sun is darkened and outside this new constellation.)

5. The moon—the new organization of soul and the archetypes—marrying the sun (with consciousness and the *hieros gamos* mysteries of inner unity appearing.)

Keeping these progressions in mind, we now turn to myth, dreams, and life experiences whereby yin's terrain becomes distinct. New instincts are born, madness or inner chaos may be encountered, and new organizing principles can lead to a new unity of being.

Lunar Rebirth

At 51, an artist/metaphysical teacher arrived at a place in the road of life where her impulse toward creativity began to dry up.[5] She felt that in order to go on, she would be producing paintings for galleries and the public that would sell when the work she valued would not, and naturally this was very depressing. A process of descent began. The meaning of many areas in her life began to change. She dreamed the following:

> I realize I am at the base of a mountain in the dark, and there is a man here (who cuts my hair in real life) who is on the mountain. He wants to cut my hair at midnight on the mountain. There is a winding road all the way up the mountain, with hot tubs at various stations along the way with archaic symbols I am supposed to work to understand at each hot tub. People soak in each tub along this winding path. At the top is a woman with a huge headdress—vines, roots, vegetables, and organic twine in her hair—soaking in a hot tub, too. I let my hair be cut by this man at midnight at the top of the mountain. Then I descend the mountain and am afraid in the dark of a man at the bottom who could hurt me. I find my dog Angel, who is now my protector, and then realize I need to stop at each hot tub and write down the symbols that are there at each one. I do so and then get in my car at the bottom, with Angel, and am safe to drive back up the mountain.

Night and midnight in the dream tell us that night rules. This is neither the sun's domain, nor solar terrain. This is neither a place nor time where the ego can rely on what it has known. Out of the night, a mountain and a path appear, with stations for soaking and changing, offering the possibility for alchemical rebirth of consciousness. In the human soul lives the alchemical pattern of initiation. It is now emerging, taking the dreamer seriously in this time of great transition, when the old way of life has lost all meaning. She must take a steep, challenging journey up a mountain at night, with steps along the way for soaking and dissolving and discovering images and symbols of these stages.

She submits to having her hair cut at midnight. The midnight haircut is a vital part of the dreamer's initiation. It is a sacrifice, and a midnight sacrifice at that. Symbolically, midnight is when the sun, consciousness, is at its weakest. The haircut represents a relinquishing of the old psychic energy. To find the new way, the darkness requires the sacrifice of old ways of thinking, living, and being. This will require an admission on the part of the ego that, on its own, it lacks the energy and the wisdom of the way.

Submitting to the inner night, the not knowing, is required, as is action. In her outer life, the dreamer had the good instincts to cut back her commitments to the galleries and let her energy retract inside, rather than push herself to create out of the wrong inner climate. In the dream, the haircut and her submission to the sacrifice at midnight parallel her outer action.

At the top of the night mountain, she encounters a feminine figure whose hair is full of bounty, soaking in the highest hot tub. This feminine presence carries the new consciousness in her hair. The mountain in the night, the dream tells her, will require a sacrifice, but it leads to connection with this new presence, a truly abundant and fertile consciousness, imaged by the cornucopia in her hair.

The dreamer, in waking life, thought the haircut had a 1950s style. We had just spoken the week before how delicious it was for her to have had 7 years to be in love with the prince, in a lovely perfect life, and that change and time were knocking on the door of her relationship. And that as the bells peal in wedding ceremonies, women have to be aware that certain paradises can turn into the pattern where the "princess" falls asleep in the castle, and may awaken to find she has turned into a 1950's housewife! So this theme followed the work, and appeared in her association to the haircut. In a way, she had to look hard into that reality, the reality of the instincts being deadened by the 1950s housewife constellation—the woman who agrees, is always fine, lives through her mate, his money, his relationship with the world, and so on. She had to look hard into the face of what can happen to her if she falls asleep into a participation mystique with her mate for too long. "So long" is great, but "too long" is trouble. When the Tao shifts, it shifts, and it is up to consciousness to listen, heed, and follow the changes, or else it will experience tremendous soul loss. Thus, part of her awakening at the midnight hour was submitting to seeing what she could turn into if she didn't watch out and take the next steps her individuation process asked of her.

Needing protection on the journey and discovering the instinct to protect are vital. Her dog, Angel, is there, so she feels safe. Protection must be established with the unconscious when an initiation becomes possible. Without protection, there is great danger. How this instinct will function, as well as her ability to turn toward it in times of difficulty, is now her focus as she drives up this mountain. That the protector is named Angel *and* is a dog is exquisite. It is a protective, divine animal, an instinct that spans heaven (Angel) and earth (dog) and guards the new way.

Artemis, the moon goddess, is often depicted running swiftly through the woods with her hounds. The appearance of the guardian dog, Angel, on the mountain in the night is a gift of grace, reflected in the Artemisian pattern. It mirrors that in the larger personality, new guardian instincts now reside close to the dreamer's consciousness, as a loving dog might. Instincts can guard her new way of going, which is connected now to the night mysteries within—not alone in the solar world of the ego, cut off from the depths.

Sacrifice of the ego partially entails the ego's recognition that it needs the protection of instincts that live outside its field of apprehension. These instincts sniff in the night and relate to what comes in the larger wilderness of being, which ordinary consciousness cannot do. Having such instincts and relating to what they sniff out in daily life *and* in the wilderness of being contributes to the birth of the new way. For without these instincts awakening consciousness is just lost in the vast unconscious, and the potential for inflation, possession, or madness is great. As the ego humbles itself to the evolving keen instincts and perceptions, we learn to differentiate experience in the psyche and psychoid and discover Self, shadow, wisdom, integration, humor, and richer humanity.

The dream announces that this transformation begins at the midnight hour on the mountain. At midnight, darkness is at its zenith, but the sun is beginning its return. From the sacrifice and the initiatory trek in darkness, she gains renewed consciousness as she negotiates her way with the powers that be.

Often we hear people say, "I am depressed." It means that the light of the ego is dim, the landscape feels like it's in a hole, there's no point of view, and affect is usually down or flat. And here the chance to turn to the soul for help has arrived. What will we meet in the dark by going within? Jung pointed out that turning consciously to the mysteries and giving energy to the unconscious illuminates a new way. The transcendent religious instinct can awaken. We see that this dreamer makes the sacrifice with the outer world and the depression makes way for an initiation. The inner world gains energy and brings her a jewel of a dream to guide her. The dream opens the way to live with the unconscious and she can make fresh discoveries of the religious attitude toward the mysteries, which is exactly what happened as her journey unfolded.

Midnight Birth of the Sun God

We discover elements of the midnight rebirth pattern in the myth of Apollo. The Apollo energy illuminates the new consciousness being born of the darkness in relationship to the moon. Apollo's mother, Leto, gives birth to him at midnight, aided by his moon sister, Artemis. Here, as in the artist's dream, the new light is born at the darkest hour, when a *coniunctio* of opposites occurs. In that darkest hour, mysterious yin principles are at work. What are these mysterious principles?

The myth gives us clues. First, Leto births Artemis, the new moon goddess, in the mouth of a watery ocean cave, hidden from sunlight and the wrath of Hera. Artemis is born close to the watery depths of the sea, the unconscious. She immediately helps her mother hold on to the *axis mundi* (which she, Artemis, also is) and deliver the new sun god. Artemis stands simultaneously between her mother's legs, pulling the sun god from the womb, and at her mother's head, as a palm tree loaded with dates. The date palm stands as the *axis mundi*, to which her mother clings as Apollo leaps forth. Artemis's role with the sun god is dual: as midwife and *axis mundi*. The moon goddess even separates the sun god from the mother after birth. Later, she teaches her brother the art of archery. This moon goddess is no simple archetypal constellation. She does not just dissolve forms in the watery depths, as we might think of the moon's archetypal oceanic *solutio* functions. No, this lunar mystery is also the *axis mundi*, the world tree, and the part of the cosmic forces in all of us which potentially helps the sun god come forth!

ARTEMIS, GUARDIAN OF THE *AXIS MUNDI*

Artemis personifies dynamism in the nature spirit, a psychic pattern that orients us to our original nature, which for the alchemists was a central goal of the work. Artemis—virginal triune goddess of the phases of the moon, great huntress—roams the forests with her hounds and nymphs. She protects all newborns in the forest, is midwife to all birthing women and animals, and guards the life of the wild forests. Untamable, true to her nature, Artemis has her killing as well as life-preserving ways. In her nobler form, she guards the life of the font, the waters of the imagination in all its manifestations. She lives in the soul and, with her keen sight and penetrating arrows, attends to the nature of the waters so that they remain true and wild.

The fierce instinct to care for life also functions in the individual soul, where the Artemisian instinctual pattern fights to uncover and bring to birth the original nature of the soul. We all know men and women who carry a visible relationship with this archetype in their lives. On a practical and valuable level, environmental activism is a hotbed today for serving this divine pattern. Protection of the ocean, land and its wilderness, and all species of the earth is pursued with vital life energy that proclaims the value of the many manifestations of psyche in the natural world and demands their right to survive. How valuable are these people who serve this pattern!

Depth psychology, at its best, serves these dimensions of the soul, spirit, psyche, and psychoid. A depth psychologist functions, in part, like a naturalist, appreciating and investigating the vast wilderness of being and not co-opting the terrain or manipulating it with too much theory or fixed thought forms. Part archeologist as well, he or she looks for the ancient contexts throughout the ages. Fate requires that some depth psychologists trek into the depths of the psyche and psychoid. If they bring back new instincts from this lunar terrain, they may discover something of the incarnation mysteries that birth the divine-human relationship anew. Then, they may be moved to bring something unique of the relationship to the mysteries to others as well.

It's no wonder the alchemists depicted Artemis as a personification of the yin mysteries. She personifies the powerful force in nature that continually redirects consciousness to the autonomous and incorruptible essence of the living soul that informs all life, where the sun god, consciousness, finds rebirth.

In the myth of Artemis, we discover that her throne on Mount Olympus is pure silver, the back shaped like two date palms, one on each side of a new-moon boat, and its seat is covered with wolf skin.[6] Silver is the metal associated with the moon in alchemy and astrology. The image of a new-moon boat points to the lunar changes embodied in the image. Literally, something of the yin principle, in its mysterious changes, is a vehicle for the soul. This vehicle is related to the wolf spirit, to instinct. The soul vehicle lives close to wolf instinct that can track trails in the wilderness, sniff out and relate to what it encounters, and take care of itself by instinctual inhabiting of that self.

It is said that Artemis was born with wolf eyes keen enough to see in the dark. Her presence in the soul brings up vision capable of penetrating darkness. Emissaries of the yin principle, as they appear in our dreams, visions, and creative work, bring alive the new vision in the darkness.

Artemis also has a throne in the starry heavens. She is sent to circle and guard the northern axis, the center of the world. She cannot romp and join with the sun god. Psychologically, this duty as guardian of the center of the world mirrors an inherent structure in the soul that lives in allegiance to an organizing principle beyond the sun—that of the world axis, around which all life circulates. This mysterious center, like a polar star in deep space, in the soul, creates unique bridges in each being, from heaven to earth. It brings us into the reality of diurnal consciousness. As we rotate around the world axis, circling the center, we discover relationship to the sun *and* the moon *and* darkness.

Artemis and the Pre-phallic Mystery of Yin

The myth of Artemis-Calliste (Artemis as she takes on another aspect of the feminine, in her nymph Calliste form, is so named Artemis-Calliste by the Greeks) mirrors the pre-phallic mystery of the feminine, where the inner center is discovered and served *a priori*. That is, an inner center is essential to the soul before yin mates with yang in a mature conjunction. The nymph longing to make love with Artemis reflects the core of existence where yin longs to be with yin, to generate more yin. Yin's heaven-earth axis comes into being from the intrusion of the sun god and the moon's insistence on his separateness. She pushes at the sun god and shows us her alignment, her inner structure, an organization of self unto itself. This pre-phallic state where we belong to the Self, the soul, core nature, must have its place within, or the solar world and relationship to the world of the ego cannot sustain the soul.

The territory of soul reflected by the virgin Artemis archetype belongs not only to teenage girls but is alive in men and women and readily available to consciousness. For life and love to carry genuine essence of soul, consciousness often must discover experience in the virginal core of existence and bring fresh presence back into dialogue at all levels of existence. If we forget to court the virgin waters of being where yin belongs unto herself, trouble arises in a number of arenas, most commonly in love relationships. When individuals fall asleep in love relationships (that is, personalistic psychology such as ego function and complexes take over the field of interaction), a bugle sounds, the hounds arrive, and the Artemisian territory of the soul calls. We can respond consciously and discover ways to court the virgin waters of being and renewal, or we can fall backward into her territory—that is, proceed unconsciously and then discover what has happened.

When relationship fields become frozen, the backward entrance into Artemisian terrain can occur in numerous ways, love triangles being one common experience. Mergers are often broken and stale patterns shaken up when a new lover enters the picture. The relationship itself is the third party. If the relationship becomes blocked, or without image or imagination, the third may be concretized in another person. Triangles create tension; no one belongs to anyone else. This, of course, is completely human, but also painful. In such experiences it is important to try to see our way through the dark. If we do not, tremendous loss of soul can occur. Splitting and then using others unconsciously can be part of the mix, as well as inane interpersonal torture *and* new awakening. Usually if a split is occurring, one person carries the stale aspects and the other carries the new "wilderness" that is unconsciously craved. Falling backward into Artemis's terrain through triangles or other means indicates that an Artemisian instinct is searching for its source and reaching to become aware of itself. Once we are aware of that, the pattern becomes more conscious and more humanity can be brought to bear on the life situations where this instinct is in need of its source.

Heart of the Forest, Heart of the Imagination

The Artemisian presence, in her archer form, is cool-minded, impersonal, and far-seeing. As such, she represents the direct-aiming instincts needed to tend to the "heart of the forest"—the watering hole where the animals drink, the sacred, secret, wild place where the virgin springs gush forth, fresh and clear as they were when the world began. The Sufis say that the heart, the *himma*, is the seat of the spirit of the imagination. To live from the heart is to live close to the imagination. To embody a relationship with the lunar terrain requires developing Artemisian instincts.

A friend of mine experienced the heart of the forest and the heart of the imagination as one and the same. In the forest one night on the Virgin Islands, after a drenching rain, this woman heard the crickets, toads, and other beings of the forest begin to sing. Her heart filled with the night song, the intricate sounds of each creature adding to the cacophony. That night she dreamed:

> My reclining body is a wilderness of rolling hills and mountain forests under a black night sky. My heart (of my reclining wilderness body) is a heart in the landscape, a pool of water where many animals come to drink. As they arrive to drink, their tongues lap in this "heart spring" that also stimulates the flow of water to gurgle and rise. A quiet, harmonious reverie permeates my body, this landscape.

The dreamer participated with the abundant, core, virginal nature teeming within and without. The rich life of the imagination informs the subtle body realms and infuses the physical body and outer wilderness. The imagination, as she listened to the night song, fed her body and soul. The dream world picked up the heart flow theme as other creatures of the inner wilderness join her and a new heart center operates inside her essence.

When we live more from the heart, we give other beings a place to gather and drink. Their thirsting and drinking stimulate the heart spring, the meaningful, life-giving flow of the imagination.

The Dark Side of the Moon

Alchemists depicted the moon as an archetypal embodiment of a field of being that participates in the suffering and transmutations of the earth plane. As such, the moon personifies the divine feminine that suffers and changes with human beings. In his research on the moon in the *Mysterium Coniunctionis*, Jung points out that as the planet nearest the Earth, she partakes of the Earth and its suffering, and functions as a mediator, just as the Virgin Mary is said to function between the people and God.[7] "She partakes not only of the earth's suffering, but of its daemonic darkness as well."[8]

As with every archetype, we must consider the shadow sides of encounters with lunar terrain. With Saturn, for example, we must watch out for "lead poisoning," a critical, know-it-all, arthritic spirit that prevents contact with the numinous. At the other extreme, without enough of Saturn's form giving, the soul's potentialities do not manifest in life. There is sun poisoning as well, when the light of consciousness burns too brightly and I-ness becomes autoerotic and narcissistic. Another shadow of the sun can occur when the ego identifies with the archetypal world and wants to reflect its majesty but does not bring out its true humanity. An ego stuck in this pattern has not yet discovered the religious instinct that helps the sun to emerge and require us to individuate into unique, incredibly *human* beings. Early on, in experience with the numinous, this is common. However, the tenacity of the religious instinct in the soul will confront us with this, with remarkably fresh clarity from within and from without, via relationships that cannot thrive in such a climate.

In alchemy and astrology the moon relates to soul, yin, emotion, creative expressions, and attachment patterns. It relates to the temporal, changeable, malleable, corruptible that eventually leads to the opposite, the incorruptible—the eternal. Moon poisoning as a psychological reality can happen in any number of ways. For example, it threatens when we shut down our emotions or are thrown into extreme emotionality or we compulsively enact instinctual needs that dominate our lives and others' without getting help to transform these dynamics. When we are enraptured or captivated too long by the spirits of the imagination or attempt to remain at one with the unconscious, swimming in the mythic "realm of mothers," we are heading toward "lunacy."

Becoming a lunatic is a common way to refer to getting caught on the dark side of the moon. Getting caught there is not a moralistic issue. In fact, getting stuck in isolated ego consciousness (sun poisoning) is just as awful as moon poisoning and is a different kind of madness. In the territory of the psyche where moon poisoning ensues, our humanity lessens over time, and we usually come to an inner experience of soul loss. Individuation is impossible if we remain in such places, for emerging consciousness has lost its way.

Here is an example of a man who got caught on the dark side of the moon: He was a brilliant, intuitive thinker who worked hard in Jungian analysis for years, and cared tremendously for the environment and created a number of great inventions to help the ecosystems of the Southwest. He worked with Native American people to solve ecosystem pollution problems; he received funding to disseminate knowledge from the Los Alamos National Lab into the community of various peoples who could use the technology for the environment, and so on. In his later years, his flight of ideas grew, and so did the lack of support and funding. The more the funding dropped away, the higher he leveled his aim for his ideas. His pain deepened when a bill he supported was shot down by the incoming Republican officials. He had worked for years on this creative bill, and it had come so close to becoming a reality. The benefit for the environment would have been a true victory for the world soul. Naturally, a depression hit him. Sadly, his feeling of lack of support in general, from friends, business associates, and others grew. It was like watching the bottom of his emotional and financial support systems drop away. His desperateness led to more manic pursuits, which took his credibility down, and began a cycle of pain and undoing. It looked to me like the moon split in two—the emotional-financial element dissolved, and the idea place flew off with him. In his despair, he moved to another town. Clinically depressed, without help, he hibernated, leaving all connections behind, and even getting into painful snares with life-long friends. He basically disappeared from a community he had served with his heart and genius for decades, and the loss to our area, and to the world in its current environmental plight was and is still immense. He was diagnosed with cancer three months after he moved, and was gone in a matter of weeks. He did emerge from the blackness to talk with a few friends briefly on the phone before dying.

His bright ideas for our troubled world, and his wish to see them incarnate seemed to split him. That painful moon split (between form and spirit, concrete implemented plans and brilliant ideas, and inner versus outer support and value of self) took him out of life in the end, at only sixty four. I often wonder what his dreams might have been in the end, and hope he found the solace he deserved there.

Moon poisoning can also happen when we swim in the waters of the unconscious and become lost there, taken over by archetypal or psychoidal forces, refusing individuation. Addiction is another kind of moon poisoning, for it enables avoidance of certain emotions, or, on the other hand, propels compulsions and hyperstimulation of the emotional body, while creating a deadening effect.

A woman I once knew fell into serious trouble after her lover died unexpectedly of a heart attack at a young age. She would call up the local escort services and would take excessive drugs and play out myriad fantasies with the escort people. An addiction demon of *false* ecstasy had jumped into her empty space where her old life had been, and in her refusal to get to the bottom of the grief, she chose the demon of hyperstimulation over soul. She lost her home and risked her career too on this sex addiction, despite tough love, or rational, loving conversations with her friends, who eventually became estranged. After she inevitably crashed, she constructed a new life with more understanding and appreciation for the psyche and its dangers.

There are much more mild versions of these troubles with the unconscious that can take hold as well, but this illustration is a case in point. The wrong relationship to any archetypal presence can become demonic. Usually we think of moon poisoning being present if a compulsive behavior takes hold while emotional/sexual avoidance or hyperstimulation is sought. So where blocked felt experience exists, or hyperstimulation or hyperemotionality occurs, we can think of this as the need to reconnect with the feminine and find the divine feminine within that seeks her own healing.

Part of the trouble is yin principles and presences have been repressed and demeaned collectively for centuries. As they emerge in the modern psyche, they can seem dangerous or demonic. The moon makes its own cycles through full light and utter darkness. The lunar forces in the psyche can also turn black and remain stuck in utter blackness for periods of time. Destructive, split-off primitivity or utter darkness settles in when "she" has been devalued and undeveloped in culture and consciousness. The care required for her emergence in human beings is not yet sufficiently known or valued. War, psychosis, disease, and mass destruction manifest this feminine core when she turns black, and remains so, in our consciousness. When yang principles in humans are undeveloped and unrelated, they can *force* yin to emerge in primitive manifestations.

Take, for example, the projection Artemis's totem animal, the wolf, receives from the collective, for the problem of madness is illustrated here. Wolves can either be romanticized or demonized, and are rarely respected for the beings they are. People who buy wolves and keep them in their suburban neighborhoods have a romanticized notion about them, and are stunned when the animals break loose and run away, or attack animals near their pens. On the other hand, others, who have projected tremendous fear and misunderstanding on wolves, demonize them because they have no other predator besides humans. On Flores Island off the coast of Vancouver, wolves lived in freedom until the late 1990s. Humans would ride across the sea inlet at times to hear the wolves and to camp on this remote, thickly forested island, but the wolves reigned there. One day the inevitable happened, and a wolf went for the food in a tent and bit a man. The next part of this heartbreaking story did not have to be inevitable. The government shot *all* the wolves on Flores Island, and today you will not find one survivor, you will not hear their howling, spot their tracks on the forest floor, or feel their uncanny presence in the woods. This kind of stupidity and atrocity to wild animals is "beyond the beyond." It is unthinkable and inhumane and mirrors the human fear of the wilderness of being that wolves represent as well as our demonic projections onto nature.

No wonder Artemis appears with the wolf! For this archetypal constellation of yin resides deep in the psyche of nature, where keen instincts mirrored in the wolves are still alive. When we link with this archetype, we bridge humanity to the core of the primeval natural world that lives within us as well. That core is not romantic—it includes the rabid and the murderous. But it becomes mad only if our consciousness has projected the demonic upon it, cut it off and thrown it out, and has not tried to humanize a link with instincts it can carry. It may be mad within us until we do the work to redeem it.

We may have to encounter and heal the mad feminine in us, beneath a polished persona, or beneath a Christian ethos that cuts out the instinctual soul, in order to get to the moon mysteries that can heal. I don't know of a profound healing crisis or transformation of any depth that does not access this yin core to some degree. When we work with this energy, a unique presence similar to Artemis often arrives as the protectress. Reconnection with the lunar, Artemisian core is central to individuation for many of us because in the development of the Western psyche, the lunar dimensions of reality have been cut off, demonized, or overly personalized, and thereby demeaned. No wonder the alchemists targeted the redemption of the feminine at the heart of their work!

The central mystery of alchemy leads consciousness into and through suffering to the divine feminine who both suffers and brings new developments. She creates inner orientation of the instinct around the Self, bringing new balance, harmony, and self-regulation within the personality and between Self and other. This promotes healing of what has been cut off, thrown out, or gone mad.

One very pertinent and potent image of the divine feminine connected to the wilderness of being is Sedna, the Inuit goddess who needs the help of humans in order to heal from her madness. Sedna falls from the heavens to the sea, then falls to the bottom of the sea, and when she returns to earth, her father tries to marry her off to someone she refuses. She clings to her father's boat, and her father cuts off her fingers to get her to let go. Her fingers fall into the sea, where they become the walrus, sea lion, whales, and other animals. The goddess has come to earth and learned *becoming*. There are Inuit images of her, mad at the bottom of the sea, her hair tangled with all the sins of the human beings.

The shamans of Inuit villages seek contact with Sedna in their visions in the crack between the worlds. She is crazed, angry, and unpredictable, and her suffering great. Some shamans try to trick her; others learn to find their way to her and compassionately comb and untangle her hair, bit by bit. To these, the goddess gives healing power, or success in the hunt, and so on. The image of combing the wild goddess hair—taking the sins of the human beings out of her hair—is a perfect image of how we humans impact the collective unconscious, and the feminine yin living at the bottom of the ocean of the human psyche. Her madness is also soothed, and she is returned to her true nature as we discover ways to untangle our troubles from the archeytpal milieu she inhabits. Then, both we and she discover healing power and grace. The psychic functions in this mythic pattern reveal the alchemists' sense that the moon, the archetypal feminine, partakes in the earth's suffering, daemonic darkness, and transformations.

A Little Light on the Moon Mysteries of the Alchemists

The alchemists said that the moon is the mother of the art.[9] "Corruptible," as they described it, the moon has ever-changing ways. Yet, during the circulation of energy through the changing cycles (which the moon represents), that which is incorruptible, eternal, and beyond change emerges.

The lunar pattern in our diurnal consciousness also opens the door to finding our place in the dance of life and death. She protects newborns and sends the death arrows. One of her lunar triune faces is the crone, Hecate. The feminine principle personified in Artemis/Diana/Hecate also functions as the psychopomp and separating and reunifying processes alive in the psyche.

The myth reflects differentiating, separating, and reunifying parts of a psychic situation occur as Hecate hears Demeter crying on the face of the earth, separated from her daughter, Persephone. With a torch and a headdress of stars, Hecate enters the underworld, finds Persephone with Hades, brings her back and reunites Persephone and Demeter.

The alchemists depicted the moon as Mercurius's other half, the yin half. As an alchemical force related to death and rebirth, Artemis/Hecate, like Mercurius, not only kills and separates but also personifies—like Isis in Egyptian mythology—a shamanic reunification of separated parts, as the following stories and dreams illustrate.

The Moon Grows a Phallus

Here is a case of a woman who, in depression, went far into the yin mysteries before new yang energy brought her back into relationship with the world. Adopted by white people at the age of two, she had lost her connection to her Arapahoe roots. When her adoptive parents died, she clung to her lover for a sense of family and identity. He left her just after she closed on the sale of a new cabin deep in a national forest. They had planned to live there with the wolf pups they bred. He took off for law school, not telling her months earlier when he had applied. She was crushed and began to fall apart. I was very concerned about her living so far out in the wilderness, especially with the harsh winter snows coming, so I poked and prodded her to return to the village and get a fenced yard for her wolf pups. She would say placating things to me about how she would move soon enough. Eventually, I stopped pushing, because it seemed fruitless.

She cross-country skied out of the woods once a week to the road near her cabin. Then she drove her car or snowmobile fifteen miles into town, as weather permitted. An introverted, sensation type with a huge heart for the wilderness, she diligently came once a week to her sessions with me. After her initial three-month seizure of fear and grief, she seemed more peaceful. She explained how she was healing herself. She had taken to snowshoeing at night in the forest when she was unable to sleep. For hours on end, she would trek with her wolf pups in the wilderness and then return to her cabin exhausted. Drowsy, calm, and filled with the sensations of the night forest, she would drop into a deep sleep, curled up with her pups, and she would dream.

An inner calm and vastness grew in her consciousness. The emptying process was remarkable. The grief and anxiety released, and the critical spirit that had been tearing her apart ceased. As the grief and loss loosened their grip, her emptiness came to be embodied in a rich way. I felt her very much taken into the arms of the moon, into the night, into the diffuse light, the dark groves of pines, the sniffing of the wolf pups along animal trails, her broad face open and clear as the moon. As she healed, she began to experience epiphanies in nature, which she expressed in wood carvings.

Dreams of her Native American ancestors guided her heart to heal. Later, when her inner self reintegrated, she moved to the edge of town, took up life with her friends again, and resumed teaching jazz dance to the high school students. An interpersonal warming occurred in her life, and she finished her work with me.

I had hoped that she would connect with her ancestors' reservation and ceremonies, but I never heard whether she did. Several years later, I ran into her on the street when she happened to be back visiting friends. She had moved to central Alaska, had taken up dog sledding (with husky-wolf mix pups), and was working as a nurse in an Inuit village. The vastness of the land soothed her soul, she told me. She also thanked me for being there as she found her way out of a scary time, "tipping on the edge," as she put it. She lived with her Inuit lover, and although she said that she was too afraid to marry, she seemed to be enjoying the love and the stability of the life they shared. Smiling, she told me that she had a carving hut with heat, next to the dog run, where she would go when she needed time alone.

I muse again and again with awe about how the Artemisian pattern literally lived itself in her life. This form sprang out of her soul and helped her heal. Her psychic proximity to the indigenous soul brought an immense wilderness of being to the healing process.

How did she not go mad? Several women who lived way out in the woods around this village went over the edge, half on the planet and half on the moon. They went into the inner lunar landscape and did not return with the boon of the journey. Some inherent life instinct that this woman learned to follow helped her, and grace arrived. Toward the end of the time she worked with me, just before moving into town, she had the following dream:

> It is night. I am standing outside the cabin with my wolf pups in the yard and a carving I was going to give to M. I turn to look at the moon above the ridge near my cabin. It is a crescent moon, just after new moon. Suddenly, the concave part of the crescent grows a protruding penis. This penis rises from its base in the moon and is made of the moon somehow.
>
> This weird moon penis then turns into a candle that lights my way. The light from the moon candle shines into the yard, around the cabin I love, and then down the path that leads to the road to town. It felt like it was loving this place with me and leading me down the path to the road, for the light moved around my yard and down the road, directing my gaze.

The psyche and the inner moon principles had taken her seriously, and she them. After her time of extreme yin, "tipping on the edge," living with her wolf pups and trekking under the night sky, new instincts arose and guided her back into life, creative expression, and connection with others. Here the moon principle is an active cradling and then guiding force that pushes for expression and outward movement.

The phallus in the moon has a remarkable parallel in one version of the myth of the Egyptian moon goddess Isis (her connection to the moon links her with Artemis) and her brother/lover Osiris. In the myth, Osiris's jealous brother Set kills him and cuts his body into pieces. Isis finds all of Osiris's body parts except his penis, so after putting Osiris back together, she makes a new penis for him. Under Isis's care, reintegration occurs, and this is exactly what happened in the dreamer's life.

Yin's Reorganization around the New Psychic Center

The alchemical rebirth pattern has its stages, as depicted on page 120 of this chapter. The emblem in figure 15 shows the steps whereby transformations in the psyche create a new organization around the yin principle, with the sun (consciousness) outside this constellation, to the upper right, existing in darkness. These steps are essential to the creation of the Philosopher's Stone, or manifest Self—that center between the conscious and unconscious—growing and incarnating in time and space in our lives. The alchemists knew that this transformational process had to go through its deep, organic steps or an unfinished, aborted, or unsuccessful transformation could result. They also understood, in addition to working with the organic steps that emerge from the *opus*, that grace was essential in that midnight hour for the true *coniunctio* to prevail.

The following dream exemplifies the moment of transformation where the yin center and new organization of the Self takes hold in a woman's life. She entered a deep *nigredo* during mid-life, discovering in the process that her life was run too much by will and power. With help from the dream world, she was busy finding her way out of the old ruling yang spirit of her life. Her career changed, her relationship changed, much to her mate's surprise, and the quality and rhythm of her daily life changed, too. She discovered deep new values emerging from within the soul regarding home and relational life—truly a profound shift from Logos to Eros. At this time she dreamed:

> I am at a gathering of people, and we are all standing in a large royal room visiting with one another. Then I am looking on with others as we all see a new queen just now taking her rightful throne. Somehow it was always hers, but for some reason this is the first time she has taken her seat. She is young and ancient at the same time, stately, fresh, and lovely. Behind the throne stands a handmaiden to this queen, who is somehow an earthy, humble angel! This handmaiden angel is telling everyone to hush, to quiet themselves. She has her finger to her lips and is gesturing the appropriate silence needed for this moment. We all stop our conversations and turn toward the throne, giving this our attention. In the stillness then, the new queen stands up and walks about, greeting individually each person who came.

The handmaiden/earthy angel who serves the new queen and tells everyone to hush lets the dreamer know that she, the dream ego, and the other participants are in the presence of a great mystery where silence is the fitting response. The ensuing "hush" and quieting of self mark a profound mystery in which both celestial and earthly realms are invested, one that an angel urges participants to witness and take into their depths. It is reminiscent of the alchemical emblem in figure 2 (on page 11) where Hermes/Mercurius gestures the same urge for silence. This element alone points to the urgent need to attend, witness, and *feel* what is occurring.

The queenly feminine is taking her rightful place in the psyche. Queens have long been symbols of the human feminine who is called and connected to the divine by royal blood to mediate between heaven and earth, to bring divine order into the human realms. Part human, part divine, the queen's presence is an expression of the incarnating manifest Self, taking its throne, its place of growing and rightful power at the center of the psyche. The queen, the angel-handmaiden, and the group gathered around depict the strengthening of the yin center and the organizing principle that has all parts relate to this center. In the image, the new ruling queen greets those gathered, one by one. This depicts the reality of the multiplicity of the psyche and the existence of the center and organization around the ruling incarnating energetic principle. And as mentioned, this woman dreamer was involved in a deep process of change from a life dominated by yang, with undeveloped yin. The dream angel heralds the moment that the yin principle is coming to center and creating new organization of self.

Importantly, the fact of the dream ego as one element of the psyche becomes clear in the dream as the queen visits each person. The queen, the incarnating Self, relates individually with all energies that gather around the center, all energies that are part of the psyche. Here the dream ego is a witness to the new ruling presence, and is visited by contact with this presence, as are the other figures there gathered. The new *valuation* of the feminine has taken her rightful place of mediation between human and divine. In a way, the ego has found its rightful place, too, in relationship to the mystery between heaven and earth and the value of the feminine as mediatrix between the worlds.

The importance of the witnessing function of the ego cannot be underestimated. By remembering and working on the dream, the dreamer helps bring this presence into her life, which marks the importance of the witness to the mysterious changes happening. Jung once said to Marie-Louise von Franz that when someone came to him to work on dreams, he wanted to know how much of the personality was listening![10] Here the image is one of the whole community gathering for this transformation, and the light of the ego as witness is as crucial as the angel and the queen, for without that witness this mystery and its fruit would fall into the unconscious. That means the ego must quiet itself and turn toward the angel and the center and witness and feel the mysterious changes.

At the time of this dream, the dreamer experienced the redemption of the ordinary, the empty, the simple parts of self and life. She began to feel the presence of the divine feminine guiding her through the dark night of change in her life. She gained new respect for everything that exists in time and space inside matter, just as it is. Her driven spirit eased and a grace came into her attitude, body, and life. With this felt presence within, her new ability to perceive the numinous in the ordinary grew. This in turn dispelled the manic energy, narcissism, and fear that had defended her against her mortality and ordinariness. When she came to experience the divine feminine residing in her soul, she felt something within open her to a genuine *bhakti* ("devotion to God") experience. She discovered immediate experiences of the divine incarnating in all beings as Eros began to grow in her life.

The reorganization of personality around the strengthening yin presence that mediates between human and divine, between what is temporal and eternal brings the feminine into her redeemed stature in the psyche. This creates in the individual the potential for a growing experiential, synchronistic field between heaven and earth, where the *opus* creates that subtle body field between the opposites. This is one aim of the relationship between ego and Self we see growing in this woman's life and dream.

At the Hour of Darkness, Will the Renewed Moon and Darkened Sun Unite?

The step in the sun-moon rebirth processes where the lunar principle has gained energy is where consciousness gives energy to the unconscious and finds a different point of view by submitting to a wisdom larger than its own. Usually it entails residing in the unknown for sometime. Alchemists called this the *sol niger* ("darkened sun"), where the light of consciousness is in utter blackness and unknowing. The entire alchemical process pivots on that moment of pregnant darkness.

Just after yin strengthens and re-centers, and the sun is in darkness is the moment the possible *coniunctio* and conception may occur between yin and yang, and between the conscious and unconscious. The *sol niger* then comes into the picture. If grace prevails, the opposites in the dark, unknown moment discover each other and new light is born from their union.

A woman in her late forties had a dream that exemplifies that most important alchemical moment. She had been working diligently with her dreams in a deep process with mid-life changes when she decided to participate in a week-long meditation retreat. Her work and calling in life were changing, her children were now grown and leaving the nest, her marriage was in complete chaos as her partner was also in radical change, and other changes as well were brewing and being made known during the retreat. She could feel the messages at the retreat telling her over and over again that she had to sacrifice her old ideals and wishes in a number of arenas in her life and try to find what the soul wanted. Feeling herself submitting deeply to these messages, bowing to a way deeper than her ego ideals, she prepared to go home. The very last night of the meditation retreat, on the night of the new moon, she dreamed:

> I am standing barefoot outside, in my nightgown, in the utter darkness. I feel the moon and sun beneath the Earth's dark horizon meeting as

> equals somewhere in the blackness, and for some reason I don't understand, this is a dangerous moment, full of awe. I realize it is rare to witness this and stand still. It feels as though all in life I could ever most truly hope for, for myself, for those I love, for the world around me, too, depends on this moment. I stand alone and shyly outstretch my arms toward the horizon line of stars and dark, silhouetted earth. A shudder runs through me. Then a voice comes to me and tells me to breathe and listen. In the darkness before the coming dawn in the woods the wild male and female turkeys are calling to each other. I hear the male call, I hear the female call, and I hear the rustle of leaves in the dark. Although I cannot see them, I feel them rush to meet one another, and the rustle of leaves on the forest floor where their feet are dancing the mating dance echoes in my senses. The dream voice says, "Everything depends upon this moment."

A synchronistic affirmation occurred with the soul of nature as she wakened from this dream. As she reports it, the first light of the predawn sky warmed the eastern horizon as she awoke. She sat up in her sleeping bag and heard an actual wild turkey call outside her tent and its mate answering back, and their cawing and chortling calls to each other in the woods made her weep.

This dream experience portrays the alchemical reality the Irish poet AE knew when he stated, "the soul is a midnight blossom." The soul-spirit moon-sun *coniunctio* of opposites happens in the darkness. This is indeed an unknown and dangerous time. The opposites can as easily destroy each other and no new union or conception in the soul would then occur. The dream speaks to the mystery happening in the unknown. Will the renewed reality of the opposites join in the darkness, seek and find each other out—like the wild turkeys before the dawn dancing their mating dance? Such a lovely synchronicity—to awaken and find the mating birds near her bed calling out in the predawn darkness! The hope of the coming dawn with that possibility right there is the gift she took home with her from the retreat.

It took a number of years to see how this potential union might happen in her life, and required she live in close contact with the darkness, the depths of the soul in order to orient within and without in ways congruous with this coming energy. For the opposites were seeking each other in a new way down deep in her soul, and had not yet joined, had not yet given off the new light. The process took her through a depression. She thought the images and occurrences that this dream heralded would lead to a renewal in her marriage; that is where her conscious wish tried to focus the new life coming. It turned out, however, that the *coniunctio* was to be only in her soul for sometime. A terribly difficult passage for couples often awaits them as children leave the nest. Each person reorients within and without, and the relationship itself must submit to alchemical processes. For this woman, the sacrifice of the hope and plan for the recovery of the marriage was necessary for a long while. It drove her into a deeper discovery of the new ground opening in her soul, related to this *coniunctio*. Her discoveries eventually led not only to sacrifices, but to vital life energy, new fructifying unions inside and out.

Her dream experience mirrors the depths of wisdom the alchemists knew. The core of renewal possible in the soul happens when the light of consciousness is in darkness and has submitted to a way larger than itself so that the strengthened yin joins with transforming yang and the unconscious and conscious meet in an embrace.

THE MOON AND MERCURIUS MARRY: FIXITY, LOVE, AND GRACE

The alchemists portrayed Luna, the moon, as Mercurius's yin half. They also said that Luna must be married to Mercurius so that darkness will disperse and new light will be born. The marriage of Moon and Mercurius is depicted in an important alchemical text, to which Jung refers, the "Introitus Apertus" of Philaletha, commonly known as "The Treatise of the Font of the Knight of Treviso."[11] The waters of this font are dedicated to the maiden Diana (Artemis). The text tells that the spirit Mercurius must not flee with the "thief" at the font but must marry Diana.

For this union to take place in our lives, a certain kind of fixity must occur (mirrored in the hermetically-sealed vessel) so that spirit does not fly off, bubble out, dissipate, or leak away. The making of the divine water, the alchemists tell us, requires that this spirit (the "winged youth") be contained.

At the beginning of chapter 4, we investigated the kinds of fixed attitudes that get in the way of relationship with the spirit of the imagination. Here, however, the alchemists point out the other side of the issue: The right degree of fixity is essential for transformation. The alchemists portrayed essential fixity through images of the vessel (containment) and arrows (penetrating power). Yin (magnetic, receptive, containing) and yang (active, penetrating) principles are mirrored in these different mediums of attaining the fixity necessary for transformation.

As we turn to the inner world, via active imagination and dream work, for guidance in an area of difficulty, pain, or inquiry, these realms can be accessed as consciousness enters into dialogue with the imagination. Like the alchemists, we learn the mystery and art of containment and penetration. Earlier I noted that the archetypal motif of the new Age of Aquarius is to learn to be the alchemist who pours the mysterious waters, rather than merely swims in them as the fish (the Piscean Age) does.

A vessel that can contain the spirit cannot be created by a concretistic mind or a leaden consciousness that thinks it knows the way things are. Either stance kills the spirit being contained. It cannot happen, either, with a *puer* or *puella* attitude that fears containment and constantly discharges psychic energy via unconscious attempts to reduce anxiety and tension.

In no way can a dynamic, pattern, attitude, or spirit transform in our lives if it does not become contained and penetrated—that is, fixed—to some degree. Over time, in experience with the imagination, we discover this razor's edge: too much or too little fixity, the wrong kind and the right kind. Eventually we can discover this mysterious, middle kind of fixity, in which containment and penetration lead to experiences of grace, the new midpoint in our consciousness, the union of elements and opposites, of heaven and earth. This is the art of inner alchemy in the life of the individual by which the latent Self comes into the manifest self. It can arrive and be tended in many forms in life—through meditation, active imagination, creative work, yoga, and so on. In fact, the idea is to find a means whereby the daily routines of life and these realms can be in a continual, flowing dialogue. This dialogue courts our soul essence to come into fuller manifestation.

Discovering the right degree of fixity requires openness to the arrows we receive in dreams, waking life, creative projects, relationships, visions, and so on, in order to discern where the larger psyche is attempting to penetrate, adjust, realign, and change consciousness. Our human experience of the arrows and our honest dialogue with the *mysterium* penetrate the barrier between human and divine.

Our inquiries into the mysteries can become our arrows, which penetrate the mystery to create a fixity for spirits, issues, or dynamics in our lives that need change, where opposites are confronting each other. Yin containment provides a magnetic receptivity in which both the human and divine participate. With yang, there is an active penetration that is, to some degree, a mutual exchange between the human and divine.

Artemis/Diana and Her Doves of Peace

Just as the new moon symbolizes the *nigredo*, the full moon symbolizes the *albedo*, where grace and insight abound. The alchemists point out a central mystery of the moon and the effects of these yin principles on the alchemical processes:

> If thou knowest how to moisten this dry earth with its own water, thou wilt loosen the pores of the earth, and this thief from outside will be cast out with the workers of wickedness, and the water by an admixture of the true Sulphur, will be cleansed from the leprous filth and from the superfluous dropsical fluid, and thou wilt have in thy power, the Knight of Treviso, whose waters are rightfully dedicated to the maiden Diana. Worthless is this thief, armed with the malignity of arsenic, from who the winged youth fleeth, shuddering. And though the central water is his bride, yet dare he not display his most ardent love towards her, because of the snares of the thief, whose machinations are in truth unavoidable. Here may Diana be propitious to thee, who knoweth how to tame wild beasts, and whose twin doves will temper the malignity of the air with their wings so that the youth easily entereth in through the pores, and instantly shaketh the foundations of the earth, and raises up a dark cloud. But thou wilt lead the waters up even to the brightness of the moon, and the darkness that was upon the face of the deep shall be scattered by the spirit moving over the waters. Thus by God's command shall the Light appear.[12]

To what mystery is this alluding? Earlier in this same text, a rabid dog is soothed by Diana's doves and transforms into an eagle. The rabid dog is thought to be Diana's lower nature; as this transforms (into a solar eagle) in the process, Diana/Artemis's nobler manifestion takes hold. If we are connected to Diana/Artemis, and her nobler spirit arrives in the work, then the animals, the important life of the imagination and the instincts, come to organize around her and are tamed. With this constellation of yin present within, her twin doves arrive. Doves are the birds of love and of peace. The twin or duplex pattern that appears in the twin doves may signify that what emerges from this divine presence is double-natured, paradoxical, can embody and relate to both sides of any duality, and thus bring peace and harmony. The two doves also allude to yin and yang attracted by love.

Anyone who has experienced the clash of opposites in relationship knows that without the grace of the spirit of love arriving amid the tension, pain, and reorganization in the relationship, there is not only *no hope* of the relationship evolving but also *no point* in it. Without love, compassion, and objectivity pulsing in the center of the change processes, all becomes inane, like making love without any moisture or juicy fluidity appearing, and the heart of the matter is lost. The "malignity of the air"—suspicion, negative thoughts, and bad feelings—continues, and redemption does not dwell there.

This principle applies to all we do, perhaps especially when we seek some form of alchemical rebirth. As the New Testament states, "Though I speak with tongues of men and of angels and do not have love, I am a clanging symbol, a noisy gong. I am nothing." Without the spirit of love and wisdom from the divine feminine manifesting in the work, alchemy amounts to nothing. Hence, the wisdom put forth in the alchemical treatise about Diana/Artemis's appearance in the work!

When do these doves descend in our work and lives? When the heart of matter becomes clear and love appears, our vision of the human-divine suffering is embodied and adds feeling to the gist of the difficulty. To come into true feeling about the heart of the matter is not just a personal insight or emotion; it is a gift of grace that comes from on high, appearing out of nowhere, and descends upon us and changes our consciousness.

Love, compassion, and peace of this sort are gifts of yin, of the divine feminine. To have divine new insight and feeling arrive for both sides of a polarity, an argument, a world crisis, or such, and to have this new presence enter into our human consciousness is a gift from the transcendent psyche, imaged here in Diana's doves. Amid the opposites, this is the presence of peace that surpasses all mental understanding.

Here is a dream example of this yin presence of peace. A woman activist who was dealing with tremendous tension in the psyche dreamed:

> I am on a rocket that is being sent into space. It takes off and I end up in space. Before me in space is a huge, silver-colored sphere with myriad facets of cut mirror or glass-like substance throughout its surface. It is spinning in space, and perfectly round. I notice all the facets of color and light appearing through these glass-like parts held together by the silver-colored substance. The peace it brings is incredible. My consciousness and the consciousness of this presence commune in a penetrating harmony. I look onto Earth and the world problems and hope this can also penetrate down into our political problems too. I see the East and West and send my hope for this peace to penetrate both sides. My mind discovers a state of peace I didn't know existed.

Earlier we considered the images of the demonic feminine who must be appeased, as in the appearance of the rabid dog in the "Font of the Knight of Treviso." Here, in this part of the alchemical text, we see her other face, the redemption bringer. Redemption comes experientially, when human and divine essences of being open to one another, and the cosmic heart of being penetrates between the mortal and divine spheres, and peace arrives. In a way, this is the entry point to the subtle body realms as well. In this dream above, it is very interesting that the sphere is silver, has many facets and brings peace. The mutliplicity present in the facets, the wholeness in the roundness of the object, the spinning around its own center, and the color silver holding together all the parts—these constitute a feeling experience of the divine Self, with yin traits. Jung points out that "Luna is the sum and essence of the metal's nature which are all taken up into her shimmering whiteness."[13] This mystery of the organizing, multinatured wholeness in the feminine brings the dreamer newly-found peace, an experience of the transcendent feminine that exists now as a growing center in this woman's life.

When her doves arrive, the alchemical text tells us, the malignity is taken out of the air, and the winged youth easily penetrates the pores of the dry earth. Diana/Artemis and Mercurius then work together, for with her arrival and gift of peace, he can descend and penetrate the dry earth. (Also interestingly parallel to the dreamer's wish for this peace to penetrate into the Earth's world political problems of the clash of the opposites in East versus West.) In the text, Mercurius's penetration into the dry pores of the earth portrays the penetration of the living wisdom spirit, the *sapientia dei*, into our dry consciousness, our inner deserts. Then a dark cloud rises up, and the text instructs us to lead the waters up to the brightness of the moon.

Leading "the waters up . . . to the brightness of the moon" is, in our terms, making an offering of the alchemical process to the source and mother of yin. The darkness that was cast upon the earthed situation is then scattered by the new spirit (that is, new consciousness) moving over the waters. Hence, God commands the Light to appear.

The dark face cast upon the Earth, if we follow the metaphor, would be the moon, as its shadow falls on the earth. Perhaps this is an image of the moon appeased. Yin, mother of all mortal bodies, is given an offering from deep in the psyche—matter mysteries as fresh spirit, Mercurius, penetrates the dry earth. This seems to suggest that when we make an offering to yin, to Eros, in expression of our submission to and participation in the rounds of death and rebirth, it may penetrate the fabric between human and divine, and she may be appeased, bringing peace to human consciousness as well.

Then Diana brings in her doves and marries the new spirit descending—which becomes a wisdom spirit penetrating into the dry, stuck, or lifeless situation. The offering of these waters to the brightness of the moon brings the last elements of change. With the moon appeased, the darkness dissipates and new light is born. From the darkness of the unconscious comes the light of illumination, the *albedo*, and the descent of this energy is taken into earthly matters once again.

The Devilish "Thief"

Earlier I noted that we may come to live closer in awareness to the movements of the Self. These movements include dark and light manifestations. Destructive psychic constellations may sometimes activate to such a degree that personal and collective forces enter into tremendous chaos. Sometimes this constellation of darkness and difficulty is *not* the dark side of the Self. Something in the process of the divine manifesting in our lives and personalities also brings with it a counterforce of chaos—one that seems to resist or even undermine the new incarnation is appearing. This is an important distinction: the dark side of Self and this counterforce.

Alchemical texts illustrate forces destructive to the new union of the lovers at the font, as we saw in the image of the thief in "The Font of the Knight of Treviso." The thief who appears at the alchemical fountain where the lovers are trying to unite is said to be "worthless" and "armed with malignity of arsenic." The winged youth at the fountain flees from the thief. The text also describes the unavoidable difficulties of this phenomenon, which serves, psychologically, to make the thief, "whose machinations are in truth unavoidable," less personalistic. The thief, they say, must be dealt with by Diana so that the "malignity of the air" can ease and Diana's doves of peace reign. Then the winged youth, Mercurius, unites with and marries Diana, the maiden at the font, and matter is penetrated anew with spirit, with the wise presence of Mercurius.

The alchemists viewed the thieving energy that can accompany the process of discovering the lovers at the font as *worthless and toxic*. This is a fitting description for those highly charged destructive voices that can be unleashed when collective forces start to play out. Dark manifestations of the Self do exist, of course, wherein the energies in the divine are not integrated into paradoxical nature but (individually and collectively) are split off from cohesive totality. Dark manifestations of the Self may be different from the thief, however. The thieving energy is also *not always* personal shadow dynamics sabotaging the Self from incarnating. Rather, on a less personal note, the thief can at times be that in nature which is struggling to make room for the new consciousness coming into incarnation in the human sphere.

Sometimes it constellates very strongly and threatens to be like a miscarriage on the part of nature. We might also look at the phenomenon of what occurs in the world with visionaries at times, as part of this phenomenon. Genius individuals rise up out of the rhizome of the human soul, and often they are cut down early in their lives. Martin Luther King is an example, John Lennon is another; every culture has them—Anwar Sadat, Ghandi, Cochise, Crazy Horse, a number of Dalai Lamas throughout time, and so on. We could think of the insane assassinations that took each of these men out as a backfiring, or recoiling of nature. Nature rises up in these individuals and something in nature also brings them down early in their lives by worthless toxic forces that seem to thieve them away from us. The thieving energy obviously manifested in very specific ways inside the human beings who did the killing; they are not taken out of the equation of responsibility. It is just that this happens so often when something rare is born that it is worth also looking at it from a less personal point of view as well as the personal responsibility view.

When this theiving (personal and/or impersonal in origin) is nearby, as the alchemists saw it, the feminine yin principle must bring in an instinct that settles the thieving and takes the "malignity out of the air." This image, on an individual level, points to times in individuation when so large a darkness descends that even a well-intentioned conscious ego in connection with the divine, with the Self, may not be enough for transformation to occur. The ego must submit that its efforts and good intentions are not enough, no matter the resources with which it connects. The process depends upon transcendent grace, the doves arriving, which may or may not happen, to turn an inhumane psychic environment into one that is life-giving, where love and compassion can reside and the inner yin-yang lovers can unite. It requires endurance, tolerance, and often a stepping back on the part of the active, well-intentioned ego. Sorting out the personal from the impersonal elements is an important differentiation to make, because the means to weather the different kinds of storms are different for each.

Examples of some ways the impersonal elements may constellate are important. Vortexes of energy may constellate that threaten to undermine and even demolish new developments of the Self constellating in the lives of various people at a crucial time in creation processes. Strings of events, one after another, that seem to point to something much larger than just the personal sphere often arrive just as a creative outcome arrives. These vortexes seem to have a darkly chaotic core that can play its way out via personal ambivalence about the new birth of the Self in one's life, and also play its way out in impersonal ways.

Does something in nature seem to counter-react to the evolution of consciousness, even when consciousness takes into account the unconscious? Our participation with this force, together with the arrival of redemption and compassion, is necessary for the transformation of toxic psychic environments and dark chaotic times.

The main point is, sometimes the difficulty of the Self's manifestation is not *just* personal in origin, but *also* impersonal. Two years after the death of her child, a woman in her fifties experienced a deep homecoming in her soul via her dreams, art, and love life. In a dream, she was given a new ring made of crystals that circled inward, pointing to the common center. A new psychic condition in her life took root; a new sense of peace arrived. Her artwork found its way into various galleries and museums throughout the United States, surprising and delighting her. However, while gathering together her art for a new exhibit of women's work at the Metropolitan Museum in New York (a highlight of her art career), she dreamed:

> A giant killer whale turns into something even more dangerous, some swimming, violent beast I did not recognize as any normal identified species. It swam for a surfer in the water and swallowed him up. I was on the shore line screaming, "NOOOOO!" Some young man goes to leap into the water to help, and I see him and can hardly believe it because what could his diving into the water with that monster do to help!

At this time in her life, all kinds of chaos unfurled. Within two weeks of the dream, the following onslaught occurred:

Multiple tax audits arrived out of nowhere which took months to settle. She owed not a penny more to the government in the final outcome.

Someone hit her parked car in a parking lot and tried to run.

Her jewelry was stolen out of her car.

Two of her animals became sick, and even with numerous vets and surgeries, the problems could not be halted. After all the surgeries, the vets did not even think that they had accurately identified the problems!

Two of her cars were repeatedly stopping for no reason, stupefying two automotive dealers after several rounds of fixing the same things with new parts.

Her alcoholic sister relapsed while staying alone at her home and had to be hospitalized.

Her fireplace caught fire in the roof of her home, and then a broken pipe flooded everything causing thousands of dollars of damage.

Family members came down with terrible illnesses, and her father died unexpectedly.

Her beloved cat went missing the day after an owl camped in the backyard.

The ensuing chaos took priority over the Metropolitan Museum exhibit. If she had fallen into believing that, "Oh, this exhibit of my work there does not ever really want to happen, this is a synchronicity and the psyche is trying to tell me that it is not ever meant to be," then she would have misread the situation. Usually, when such series of events fall upon us, our first response is to attribute them to the gods or ourselves, but it is often more complex than that. This woman realized that she could not tend to her life and the exhibit at the same time, so she notified the museum of the delays. Then, somehow, she kept to the daily tasks in front of her, in a spirit of amazement (and with some exhaustion). Everything eventually settled down. Because of unprecedented delays on the museum's part, she even managed to get her work into the exhibit. Vortexes of this magnitude are larger than personal.

The alchemical text referring to the worthless thief parallels the dynamics of these vortexes. It is not as though we need to always blindly try to "transform" this kind of dynamic (that is, personalize it, become more involved trying to "solve" it). Sometimes these dynamics can be like flypaper: the more we try, the more stuck we get in the problems. Instead, at times the process requires we find a way to survive, and even detach a bit from our personalizing through observing "the time of it" that *nature itself is having* in our lives as the birth of the new attempts to come into consciousness. Such an attitude does not need to relinquish responsibility for whatever in our own psychology might be contributing to the trouble—it is not an either/or situation. It is just that it helps to recognize the parts of the storm that are not personal, not our own. Having owned the parts that are our own, then we can afford to look with detached curiosity and even compassion on the difficulty nature itself is having in our lives.

Then, of course, we await the doves, the calming love instincts of yin. At a felt level, we easily recognize their presence when they constellate—the "right spirit," the sense of meaning and peace. These doves are like redemptive heart instincts born in us at the inner fountain during transmutations—instincts that can get past those personal and/or impersonal constellations that steal from us and remain with the heart of the matter. We assist this love in being born into the human sphere, where it can live, dance, create, and heal. These heart instincts are also like the felt devotion to which Jung referred, born of our attention to the flow of energy in the psyche and psychoid.[14] Interestingly, Jung thought this thieving energy was the same as the rabid dog—Diana's lower nature. However, I disagree. In the text, the rabid dog transforms into an eagle, a valuable solar creature, while the thief is worthless and does not transform.

Integration of Sun and Moon: Night Vision, Day Vision, and Binocular Vision

Integration of psychic experience into living wisdom that operates as an alchemical stone in our daily life goes hand in hand with the motif and imagery of *re-embodiment*. Both shamanism and alchemy refer to this theme. The old way of being is separated, cooked, and reunited with the source of original life and spirit, and then the parts are joined and embodied anew. Alchemical texts intermingle with astrological material in the archives of numerous cultures and depict the archetypes integrating into the field of humankind and the body of the great cosmic human. In India, the alchemical texts describing medical astrology portray the sun and moon residing in the embodied field of a human being—located in the eyes. The left eye is the moon eye; the right is the sun eye.

If we play with this metaphor, the sun (or day) vision perceives the rational delineations of separateness. We learn to see with nonpersonalistic wisdom from this eye.

Vision that comes from beyond the ego and is born from the irrational (or nonrational)—from the vast multiplicity of the psyche and psychoid—we could think of as night vision. In Greek mythology, the moon goddess was viewed as the "Giver of Vision." Both the full moon and new moon goddesses, Cybele and Hecate, were called Antea, which means "sender of nocturnal visions."[15]

We could think of sun and moon as residing in the psyche-body field as our two metaphoric eyes. When the two principles marry, vision becomes binocular; that is, two visionary bodies of being integrate into one mysterious whole. Based on each one's unique vision, they bring in different information that contributes to the vision guiding our life.

These visionaries continually go through rounds of death and rebirth in us as new, more advanced organizations of psychic life (new harmonies between sun and moon) seek fulfillment.

The interplay of sun and moon vision takes place in numerous life arenas. The awakening of the diurnal nature of the psyche, of the sun and moon principles within the individual, is the opus of depth psychology. Creativity and the healing arts make room for the binocular visions of sun and moon to play.

As the sun and moon principles mature within us, we become related to both Logos and Eros. As M. Esther Harding saw it, with Logos we acquire a relationship with a nonpersonal *truth*. With Eros, we gain relatedness with that which transcends personal ambitions as we gain relation to a nonpersonal value.[16]

The integration of sun and moon appears as the ability to see with both the rational faculties and the eyes of the soul. The integration of night vision and day vision is tantamount as we step into life with the fruit of the alchemical work. Then a spirit of "analysis" eases, self-consciousness releases, and we inhabit the newly-found ground of being in our life. We enter into new dynamic interplay with spirit in the world of forms. Rationality has learned respect for the vision of the soul, of the night world, and of multiplicity. The wisdom gained from the night world joins with the day world; wisdom is enhanced, not destroyed by the sun's adjoining vision.

FRUITFUL STRUGGLE BETWEEN SUN AND MOON

Whereas Apollo's mythic fate was to kill the great snake in the crack between the worlds, his heir, Asclepius, was fated to rediscover connection to the healing snake. Asclepius's dubious beginnings reveal the archetypal pattern of the sun-moon/brother-sister pair. Apollo's trickery duped Artemis into killing her own lover. In retaliation, she killed her brother's lover but allowed their child, Asclepius, to be born and sent him into training with Chiron to become the god of medicine and healing. The birth of medicine and the healing arts into the human realm, personified in Asclepius, emerges from the sun-moon struggle of opposites personified in Artemis and Apollo. As their fateful struggle unfolds, neither marries, and they remain in an archetypal brother-sister bond. In alchemy, Asclepius parallels the *filius*, the child in the soul who is born from the *coniunctio* of sun and moon.

At the ancient Greek healing center of Epidaurus, I was stunned to discover a curious phenomenon connecting the hero-god of medicine and healing arts with his mythic aunt and career director, Artemis. Epidaurus, dedicated to Asclepius, was built in the woods just above the even older Artemis shrine. A lovely stroll through a pine forest on a hill leads you to the perfectly preserved remains of the amphitheatre, where healing arts in Western civilization were first exchanged. Walking back down the hill, to the right, is a small shrine you could easily miss. There, in a crypt-like hovel, the remains of Artemis's shrine now house relics, including ancient bear and large cat skulls used in divinations by her cult followers.

The geography at Epidaurus rings true in the great human soul because medicine and the healing arts have at their foundation, *a priori*, connection with the life-and-death mysteries personified in Artemis. The healing arts and medicine are alive as mediums when they serve the mysterious life force, the wilderness of being as it incarnates in any being, helping it to survive and thrive. As such, medicine and the healing arts serve life itself. Like Paracelsus and the alchemists, medicine treats nature with nature, serving the light and life in nature. Ultimately, medicine also knows to release the body to death when it is time. This domain of medicine enters the territory of Artemis, goddess of the wilderness of being, protectress of newborns in the forest, and slinger of the death arrows.

The death territory of Artemis is not a romantic idea. It encompasses life and death and all the ultimate questions underlying our mysterious, brief lives in the web of creation. Being on the edge of death often reveals the mysteries of incarnation and healing to us and prepares us for death. Of course, death does not come only once in life; in alchemical terms, death-transformation arrows come often. It is no surprise that Artemis's presence appeared to the alchemists as they pursued the death and rebirth mysteries.

When the conscious and unconscious struggle in us to bring about a new unity of being, we can turn to Asceplius's arts. In medicinal dreams, we can discover the healing spirit of the snake between the worlds of conscious and unconscious, sun and moon, manifest and hidden realms and discover transcendent peace.

The Garden of the Alchemists

In figure 16 (page 152) Saturn waters the sun-moon trees in the alchemical garden, while the alchemist looks on. The image shows us the goal of the work. To bear the fruit of the sun and moon principles within is to live a life with imagination, where the fruit of yin and yang can multiply, while the religious instinct awakens and guides our life. The Self is born in this garden and multiplies. *Multiplicatio*, as the alchemists called it, is a fundamental mystery of the Self, wherein it has a life of its own that affects the world. The ego learns to carry water for the Self, to partner the life in the secret garden of the sun and moon mysteries.

We have been exploring how to live with the spirit of the imagination, the metaphoric snake living in the crack between the worlds. One way is to join in the rebirth patterns that spirit brings. This way leads us into the territory of sun and moon, of paradox, of rationality and soul, day vision and night vision, singularity and multiplicity, and so on.

Fig. 16. Alchemist in garden of love, with Saturn watering multiplying sun and moon flowers. Michael Maier, Symbola Aureae Mensae Duodecim Nationum *(Frankfurt, 1617), p. 555. In De Jong,* Michael Maier's *Atalanta Fugiens, p. 437.*

Here, in this alchemical emblem, the alchemist stands content in the garden of love, with Saturn (and his prothesis!), watering the multiplying sun and moon flowers. The *coniunctio* mysteries of sun and moon learn to multiply of their own accord when one comes to live close to the Self. The wounded masculine character in each of us who can discover means to serve the larger mysteries of the psyche is an important figure. The alchemist has his eye on the figure, and this figure is watering the sun and moon flowers! This seems to refer to how our work with these mysteries is linked with the gimpy side of self, the wounded one who is also essential for eventually bringing the water—or feeling—to the work and the ground of being where the life force of yang and yin dwell. When the wounded side learns to be a water carrier, that water, by definition, has to come from the work with a higher source. The fruit of the work appears in these organic mysteries of yang and yin grown in the alchemical lab of our life, with the invaluable wounded one serving these transpersonal processes.

Meditating on these figures of yin and yang, light and dark, that arise within, we can discover the development of the inner lovers, the *coniunctio*, that dynamic ecosystem within which the flow of the Tao between the opposites brings the soul's life into wholeness. Each of us is a carrier of this potential. Here the names of the divine within are discovered emerging from these inner ecosystems. The soul of the human being is that garden the alchemists discovered, where the fertility of the sun-moon mysteries comes to fruition in time, with great work and skilled cultivation.

PART II

THE *ALBEDO* & *RUBEDO*: REBIRTH OF CONSCIOUSNESS, SHINING RENEWED

. . . from the dry dock of mute old men
bring back the miracle of a tear,
from the delta of good intentions
bring back a seed that will change a life.

From the fields of the dispossessed bring me a donkey
with Byzantine eyes, from the wells of the mad
bring the bell and lantern of heaven

From the bay of forgetfulness come back with my name,
from the cave of despair come to me empty-handed,
from the strait of narrow escapes come back, come back.
—Lisel Mueller, "Spell for a Traveler"

6

The Divine Transforming in the Human Soul

Even if we are unconscious of it, the god lives in the vessel of our soul, of our psyche, as in the jar of Osiris or that of the Grail. It is up to us to pay attention and to allow the development of that which within us seeks to fulfill itself.
—Marie-Louise von Franz

Relationship with the numen develops and changes throughout our lives. These changes bring about new perspectives of what it means to be human and how we experience a sense of both time and timelessness in that human unfolding. In the alchemical image of the ouroboros, the snake holds its tail in its mouth, forming a circle—an apt image for this evolving relationship, for it is both linear and circular, mirroring that although we go through stages in life, something nonlinear and circular in the life of the soul can reveal itself. For example, if you think of a young oak tree in the forest, you don't say that it becomes the oak only when it is old and stately; the young oak had its hologram in it from the beginning. The unfolding growth brings forth the potential into reality, where wind, the angle or intensity of sunlight, lightning, rain, and such all play a part in the unfolding growth of the tree. The same is true of the human being. Watch any child and this becomes visible. The potential adult is latent in the child's personality and soul from the beginning, and the life experiences of love, nature, creativity, community, and so on will play their roles in the development or unfolding of the Self.

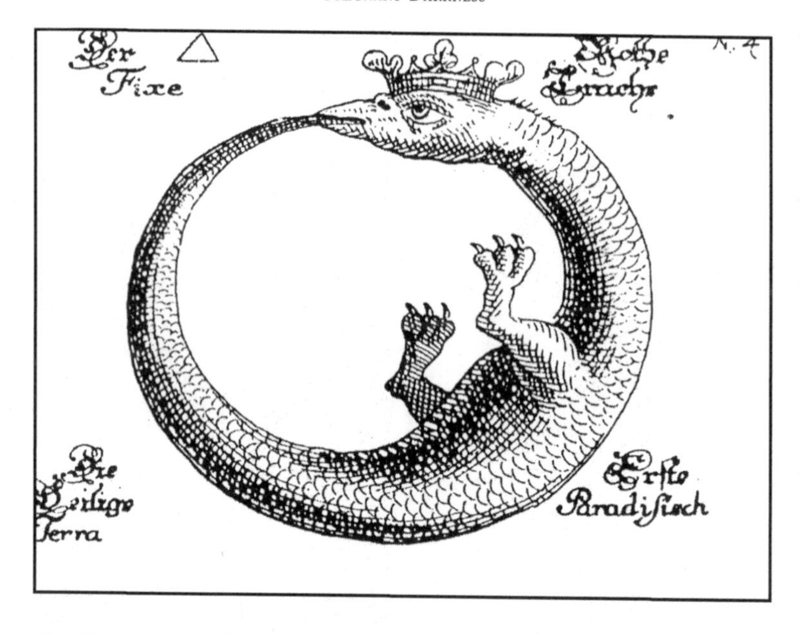

Fig. 17. Ouroborus. A. Eleasar, Donum Dei *(Erfurt, 1735), reprinted from Alexander Roob,* Alchemy and Mysticism, *p. 403.*

Sometimes we get an experience of where the latent Self in early life is linked to or mirrors the manifest Self that our life works to bring forth. If you think back to what books you loved to read as a child, and then look at those motifs that attracted you, most likely you will see those motifs still active in your soul and adult life now, and these motifs still bring your life meaning and richness.

A friend of mine who loved to read nature adventures as a girl spends her life both living in the wilderness and writing nature experiences, including a novel about a woman surviving in the woods alone for years. As a girl, one of my nieces loved *Star Trek* and science fiction and grew up to become a physicist in love with the mysteries and science of spirit and matter. I recall once when she was staying at my cabin when she was 12, she said she was going to read her favorite book for the third time. Just as she was about to disappear upstairs to read for a while, I caught a glimpse of the book under her arm. I was stunned when I looked down to see what this book was, expecting something like *Black Beauty* and seeing instead *A Brief History of Time* by Stephen Hawking!

Another of my nieces was both attracted and terrified by the book and film *E.T.* She had to draw E.T. over and over again and talk to him to turn her connection to him from fear to eventual friendliness. She grew up to become an astrologer and an intuitive in touch with psychoidal phenomenon.

Following in life what we love, what we are attracted to (and may be terrified of as well), brings forth the manifest Self, the fruition of the personality, the life force within.

The alchemical symbol of the snake eating its tail represents the self-transformations that can occur in a human life. The shedding of the snake-skin is a profound symbol of self-renewal. If you have ever come across a snakeskin "shell" in the wild, you know how strange it is to see the entire shell, with all the definitions of each scale left intact as the snake slithered out of it, its new skin tender, sleek and vibrant. Human life is invested in the creation and shedding of self, to bring forth the transmutations that reveal the manifest Self. In order to accomplish this, the life force requires that we consciously participate in shedding our outer coverings in various ways and in varying degrees.

Among alchemists, the ouroboros symbolized eternity.[1] The alchemists used the symbol to portray the divine circulation of psychic energy that brings about the creation of the Philosopher's Stone, the divine child. Psychologically, we would say that the circulation of psychic energy, which brings about the new center of the personality formed between the conscious and unconscious, carries new possibilities of initiation and renewal, as the mortal and immortal transform together.

The beginning of the journey of awakening often carries the innocence and naïveté of the fool archetype, whose emblem is the circle, the zero, the void. Walking with freshness into the unknown, we relate to life and the mysteries with our beginner's mind. Our initiations can take us far into territory of the psyche and psychoid as we encounter forces larger than the ego, perhaps exposing us to the death and rebirth mysteries. These experiences bring to light the divine core, the spirit in nature living itself out in human beings. Along the journey, as we become aware of the limits our mortality brings to light, we may link with the tail end of our evolution. This can bring alive a prescient feeling of the totality, that can be comforting, nourishing, and fulfilling.

As the soul expresses itself in time and space in the many manifestations of our lives, life energy comes full circle. Here our awareness of innocence, experiences of hardships, and accompanying wisdom, bring a sense of time shifting out of the ordinary or linear into circularity, synchronicity, and wholeness.

Alchemists such as Michael Maier imagined the alchemical *opus* (in psychological terms, the individuation process) as a *peregrinatio*, a wandering or odyssey. The alchemists found that the circulation of energy stimulated by inner reflection brings psychic energy back to the individual's life. The restoration of energy takes the linearity of the journey into a *circulatio,* where insight, freedom, and healing flow.

A man in his late middle-age years, an intuitive thinking scholar who studied Middle Eastern religions, had begun a deep process of life reflection in order to prepare for death. He had been in analysis during his forties, and wrote on related topics, where Jung's writings and his own scholarly work intersected. At this later time in life, he dreamed:

> I had turned my head toward my chest, and there in my heart I saw a light coming alive. Then I heard an alchemist tell me he was very happy for me, for I had learned how to circulate energy from the mind back to the heart. The alchemist told me that he . . . had been walking the road of my life from south to north. Now this road had a heart at the middle, which was growing and glowing in all directions. Some being lived in the heart-light, but I couldn't make out the shape, for the light was so bright.

When a dream like this arrives, it is difficult to use words to address it. For living the energetic mystery of it is more important than any words or interpretation. And indeed, for this man, he needed to live with the felt experience and reality of this new discovery in his body, psyche, inner attitude, for the dream is about ushering in how to live from a different center of consciousness—a change in which the soul is quite invested in this man's life.

Discovering from within the value of the circulation stimulated by psyche and reflection, the dreamer encounters the inner alchemist, a Self presence who has been with him his whole life, trekking on his road of enlightenment—the road from south to north.

Interestingly, the inner alchemist on the road of enlightenment needed the conscious personality *not* to take all energy to the head—to conscious mental awareness—and leave it there. Instead, he needed him to take the flow of energy—and all that is gained in terms of insight, understanding, awareness, and such—and bring it, submit to the flow of it, back to the heart center. Here he discovers a new way to live.

Perhaps the best way to have a feeling for this dream's impact is to take on the energetic flow of libido present in the dream's medicine. The dream prescribes a profound meditation of libido circulation that we, too can experience. Taking whatever insight or understandings we've gained in our lives and bowing the head to the heart, and discovering inside a felt, open-hearted way to live the mysterious incarnation we are, would be one way to honor this dream. This energetic meditation brings acceptance of the totality of our life, a religious attitude from which we can live. It is of course the dreamer's dream, and his psyche is ripe for the enlightenment brought forth from his work. Yet, we can honor the depth of the psyche as it appears here by acknowledging the universal truths appearing in the dream.

The dreamer's enlightenment comes as the energy circulates back toward his heart center. We speak of taking something to heart, meaning, to the deepest self. And there, a conversion in attitude and feeling occurs that centers us in a religious mystery that includes profound acceptance of Self, of life, and of the road we walk in life. The Sufis tell us that the heart (*himma*) is the seat of the imagination. Here in the heart center the dreamer finds the dazzling light, and the being residing there, although he cannot make out the shape of the figure through the light.

What does it mean to bow the head, the mind, toward the heart center? Insight, mindfulness, and conscious realization are not enough. They are not the goal, not the end of the road. Enlightenment is defined as insight fed back to the heart center, with the mind bowing to a center it serves. Circulation of the psychic libido, when taken to heart, becomes more than mental awakening. It becomes an embodied "religious" instinct, an indwelling, a felt experience of the divine as the basis of existence. Bowing the intellect and insight to the heart center, the dream tells us, brings a circulation of psychic energy the alchemist is very interested in. This would mean in simple terms the way of individuation at this point is moving from one of understanding with the mind to living with the mysteries also from the newly-born felt instincts of the heart. That the insights and understandings gained feed the life of the heart, the felt center of devotion where the divine being is born. This is particularly important, for the thinking function alone is not the carrier of the birth of the divine. The mental work and understanding feeds another mystery, the mystery of the heart, where the being of light resides. This truth cannot be underscored enough when it comes to life and work with the imagination. The insight or images are nothing in themselves if we do not take them to heart and allow them to change the way we live with the divine and with the world around us.

Paralleling this dream wisdom about the heart, Mercurius, as the alchemists depict him, often comes in a "dazzling white light"; as Paracelsus saw it, the inner star in humankind dwells in the heart. This appears in the dream as the dreamer's head drops toward the heart, he humbles himself and his thought processes to the way of the heart, and discovers this is where the divine is born and resides.

The alchemists spoke of the *filius*, the divine child born in the work. Looking further into the figure of light, in Christian iconography, Mary is often depicted with a full grown figure of Jesus, blazing in light, dwelling in her heart and solar plexus area. This stands in contrast to the literal pregnancy images of Mary with Jesus in her womb. For here Mary has discovered the divine Christ living in her heart. Similarly, this dreamer has discovered an experience of a true religious mystery, one his life's work has brought to fruition.

This experience of the figure of light in the dream can be seen as the divine born from the work. Through active imagination, the dreamer found that this mystery was something he could participate in during waking hours. The presence of his heart center grew and his life changed. Heeding his call to a fuller, more inhabited life, his focus on mental pursuits changed and interests in soul deepened. In the face of death, the dream world tells the dreamer that it is happy with this man's work and his discovery of the *circulatio* mystery. The concentration of the heart energy, the heart center—getting to what really matters in life and death—is the gold the dreamer discovers in his life-reflection process. As a thinking intuitive, the dreamer also discovered the divine that lives in a less developed side of the Self, the felt experience of the heart center. He came to hold the value of life, love, and creative work differently, and relational life changed, for his attention to felt experience and embodiment of his essence increased. Acceptance and compassion flowed out to those around him, as did his ability to tolerate the truth and engage in honest dialogues with others regarding love and life. He began openly discussing with his loved ones what had been missing in him, or what he felt he had done or not done, as a result of his unconscious wound, that affected others. This led to more fruition of the heart center, healing with those around him and inside his own religious conscience as well.

Interestingly, in the dream, the spirit of the work is blessing him with inner freedom in the dance of opposites, which in the long run also makes his passage through the end of life and from life richer. The dream image speaks of the path the alchemist has been walking. The alchemists' god, Mercurius/Hermes is known as the lord of roads, hence the god of enlightenment and individuation. Hermes is also known to be a guide into and through death. He appears in myth and dream at graveyards and crossroads as a guiding presence. When we reflect on the death and rebirth mysteries Mercurius/Hermes may appear. This is true in the case of this man, for his reflective process brings him in touch with the mysteries the alchemists knew, and with the birth of the being of light the alchemists sought. He has discovered the birth of the divine in his heart, at the center of his incarnational path.

These *circulatio* mysteries require being in touch with limitation, with mortality. They require consciousness entering time and space and yet also reaching out to what is eternal. These *circulatio* mysteries have been known through the ages in various traditions, and underlie psychic and physical yoga practices that lead to experiences (such as the one this dreamer was shown) of freedom and of the divine living in contact with our mortality.

The alchemist Albert Magnus used symbols to communicate the riches of the discovery of the *circulatio* mysteries, and refers to the presence of Hermes and the death-rebirth mysteries in his symbols. Magnus speaks of the *peregrinatio* (the process of individuation) as it ends with the discovery of Hermes' tomb, where a certain tree grows with a glorious greenness inside and a stork is perched on the tree. The stork is an *avis hermeticas*, a bird associated with Hermes himself and the adepts. This bird, Magnus tells us, calls itself "the circle of the moon." Here the sojourner shall build "golden seats and put a fitting end to his travels."[2]

When in touch with the mysteries of death (Hermes and his grave), we can experience a sense of Self (the tree and the bird) as it goes through the continual flux of dying and rebirthing, like the moon and her cycles. The stork is the "circle of the moon," meaning this presence at the center of the life tree is the great life spirit itself going through the waxing and waning cycles of change in our lives. The totality of the circumference, the circle, holds all the changing cycles within it. When we are in touch with death, this spirit, this circulating energy can reveal its mysterious presence throughout stages, elements, changes in our life. Then the ego becomes freed from over-identification with time and space and the changing spheres. We can then discover the light of nature, the energy of the life force, coming full circle. Something of the life force that is dreaming us shows itself in its totality, in its original or eternal nature, which brings peace. The alchemical image says this is where the sojourner can make golden seats and make a fitting end to his travels. This points to the golden seat between the opposites, the incorruptible experiences of Self where we are not unduly thrown around by life changes, though we experience these changes. The circle of the moon becomes an inner, felt reality, an ability to feel and experience the totality of life with all its changes, while wisdom grow within us.

A client of mine once brought this awareness to my door in a most immediate way. She was struggling with a life-threatening illness, and her son, a Navy SEAL—her only child and her only immediate family member—was shipped off to fight in the Iraqi war. Feeling perched on the edge of life and death—her own and the possibility of her son's—she was rushing to her session in a near panic. On the way, however, something else happened. Driving the winding road through the mountains in a snowstorm whiteout, as she made a hairpin turn, an unusual tree caught her attention. She slowed down. The tree was half alive, half dead, and a bird was perched in the middle of it. In the snowstorm in the middle of nowhere, the bird sat there singing its heart out, releasing a most lovely melody. This woman's eye connected with her soul, and in an instant an inner recognition, a snapshot of the image transmitted itself to her heart. The half-alive half-dead tree, the snowstorm, the singing bird perched in the middle all became like pieces of a dream.

She felt the bird within, sitting in the midst of the snowstorm, the chaos of life, all that is unknown and uncontrollable. And perched in the branches between life and death that soul bird was capable of singing with all its heart. She discovered inner peace amid these difficult realities of life and death, and discovered the soul's song as well. It is remarkably fitting with the imagery that the alchemist Albert Magnus uses to portray the way of the soul.

I believe mid-life is all about discovering this tree, this bird, these seats of gold, before we die, and living differently with what time we have left; living differently because of this immediate and individual contact with the alchemical mysteries of the divine-human marriage, as it has been informing our lives.

Life is then a flowering of the soul's emanation, like an oak tree or a rose unfolding, and not just a linear developmental trail we walk. In this way, the body of the snake in the ouroboros circle represents all the other embodiments of relationship to the unknown we have worked with in our lives—the peak experiences of illumination, *nigredo*, descent, struggles with demons/complexes, ecstatic experiences, the times of serenity and peace. The psychic energy circulates through all our phases, experiences, and embodiments, bringing a sense of timeless totality, wisdom, and innocence. Like the bird that is "the circle of the moon," something of the soul emanates in and beyond the specific phases of our lives.

Experiencing the ouroboros mystery can give us peace by bringing us full circle to the fresh openness of the beginner's mind and heart. There is a time for innocence, a time for diving into the *nigredo* of the journey, a time for working with demons, a time for being lost, a time for being found. The time for each springs out of the individuation unfolding uniquely in each person. The latent ouroboric Self incarnates in the manifest Self as we live in dialogue with the psyche. Dreams guide the way and express this unfolding individuation, bringing our awareness full circle into a psychology of synchronicity instead of linearity. No matter what we must consciously contend with in the dialogue with the unconscious, in the background is the ouroboros, the circular totality of the soul, bringing itself to fulfillment in our manifest lives.

Encounters with the Divine Transforming in the Human Soul

Sometimes dreams, active imaginations, creative urges, and the like, reveal how the spirit seeks us, chooses us, wants us to come build a bridge into a life lived near it. A man dedicated to suspending the dominance of rational thought in his life and to opening to psyche and psychoid, once dreamed the following:

> I am walking through a desert arroyo with my companions on some journey in a deep canyon with steep cliffs on either side. It reminds me of images of the intricate canyon systems in the desert of Jordan. As I pass one corridor in the canyon, I happen to look down it, and there, looking back at me with incredible feeling and interest, is a winged being riding a winged, horse-like mythic animal. We both pause and gape. We stare at each other through the canyon's stone walls with awe and pleasure. The glimpses take us both by surprise and bring such delight. There is an energetic field between the being and me. Somehow our attraction creates an energy between us, a communion. I feel connected with this being. Did we happen upon each other, I wonder? Did it choose me? I feel like it was following me, looking for a moment to get my attention.

Here, the dream world gives a glimpse of what seeks the dreamer and wants a dialogue with him. There are presences that seek us out and desire to transform with us as well. This dream marks the calling to the dialogue and illuminates the otherness of what needs attention, what wants a relationship with the human. In the Old Testament, the land now comprising Jordan and Israel was described as the promised land of milk and honey. By the dreamer's navigating the "intricate canyon systems" within himself, the "promised land" of the imagination takes hold. Later on, active imagination led him to a spontaneous, felt relationship with his helping spirit.

Love's Penetrating Spirit Contacts the Life Essence

The dialogue with the incarnating Self stirs when we experience deep love for another person. Love is a most important experience in the life of the soul, and how we hold the mystery of love plays a crucial role in our individuation. Jung points out that the alchemists found love to be the supreme uniter of opposites and the "final consummation" of the work.[3]

The archetypal constellations that inform personality are often noticeable when we are under love's influence. We may perceive specific archetypal qualities in a person's body presence and language, values, and ways of thinking and interacting. We may witness divinity and humanity working out their union in another person. When we engage deeply with another, additional archetypes constellate, and a unique spirit is born there as well.

Dwelling in a spirit of love (beyond merging with another) may bring insight. The tighter, neurotic sides of our personality often relax or release under the warm glow of love, and the true depth of the well we embody becomes more evident to us and to the beloved. Love's mysteries can open us to the soul and the divine core mysteries within us, including heavenly and hellish realms. Living in a spirit of love (not necessarily the same as "falling in love," although these are not mutually exclusive) is a classic way to release the tight bounds of ego consciousness. What does the divine core experience when we live in a spirit of love? Potentially, the divine core is loving the divine core in the other, whether human, animal, spirit, or otherwise.

A man in his fifties and his longtime lover visited some friends. He was delighted to find that as everyone started dancing to music, the two of them could not stay away from each other. Without thinking, they would find themselves erotically drawn to each other, courting and dancing up the energy between them. They would stop, separate, and have lovely conversations with others but again find themselves magnetically drawn to the soul of the other through the music. The experience, he reported, was one of feeling the core within drawn, of its own accord, to the essence of the beloved. People at the party noticed the energy of their connection and marveled at its immediacy after all those years.

At one level, love is our divine core attracted to the divine core of another. In the process of loving another, a mediating third spirit, which is more than the two combined, plays between the two individuals, and relationship is born. Of course, on a personality level, the two will also encounter the rough road of humanizing their complexes, dealing with merger fantasies, and so on, so that the souls can continue to love each other freely at the well of being. For love to thrive between two lovers, they must tend to their own evolution, and pray for grace as well.

The personal and impersonal dimensions of each being are two poles between which psychic libido and the spirit of love flow. If we take love so personally that we forget it is a divine mystery, the flow of love may stop because it needs the impersonal pole as well. On the other hand, when we experience the transpersonal dimensions of love but don't find a good vessel or form for it in our life, then love suffers.

If we think of love as informed by Aphrodite and Cupid/Eros alone, we miss out on the whole pantheon of energies that bring about love. I am partial to the truth in the mythic image of Hermes, lord of death and rebirth mysteries, trickery, alchemy, and the like. As the "lord of roads," he plays his tricky hand behind love relationships. In this mythic tale, he looks in on us mere mortals and, seeing our paths through life, makes plans to have this person's road intersect that person's road so that they fall in love, *for the sake of soul development.* It is not a moralistic impulse he has (not Hermes-Mercurius!), but a tricky, initiatory impulse coming from the shamanic qualities he possesses. With the "help" of this god magnet, functioning under the roads of our lives, we find those with whom our own needs to develop and grow will become apparent. The person we can usually dwell with is the person we can individuate with and, at the same time, engage in the mysteries of love. Love carries an incredible grace that helps us embody the nuances of life when we open our hearts to the full experience of the opposites, and to the divine life of love that attempts to grow between two people. Love is its own presence; it is a living spirit. Human experiences of trying to embody this spirit usher us into love's territory of heaven and hell. Getting caught in a split and ending up on either side—between the suffocatingly personalistic or the starkly impersonal dimensions—can be hellish. Love needs both these poles to flourish, or it weakens and dies.

Down river from my cabin lives a woman in her eighties who was an architect and poet in her youth. In her story, she gets caught in the personal polarity, and the more impersonal dimension arises to help her heal and to bring her balance in her old age. After her husband's death, she had been living alone for 15 years. One afternoon, while I was sitting with her by the river, she spoke to me—as a matter of course, half muttering to herself:

> I wandered the river shore yesterday aimlessly at sunset, enjoying the changing colors of light falling on the water and stones. I sat on various stones, enjoying different perspectives. I discovered an old swing from fifty years ago that my husband and I put up before the house was built. I hadn't visited this swing since we completed the cabin forty-eight years ago. I forgot it was there. Anyway, I dared to climb up into it, and it managed to hold my weight. As I swung in it over the river shore, I felt the young lovers we once were, with our lives ahead of us, swinging here and dreaming of the house and life we would have. It was painful to let these spontaneous fresh memories in. It made me see how crusty I have become, guarding my heart in a terrible way, really.
>
> As I opened to the pain of seeing this about myself, suddenly time changed. I was that young woman, innocent and open, wide-eyed, all the love to share, and as I swung back and forth, I also felt the old crone I am, the sorrow and constriction that bind me. Swinging between the young and old me, something happened. I changed. Something came full circle, and I found peace in myself with my life and love story—my stillborn child, the other lovers my mate needed in his life, my own loneliness, and all the good life impulses, too, the years here alone, loving the river and the solitude after his death.
>
> All these parts found a place in me in some new way. When I got up, I felt I was different, at peace. I was released from being *only* the "sour old woman" I have been, and I felt my love story as just right somehow. Somehow it was all less personal. The pain opened my heart, like it was part of a beautiful melody I wouldn't want to miss. I shook my head as I got up, caught my breath, and wandered home.

With old age, wisdom came in the door and brought her around again to the heart of innocence, healing, and renewed love. A wonderful picture of the ouroboric totality, her experience in the swing mirrors how the psyche brings the life story full circle. She mentioned, for example, that the sour crone in her carried many unnecessary resentments about the ways she thought life was "supposed" to go. The ego requirements for a less messy, less painful life had hardened her heart against her mate in the last year of his life. When in pain, we often compartmentalize and split off our experiences (both ecstatic and difficult). The divine, however, takes its course through all elements of our lives, loves, and struggles, and can bring a fresh inner sense of peace in response to the totality of the life we have lived. A courageous heart can open to the impossible pain in a human life and discover something beyond our ordinary human capabilities.

When we allow such experiences as this woman's to open us to the dimensions of time as synchronous instead of linear, something of the divine Self appears in our midst, and an inner harmony arrives among all the seemingly discordant parts. We may then drop into the awareness that our existence is organic, circular, like a unique flower unfolding its petals and revealing soul essence, petal by petal. The petals are, at one level, like the different manifestations in time—the child we once were, the maiden, the woman, and the crone—each open to allow the entire essence beyond time to come forth into the world. From the feminine point of view, from yin, this is the soul's goal in life, to draw the unique essence from the core, out into interaction with creation, and into our own creations, love, expressions, solitude, and so on.

As we work to contact the numinous and bring the divine essence to the surface of our daily lives, we may find ourselves sidetracked or even sabotaged by our attitudes toward our wounds, limits, and character difficulties. Our unconscious pain, avoidance, self-hatred, or disdain for what is wounded or "misshapen" in us can block the flow of psychic energy present in the ouroboric consciousness that heals. We often become blind-sighted or one-sided when we guard against our wounded or misshapen sides. The healing flow of psychic libido between the personal and transpersonal realms bathes us when we face, accept, and turn toward the wounded or misshapen in us, rather than unconsciously guard against awareness of our vulnerability or our ugliness.

David Whyte addressed this reality in his brilliant poem "Faces at Braga":

> If only our own faces
> would allow the invisible carver's hand
> to bring the deep grain of love to the surface.
>
> If only we knew
> as the carver knew, how the flaws
> in the wood led his searching chisel to the very core,
>
> we would smile too
> and not need faces immobilized
> by fear and the weight of things undone. . .
>
> If only we could give ourselves
> to the blows of the carver's hands,
> the lines in our faces would be the tracelines of rivers

Fig. 18. Penetrating spirit Mercurius, from "Speculum Veritatis," Codes Vaticanus Latinus *7286 (17th century), Biblioteca Vaticana, p: Inst.*

> feeding the sea
> where voices meet, praising the features
> of the mountain and the cloud and the sky . . . [4]

The "invisible carver" is like the penetrating presence of the unfolding Self as healer, lover, and carver. The hands of the invisible carver follow the "flaw" in our character to bring the searching chisel—the penetrating light of experience and consciousness—to our core, which can bring the deep grain of love to the surface in our lives. As the poem suggests, along with this penetration to the core comes a profound flow of energy that heals the neurotically tightened small identity, and allows us to see and praise the profound beauty and presence in the elemental world. This penetrating spirit of Mercurius is portrayed in figure 18, above.

The emblem shows double-natured Mercurius impaling both the snake and the king—an ouroboros image—on the philosopher's tree (in Coptic, *ouro* means "king," and in Hebrew, "*ob*" means "snake"). Here Mercurius penetrates into the secret of the king and the snake and pins them in their separate forms to the philosopher's tree. The *avis hermeticas*, the bird of transcendent wisdom, nests above, in the tree. The processes of penetration into the ouroboros mysteries support growing wisdom. The beginnings of creation (represented in the primordial snake) and the later developments of creation (human consciousness crowned with its link to the divine) are separated, penetrated, and eventually reunited. When the fruit of these processes occurs psychologically, consciousness comes full circle, and we return to healing experiences of original nature.

Jung pointed out that the alchemists felt that the acquisition of the nobler Mercurius who knows how to penetrate the secrets of matter is a gift of the Holy Spirit. And to possess him brings illumination. In the poem, the carver's hand is that nobler spirit whose penetration in depth psychological terms brings forth the soul essence through the flaw or wound. The carver's hand brings original nature and love to the surface where humans remember their place in relationship with this elemental majesty in which we live.

What Does the Divine Experience with Incarnation?

What does the divine, or impersonal, undergo as it attempts to find a life with us humans? How does opening the heart to inner experience, including suffering, free the divine and human dimensions within us? How can we support that freedom by the way we live? We can tend the mystery of love so that it has a life with us, or in our pain and neurosis, we can turn from love's transforming presence in our lives. How does the divine suffer when we extinguish love from our lives and consciousness? What if we could hear the divine's pain and respond to the angel of love with what *it* needs?

So often our dialogue with the unconscious is more of a supplication than a conversation. The psyche and psychoid, however, also seek us, need us, for their own life and transformation. When we listen to the nature spirit's need of us in all of life, when we listen to psyche's need of us in our own development, when we listen to the divine in the core of our being, then we begin to evolve. The transcendent function is the bridge between the two points of view—human and divine, personal and impersonal, symbol and history, time-bound and timeless. In order for that bridge to take form within us, penetration by realities beneath, inside, *and beyond* the personal historical referents is often necessary.

A renowned New Mexico artist, who painted in solitude, was undergoing deep analysis. In this soul-rich process, he discovered a new instinct for the craft; a new body of work began to emerge. At this time he dreamed the following:

> A merman is swimming about the ethers nearby me. I can feel him and see him at times as he appears in the mists. Does he swim in the ocean

> or misty air? I cannot tell, maybe both, or maybe there is no distinction in the dream between ocean and air. I am standing on a shore and see him to my upper left at one point, swimming. He was suffering because he had to come in from the depths and relate to the new central light—a lighthouse beacon of sorts. He was doing so willingly, as it was being asked of him by some higher law that had to do with this light. His suffering was apparent in his visage. The anguish showed in his mature, lined face. On his head, as he turned toward the central light, a circle appeared with a cross in it that formed a halo around his head. This seemed to pain him somewhat, but he submitted to the experience he was commanded to undergo. He would continue to swim the depths, but now he also had this halo structure that connected him to the beacon light, to which he had submitted.

The psychic changes this dream depicts brought much energy to the dreamer's artwork and life. The dream ego, similar to the merman, found the new way unfolding in his changing art and life scary, not knowing whether the inspiration in his imagination would survive the journey between the realms and come into form. At this same time, the man began a new love relationship, which his heart and soul seemed to take very seriously. He hoped that he could remain true to himself in the love relationship while letting the love flourish. Yet, to overpersonalize such a visitation as this merman would deplete the spirit of this dream, which carries an uncanny universality to it and speaks from a deep stratum of being. The dream message clearly applies to the dreamer's process and his new psychology, yet this being from the dream world is also mysterious and ancient, transpersonal, and cosmic.

In this dream, a center of consciousness beyond the ego is forced to change while the new center, the lighthouse beacon in the dreamer's consciousness, is constellating. This light is not ordinary ego consciousness; it is the new center born in the artist's psyche as he comes into dialogue with the unconscious. The transcendent function is developing this central light—an image of the successful incarnation of the manifest Self. The transcendent function also carries an *organizing principle* in the psyche. According to the dream, the beacon, representative of the transcendent function, carries an authority of a *higher law*. The swimming etheric merman now must submit to this beacon and allow ego consciousness (the dreamer) to see it do so.

What is the dream ego's role? The dreamer's ego consciousness is not meant to integrate the archetypal stratum itself, for the ego never really integrates the archetypal strata, it can only integrate its experiences and

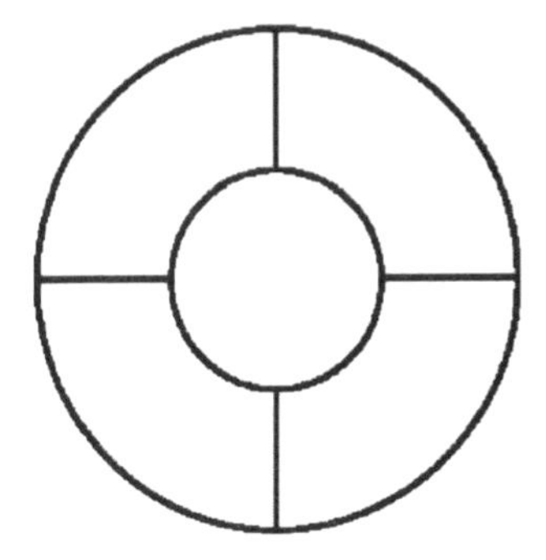

Fig. 19. Circulatio *diagram, double* quaternio.

develop wisdom and differentiated relationship with psyche. The ego in this dream is meant to stand between the new center and the depths of the psyche and psychoid and relate to the mysteries it finds itself a part of, through image and experience. This brings the dreamer in waking life into a process of integrating these experiences and images into a wider sense of reality.

In fact, the dreamer's consciousness expands as he witnesses the beacon and the merman. He is learning something by taking in both of these realities from the human point of view. In the dream, his humanity literally stands near the beacon. From this standpoint, he can also see, feel, and appreciate the fate of the merman, who is able to swim the depths and mists and is also drawn to relate to the new center of light. This is the modern plight. The dream gives us windows into the psyche at large. We moderns stand just so, poised unsteadily between the primordial consciousness of the deep and the new center of consciousness growing in the psyche.

Who is this merman, this being from the depths? We could think of many archetypal patterns that relate to this figure, for example, Proteus or Neptune. However, suspending classic mythological associations and personal psychological material may be helpful to appreciate deeper aspects of this phenomenon.

A watery, misty being who swims freely in the mysteries and survives on his own is now beckoned into submission to a new order. He must acknowledge the central light emerging in the dreamer's soul. The new order is mirrored by the halo on his head, which signifies some change of consciousness. On the surface of his features, suffering is apparent, for relinquishment of an old familiar way usually brings pain. Importantly, the merman is not dying or turning into a modern mortal figure. He clearly remains merman in nature, but he now has an established relationship with the center, indicated by the acknowledgment of the beacon and the curious halo structure around his head. The dreamer drew the halo as two concentric circles, the outer circle divided into four parts (fig. 19, p. 173).

After hearing this dream and musing on the nature of this image, without looking for anything in particular, I opened to the image of the same halo the client had drawn. It appeared in Jung's writings. The image originally comes from an alchemical text, *Tractatus Aureus Hermetis*.[5] It is a double quaternion, which Jung says, "stands for a totality, something heavenly and earthly, spiritual or corporeal, and is found in the ocean, that is the unconscious. It is without doubt, the Microcosm, the mystical Adam and bisexual Original Man in his prenatal state, as it were, when he is identical with the unconscious."[6]

According to Jung, the emblem of the double quaternion is united into one form by circular distillation and is named the pelican. The alchemists used this symbol to depict the circulation of energy between the worlds and between parts of the worlds. There is an outside, an inside, an origin from which all flows out and to which all returns, and an inferior and superior delineation (meaning that which is developed, and that which is less developed). The central circle is the origin and goal, the "Ocean or great Sea." The alchemists saw this center as connected to Bythos, the father god who is more primal than all other gods (who can be male, female, or neither) and whose name means "the abyss." This center is also known as the "mediator making peace between the enemies or the elements, that they may love one another in a met embrace."[7]

Thus, it appears that the merman, perhaps a representative of the spirit of Original Man in his prenatal state of identity with the unconscious itself, now suffers the incarnation of consciousness, with its delineations of the opposites. Original Man and Woman experience the creation of consciousness in each one of us. We can participate with this original presence if we discover ways to stand in relationship with the new center of consciousness wanting to incarnate in us.

The central circle of this halo structure, the alchemists say, also shows the mediator of opposites, which creates a circulation process among the elements of being that are inherent in all creation. This primordial layer is neither killed off by the light of ego consciousness, nor by the light of the Self. In fact, as the primordial being comes more into consciousness, it brings along the mediator of the opposites, Mercurius, also present in the central halo. The new lighthouse illuminates the depths and this incoming ancient wisdom.

As Jung also points out, the inner circle of this structure is ancient, and the universal archetypal structure corresponds with the Mercurial Fountain in the *Rosarium Philosophorum*, the text calling it "the more spiritual, perfect, and nobler Mercurius," the true arcane substance. With consciousness also comes the spirit able to unite with and transform the opposites. This spirit dwells at the center and flows between all realms, unifying opposites.

The primordial character in his suffering is illuminating, too. With this haloed double-quaternion structure, he is crowned by the "spirit of truth" residing at the center of creation. This spirit-center participates in the circulation of the elements and returns energy to the original source. He is the spirit of the fountain of renewal.

The alchemists' Mercurius is also a spirit of truth, a *sapientia dei,* but one who, Jung tells us, "presses downward into the depths of matter, and whose acquisition is a *donum Spiritus Sancti* [a gift of the Holy Spirit]. He is the spirit who knows the secrets of matter, and to possess him brings illumination . . ."[8]

In essence, this stunning dream reveals the original primordial being swimming in the depths of the human soul. In submitting to the development of consciousness, he now carries with him the circulation process, which is the mystery of renewal. He mirrors this primordial renewal of consciousness that is available in the human soul. The four components of the outer circle are like the four cardinal directions, the four functions, and the four elements (earth, air, fire, and water). Many aboriginal systems describe the cosmic order as having four essential parts, through which—like the sun through the four seasons—spirit and consciousness circulate. The spirit that circulates and brings oneness is the fifth element, or quintessence.

The alchemists found that until the illumination shone in "all four parts of the house," the light was not yet incarnate. The merman and his halo show the way. Consciousness will learn to grow, differentiate, and circulate for the latent Self to become more manifest in this artist.

The reality of the Anthropos, the Original Human dwelling in the human soul beneath conscious adaptation, is alive and well and valuable as it is, in its own transmutations. An anesthetic ego fantasy might compulsively personalize and pathologize the contents of the unconscious. However, if we let the depths of the psyche and psychoid show themselves to us, we can enter into relationship with the Anthropos, the primordial essence. This was the alchemists' goal. Indeed, contact through dreams with the Anthropos helps restore our experience of our original state before incarnation. This restoration gives us the sense of totality; now we can tap into the circular flow of energy infusing our lives that is imaged in the ouroboros. Energy does circulate between modern identity all the way to and from the bedrock of the human soul, where the Primordial One still peers through in dreams and other experiences. At the basis of existence, the human experiment is trying itself anew, and the raw material of primordial humankind lives in each of us.

In this artist's case, his work as a deeply intuitive painter needed to find its place in the larger totality of his life. The double-quaternion image of the merman's halo points out the need for circulation between the superior *and* inferior. The artist began to muse over this teaching, pondering the tail of his life as the inferior part he dragged around, afflicted with all he had neglected—his relationships, finances, physical body. He discovered from this dream character that his own intuitive side could no longer run off with all the energy in his life without depleting him. Relational, physical, and factual needs arose as the dream world began to bring these into higher places of value. He was being asked to balance his dominant function of intuition with the rest of life. His old psychology demeaned much of the natural world and the details of life. He began to marry his intuitive, spiritual side into the family of earthy elements, creating beauty and peace as he had the courage to inhabit more of the various paradoxical experiences that life entails.

The Greek alchemists illuminated these mysteries in their symbol of the ouroboros. In her book on alchemy, Von Franz points out their statement, "Unless the head has integrated the tail, the whole substance is nothing."[9] This refers to the meaningful flow of life energy through the different psychological functions of personality, through the elements, the chakras, the levels of being, and so on. This circulation brings the head, the dominant, into relationship with the tail, the inferior. Then begins a flow of the ouroboros mystery, like that in the merman's halo. This circulation process also illustrates conscious realization and the reapplication of conscious insights to the unconscious.

Often I discover in an analysis that when we take the flow of the Self seriously in mid-life, we soon discover the inferior tail we drag about in daily life. Where does the shadow of our dominant attitude of consciousness fall? If we discover and honor where the shadow of consciousness falls onto the inferior, less developed functions and parts of our lives, we may discover compassion and recovery of soul. Often, wherever our devils appear, the inferior is demanding attention. This is not an ego-psychology moralism placed on the life of the soul. Rather, this mystery grows in awareness as a natural process of individuation that issues from inside our dreams and lives. If we want to take the Self seriously and discover the freedom in incarnation with the divine, when dreams and life experiences "bring the tail around," we can respond, let them join, and honor the inferior. Then we can discover redemption in a meaningful flow of energy in life.

The world situation mirrors this interplay of "superior" and "inferior." The dominant value of rationality in ego consciousness has thrown into the shadows matter, animals, indigenous peoples, ancient ways, and even nature itself. All have been deemed inferior, inconsequential, of little or no value. Unless the head of the snake (the dominant consumerism and power value of modern consciousness) turns to take in the suffering of the tail (how matter, embodied nature, is faring under the imposition of these "superior" developments), the whole human experiment will teeter on the brink of extinction.

In our own lives, as we become aware of what it means to integrate the tail with the head, and the circulation of psychic energy of the divine this joining brings, we make a contribution to the plight of the modern world. Each of us must "listen" for the voices of the indigenous people living in the soul, for Primordial Man or Woman, who lives in sync with creation and can awaken that synchrony in us. What god dwells at the bottom of the human soul and transforms there? There is infinite, divine uniqueness in each being (human, animal, and otherwise). Humankind harbors a basic fundamental mystery. Original Woman, Original Man, or as Jung put it, the Great Man, Great Woman, the divine Anthropos, dwells at the core, the living archetype of the human being. The divine-human form is working to come into the modern world, working to incarnate into our fields of consciousness. By experiencing the Great Man or Great Woman working its way out in our lives, our ability to feel, express, create, and emanate this profound core energy unfolds.

The experience of consciousness and of the ego—the "I" that can make choices, shine its light in certain directions and not others—does not have to cut us off from the experiential root of this profound mystery. Look for "Her" or "Him" in your dreams, in your experiences in nature, in love of food, sex, starlight, passion, wisdom, loneliness, heartache, urges for unity with the world soul, and urges for cosmic consciousness. For Original Man, Original Woman, is the star in us, living behind each modern face. However, without experiential connection of our roots in the primordial, the divine core in us can become lost to consciousness.

How we live helps create the bridge to the transpersonal, which makes it possible to bring the Anthropos into incarnation, instead of some human mutation that asserts power over nature without keeping track of the cost. Each of us who is in touch with the Primordial Man or Woman within us must tend to this layer, asking it how it needs to live in this modern world, in our own individual lives, and see whether we can make some movement to access and accommodate this core. The Anthropos lives closer than modern ego consciousness to the essence and family of all life forms, and contact with it can enliven our lives tremendously. Jung called the dream source the Great Man inside who is redreaming life now. With growing relationship to the unique indwelling divine, we can learn to consult with the Great Human Being throughout life and respect the truth the Great Human Being brings.

Resisting the Divine Incarnation

In contrast to the dream of the merman, the following dream shows the collective mass consciousness having trouble integrating and honoring the birth of the divine into the human realm. It picks up the evolution of the Christian myth, which is so important for our times. So many flee collective religion nowadays, yet they do not discover the individual bridges to the divine to replace the old collective path. A thirty-year-old lapsed Catholic client experienced a tremendous opening to universal consciousness during a crisis in her life. At this time, she dreamed:

> I was walking into a walled city with many other humans. The walls were flimsy, as though of cardboard and paneling. They were pulling the walls in closer for some strange reason I didn't comprehend. I realized that Christ walked in with me, in his resurrected state! Then I saw that the masses were scared and wanted to grab the body of the Christ. They did so and began throwing him over the wall, thinking to protect themselves against his consciousness. I wanted out of there and was leaving through a crack in the fortress. The others, feeling safer with the Christ figure gone, pulled the walls in tighter and huddled together. I woke up anxiously, screaming "No!"

As an image of her inner collective, this dream did not bode well for an easy integration of the heights of consciousness she had experienced. In fact, parts of her inner community were obviously adamant about defending against her cosmic—to them, Anti-Christ—experiences. Her dream response showed that she could not go the way of inner *or* outer collective.

She would have to find another way, over time, to integrate her experience and help along other parts of her that were scared of what she had brought back from her sojourn. Often individuals who have sudden blasts of heightened cosmic consciousness suffer when they "return," for reasons just like this. The rest of the inner community must come around as well, which may or may not happen, depending on the diligence and steadfastness of the person and on grace.

This dream is remarkable for showing what the incarnation of new consciousness goes through—it is *thrown* out and resisted by the fearful inner collective. Then it is left to wander in the outer regions. Luckily, the ego left with it, rather than identify with the flimsy but tenacious defenses.

Universality exists with this dream—it applies to the plight of modern consciousness at large. Parts of the tiny mind, the fearful defenses of earlier constellations of consciousness, may try to throw out the "Christ consciousness"—illuminated consciousness that has suffered the connection to spirit, has risen into a place of enlightenment, and wants to return to incarnation. The tiny mind may want to throw this out and pull in the walls for comfort against these mysteries. "Jesus" is not betrayed only once, a long time ago; modern consciousness ditches the death and rebirth mysteries of the god-man at every turn. The mass denial of mortality and the gargoyle-like advocacy of materialism in the Western world is proof of this ever-repeating betrayal.

However, the opposite is true as well. We can turn to psyche and learn to open to the divine-human mysteries. Somehow we can, with help from the transcendent realms, shape our human lives so that we make room for the birth of the Christ—and room it does require. As one Swiss analyst, Gotti Isler, put it, "We are but a *manger* for the birth of 'Christ.'"[10] The Nativity, in fact, mirrors the revolution the self attempts. The manger, made from old wood and full of straw, houses the animals and an exhausted couple who would do anything to guard the birth of their anointed child from the threat of Herod. The manger shelters two simple human beings, who had made their way to Bethlehem as best they could, on an ass, with a little water and food. They were fulfilling the Roman order to return to the town of their birth for a census. While a guiding star flickers overhead, wise men from the East, astrologers, witness the humble yet world-altering birth.

We are humbly called to relate to the mysteries of heaven and earth. In answering the call, we go where we must to get out from under the *domination* of the shadow of consciousness that seeks to destroy the valuable birth of the new "king." The shadow in human beings is lazy or power-ridden or demands false simplicity or instant gratification, tiny-mindedness, and so on. Yet, out from under the shadow's dominance, what a humble king is born. No roof, no home, no wife, no power, no money, no career, no status. Just a connection to spirit, an open heart, and the dynamic ability to emanate the mysteries, eros, and truth in his presence and teachings—and he brings in the new order.

The birth of the new consciousness does not mean an inflation of instinct or spirit. It can come to us through the ordinary events and moments in our humble or troubled lives, into the manger that we are. In fact, it seems to choose just that setting.

What is interesting about this dream is that the community rejects the *risen* Christ! It will not let the Christian myth evolve, and it will not allow the sublimated Christ to come into human life. Very curious, indeed. Part of what is difficult about the Christian myth is its need for evolution—"Jesus" is still in the making. The risen Christ is not just off in heaven, where we will join him one day. It is an inner reality, dwelling in the heart of us all, and can become more and more incarnated and draw more and more libido to it as the divine becomes part of every facet of our life—the opposite of what happens in the dream. This dreamer did "stick it out" and her inner receptivity to the new value took hold over time.

The Evolution of the Divine in Our Life Journey

One man in his seventies reported a dream he had had when he was thirty-five, a dream he never forgot. At the time he had the dream, he was settled into marriage with his college sweetheart. They had six children. He worked at a steady job, went on planned annual vacations, and was part of the local community, an active leader in his Catholic parish. He was unaware of sensing any change in his life at the time of the dream. Many years later, when each of these manifestations in his outer life had all radically changed (he divorced, moved out of his community, retired early, left the church, and so on), he thought back to this dream. The dream seemed to portend the coming changes. What moved me most in hearing the dream was that it showed how, beneath the surface of his life, the god he loved was changing, too:

> I am in an old abbey. I go downstairs, below the great library. There, a hooded monk waits for me in a boat on a river that runs underneath the abbey. He motions for me to get into the boat. I do so. It is kind of eerie. He puts his oar into the water and says to me in a deep, quiet voice, "You

> know, Jesus will have to die seven times seven, and this is just the beginning." There was warning and concern in his voice. He then rowed on, taking us into passageways in the dark beneath this abbey.

The numinosity of the dream made it stick in his memory. He viewed that dream as the key indication of what wanted to occur in his life and *was* occurring, beneath all his outer-world changes. The messenger comes cloaked as a monk, but interestingly, a monk of the soul, not necessarily related solely to literal Catholicism. He is a psychopomp, a guide who is telling the truth and leading the dreamer into the journey of transformation, deep down in the foundation of his psyche. The guide also has a sober message for the dreamer. There is a descent to be made, and several evolutions of god will take place. Jesus must die "seven times seven."

It is easy to fall into thinking of the Jesus mystery as a historical event that happened a long time ago instead of a living reality in our life. This is the curse of dogma. It fossilizes the mysteries into something historic, something outside the self, a past event happening to someone else instead of a living dynamism always available to human experience. Jesus instructed us to pick up our crosses and follow him, with the knowledge that others to follow him would do works even greater than his. Psychologically, he appears to be instructing us who follow in time to pick up the individual path of incarnation, the fourfold path of coming into time and space (the cross), and to bring the human-divine dialogue in our lives to fruition.

Nonetheless, this dream essentially announces to consciousness (fixed in dogma at the time), that dogma, or fixed consciousness, is dead. The dream also seems to say, "Long live the divine-human mysteries!" And long may the divine live and transform in the foundation of the dreamer's life! This god he loves is closer than he realizes—he is in his soul, transforming, and the death process will take place a number of times.

Seven is the number of the descent. There were seven gates in the Sumerian myth of Inanna; she leaves a piece of clothing at each gate until she enters the underworld naked. In ancient astrology, there were seven lords, seven planets, seven metals, seven rungs to the planetary ladder, and so on. In the New Testament, people are told to forgive seven times seven. This sounds like a command to forgive endlessly. It also suggests an underlying cyclical transformation process to which one must submit. The alchemist Trismosin, in *Splendor Solis,* stated that the alchemical art has seven parts and that the processes of dissolution and coagulation should happen seven times.

Most importantly, this dream speaks to the nature of the religious function in the dreamer's life. It attempts to awaken within him the reality that religious life is not a static, historical, or collective road. Instead, religious life is envisioned as a living dynamism, a journey we must take if we follow the guide of the soul. This life entails an inner process in which the god we love and suffer is *within*, changing with our humanity at the foundation of our life.

As mentioned at the beginning of this chapter, von Franz envisioned the religious function like this: "Even if we are unconscious of it, the god lives in the vessel of our soul, of our psyche, as in the jar of Osiris or that of the Grail. It is up to us to pay attention and to allow the development of that which within us seeks to fulfill itself."[11]

Going along with the inner guide, yet remaining differentiated, allows us to participate more individually and consciously with these forces as we, and they, transform. The drama of our lives is inexorably linked to their stories. When the religious function is operating in the psyche, the inner guide is activated. Encounters with the inner guide enable us to connect with the numinous, expand our consciousness, align ourselves with the soul, and find an inner harmony. When von Franz mentions the jar of Osiris and the Grail, what does she mean? Our devotion to the soul can create the vessel for conscious experience and participation with the divine as it is transforming within us. The myth of Parsifal and the Grail king captures this theme. Poor Parsifal is a lost soul in search of the Holy Grail until he is asked the question, "Whom does the Grail serve?" He realizes that it serves the mysterious Grail king, the divine-human consciousness that has been living within the castle all along. At this moment, he connects with the divine counterpart living in his soul and is no longer lost. Thus, the "Grail" is found, and its mystery is brought to life. It is the carrier of the connection between the human ego and the divine Self.

The man's dream is pointing to a similar mystery. It is telling him that his life is more important and more immediately linked with the divine than he is yet aware.

"Atheists" Find These Mysteries, Too

Marie-Louise von Franz's statement distills the gist of the religious function in one line. Interestingly, she says that the god is present within us even if we are unconscious of it. Our conviction is not necessary to host these mysteries, nor is even a dim, conscious connection with them. There is no dogma, and we do not have to believe in order to experience these mysteries.

They are ancient; they underlie the organic living structures of the psyche. They simply bubble up of their own accord, expressing themselves in psyche and matter every day. Yet, with attention to these mysteries, we give the latent Self a better chance of incarnating into time and space. These mysteries have provided the inspirations present at the beginning of all world religions. They still spring to life in psyches devoid of belief. The following example plays with the reality of not having to be a "believer."

A young woman worked with me for years and went on to become a psychologist. During the time we worked together, her "irreligious, practical-minded" (her description) father was dying. He was having great difficulty emotionally, although he could not talk about anything he was experiencing. He was an introverted, sensation, thinking, judging type. For decades, in his career as an engineer, he had traveled all over the world repairing broken satellites. She was wondering how she, as a feeling, intuitive type, could talk with him about death or what he was feeling. He always pushed away feelings, and certainly anything to do with spirituality, with mockery.

At the end of his life, her father, "without a single religious bone in his body," whispered to her, "There is a very special Guest in the room, and could you all please be quiet and make room for the Guest's presence?" Each person in the room felt the reverence and stillness emanating from her father in his last moments. Later, his daughter and I had a deep laugh together over the irony of it all. The nuts and bolts of the satellites, which he spent so much time tending in his outer world, in the end had an inner parallel! The divine touched him at death through his undeveloped intuition. An inner satellite picked up the clear intuitive signal in an experience of reverence—devotion to the very special Guest, which ushered in the need for quiet—and brought him profound inner peace.

When the dimensions of the ego and personal layers of the unconscious open at death, the divine spark may ignite. Communion with the "other" often becomes very possible as the realms of consciousness become much more fluid. The death process does not occur only at the temporal end of life but can, instead, appear in degrees, whenever the ego relinquishes its attitude of supremacy and allows itself to be penetrated by the counter position held in the psyche.

Jung describes how the ego must encounter the "other" in the unconscious for transformation of consciousness to occur: "This continual process of getting to know the counter position in the unconscious I have called the 'transcendent function' because the confrontation of conscious (rational) data with those that are unconscious (irrational) necessarily results in a modification of standpoint. But an alteration is possible only if the existence of the 'other' is admitted, at least to the point of taking conscious cognizance of it."[12]

This recognition of "other" places the personal ego in relationship with larger reality and makes connection with the infinite possible—and connection with the Guest, the Grail king inside one, as well.

WHICH INNERMOST VALUES ARE ON THE THRONE?

When we leave collective religion behind, we put *something* on the throne instead. This is the nature of consciousness. Whatever prevails in our inner attitude and outer actions is put into the place of value. What we value most deeply and how we actively live out these values in our lives determine the shape and quality of our existence. We can say that we espouse one value and yet have another sitting unconsciously in the dominant position. In fact, we are often unconscious not only of the "god in the vessel," as von Franz put it, but also of the secret value ruling our lives. Dreams address this unacknowledged territory by showing us the conscious attitude affecting our connection to life, love, and the mysteries. This can be any attitude in which we become unduly caught—attempts to control life, excessive rationality, security needs projected onto relationships or money, one-sided power drives (or refusal to take up our power), addictions to stimulation and distraction, regressive childish fantasies of how life is "supposed to be," and so on.

When we turn to the dream world to discover the soul and our connection with the mysteries from inside our own experience, these old attitudes become dethroned, and a deeper inner value, the transformed value, begins to emerge. Jung addressed this inner situation of discovering the deeper value:

> But where shall we find the risen Christ? . . .
>
> I am not, however, addressing myself to the happy possessors of faith, but to those many people for whom the light has gone out, the mystery has faded, and God is dead. For most of them there is no going back, and one does not know either whether going back is always the better way. To gain an understanding of religious matters, probably all that is left us today is the psychological approach. *That is why I take these thought-forms that have become historically fixed, try to melt them down again and pour them into moulds of immediate experience.* It is certainly a difficult undertaking to discover connecting links between dogma and immediate experience of psychological archetypes, but a study of the

natural symbols of the unconscious gives us the necessary raw material. . . .The fact that only a few people see the Risen One means that no small difficulties stand in the way of finding and recognizing the transformed value.[13]

Discovering the Ally from the Psychoid

This following dream speaks to how the divine seeks its reflection in the alchemical laboratory of the human life; our lives can also mirror the nature spirit's transformations. A woman who had undergone abdominal surgery early in life that led to her inability to bear children, experienced twenty years later the following dream:

> I am lying in the mountains somewhere. I feel how my body is like the landscape. And my belly becomes a lake. Then it is like I am deep inside a mountain, and I am looking upward toward the sky, and my body is this high mountain lake deep in the mountain. I look upward and see a circle of sky, the lip of the mountain ridge holds the lake in a circle. Suddenly it is nightfall. I see the face of the divine appear over the edge of the mountain lip.
>
> The divine is curious, and attracted, and looks in to see what is going on down in this mountain. The divine seems a little nervous about looking, like it knows it will require a commitment and action on its part. Then the divine has the courage to look. My belly is now a lotus with water in the middle, and the divine is drawn through love and mutuality. The divine reaches over the lip and looks in deeply, and recognizes its reflection in the lake, and its transmutations in the depths of the water too—that is also somehow my belly.

An active imagination then led the dreamer to experiencing a development of this theme.

> I go into the woods, to the secret path I love to walk. Suddenly I realize I am lying down on the path along the river. I feel the winding path stretch out ahead, and I look up at the sky. Out of the sky comes a lover, to unite with me. He is beneficient, and also snake-like, and he wants me to dare to look at him. I look at his body above mine, and see that his tail stretches on down my path, and is immensely long—it takes my breath away. The tail stretches on out into eternity. It goes out the window of our atmosphere, and on out into the regions beyond our galaxy, where his home is. I ask him, "Where do you come from? What is your name? What have you got to do with me?"

> He shows me where he comes from. He says it is like this. And then he opens up my belly, and the belly of the earth. Then the sky cracks open, too. And I see him then come from the sky, down to the earth. The crack in the earth is shown as the mythic crack in the Celtic world, where the lovers Igraine and Diarmud emerged, and where at times of the year the spirit worlds are said to open. Somehow lying down and being the earth, (and being open to cracking open) allows the sky to also open, so he can come in.
>
> He tells me his name. And then he wants to answer what he has to do with me. He shows me his fierce protection of what I love. He crouches his dragon body on my secret path in the woods, and wheels his head around snorting and breathing fire, sparks of color emanate from his head. He lets out a fierce roar of protection of this path, my path! Somehow he is my companion and protector.
>
> I feel such ecstasy with him it is beyond anything I have experienced. I then talk with him and realize he doesn't rescue me from anything I need to do in life, but he will come as a lover, companion, and protector. He breathes into me, and with me, back and forth in the sweetest experience of life and soul, it is indescribable. He says, "When you feel I am far away, all you have to do is breathe like this into your true felt self, and I am here." This breath melted away all cares, all thoughts, all falsities, and brought ecstasy and sweet peace, a most profound communion between cosmic being and human being. I felt no violation, but quite the opposite, a felt-experience awakening of my own soul and simple humanity.

This dream and active imagination bring in the immediate experience of the divine in relationship with the generative psychic-emotional-physical wound, and in relationship with the path of individuation. It reveals how the god image is changing in this woman's life. There is an autonomous force, from the psychoid regions, that accompanies each of us and is capable of becoming personally engaged with us as a companion and protector. Jeff Raff calls this companion "the ally." This cosmic companion is drawn toward us via the alchemical working out of our own wound. The wound can become generative, that is, capable of carrying the living alchemical waters where the divine and human discover one another. Here both human being and the divine change together in surprising ways.[14]

Interestingly, in this woman's life, the felt experience of soul became alive like she once felt it in childhood. A simple, open presence and love of life came to her again. At this time the false-self problems in her life and relationships also rose up to the fore, which let her know the appearance of the dragon lover who protected her path was also calling her to her truer self and path through life. The being seemed to need her to get more real

Fig. 20. Alchemist explores beyond known star regions. From Maier, Atalanta Fugiens *(1618).*

in a number of ways, and brought these to her awareness in daily life. As she confronted these one by one, through her breath the love connection with this being and her soul grew.

She also found he wanted her to sacrifice previous kinds of relationships with the imaginal world that did not serve where she was now heading. One dream showed her visiting a certain animus character who was dying; she grieved his death and left him. And when in the dream she got into her car to leave, her sister and a friend were in there with her. The friend said, "Good. Now look, when the water settles the snake will have something good to drink!" As the dreamer looked, there was the snake next to a pan of water, in which the sediment was settling.

The working out of the wound so that it becomes a carrier of the living water is central to alchemy, and to Jung's work, and to our own healing and development. The refinement of our connection to the living water of life never ends. The alchemical work takes us into contact with what exists beyond the psyche and archetypal domains, into contact with the psychoid. The alchemical image in figure 20, page 187, shows the alchemist looking beyond the veil, into the nether regions of the psychoid. Being open to experiences such as this is crucial as the god image is evolving in us all.

The Ally as Erotic Healer

A young woman in a deep depression was feeling no inclination to live. Worried that death would come in some unconscious accident because of her lack of attention in life and her emerging death wish, she sought the help of an analyst. She expressed the fear of just letting go of the steering wheel on the freeway some time. The analyst said to her, "What if you did?" This jarred her consciousness. Clearly, the analyst thought of this fear as a metaphor. She tried on the idea and found it very freeing. In an active imagination she let go of the wheel and experienced the car slow down to a stop. As she let go of control, she wondered whether something else would come along to help her.

The depression consuming her life stemmed from a mother wound so deep that her existence was in question. She was unable to feel the value of her essence, the value of living. The inner world was not yet real to her. This woman's libido was blocked in her depths while flowing too freely on the surface of her life. She gave herself away in her relationships. She was without boundaries. At the same time, her core self was hidden and frozen within. She had had only a few orgasms in her life with a man. She had no idea of what it would mean to feel her own hunger and enjoy her sexuality. Her true feelings were also an enigma to her, buried under the rote, collective patterning of her roles in life. Her shadow was split off as well, making the persona even more deadly. Very little instinctual Eros was allowed into her life, because of the repressive collective norms that ruled her. Very little Eros or energy was present yet in her dreams, which was a grave concern. Then she came in with the following dream:

> I am on a stage with a number of people. There is no audience, just the people on the stage in some old theatre. I do not know what it is I am doing there, but then I kind of just find out. I am walking to the center of the stage, where the story is taking place. My pain is immense. I am overwhelmed with feeling utterly lost. I don't think I can go on. In my pain I throw myself off the stage, thinking I will die, hoping I will die.

> Then, to my surprise, there is a net there that catches me. I am dangling on this huge thick net now, wondering, *What the hell?!* But then I realize I am stuck in fear, my legs shaking. I cannot move off this net, up or down. I need help. Suddenly, a lion man appears. His fur is sticky, glistening with some substance like honey or oil. He comes over to me and holds me and helps me. He meets me on this net. The attraction is strong.

In looking at this dream, it becomes clear that psyche sends the exact messenger she needs. This sticky, furred lion-man is such an erotic and courageous creature. One might imagine that the stickiness is like the field of Eros. The honey or oil notion is lovely, also, as honey is the food of the gods and oil, the most precious of substances, was used in ancient times to venerate the gods. The glistening substance on the lion-man's fur might also suggest semen. The messenger's essence is in perfect dialogue with the void in this woman.

The erotic lover, the rescuer, the solar, lion-hearted strength of the chthonic part-animal part-man, is the god her experience of the vast emptiness called forth. Grace arrives just in time in her story's unfolding. In her pain, she wanted suicide. In James Hillman's genius work, *Suicide and the Soul*, he speaks of how suicide is a hasty attempt at transformation. However, the urge for the death is the urge for the state of consciousness to change; it is a cornerstone in transforming the suffering and initiating the sufferer into the life of psyche, where healing waits. Her urge for change is played out on the stage of the dream world, and of life, and help arrives.

Most interesting is the connection between this grand net and a mythic reference to Cretan Britomartis, a form of the huntress goddess that predates Greek Artemis. Britomartis becomes one of Artemis's nymphs and is later incorporated to such a degree that *Britomartis* becomes one of Artemis's names. Nor Hall tells us:

> Once Britomartis . . . ran and hid from a pursuer for nine months until, unable to hide any longer, she threw herself into the sea. Her escape is not unlike the chilling historical account of the Greek mothers and daughters who, when faced by enemy Turks, sang and danced the sacred *romaika* and hurled themselves one by one into an abyss. They would rather throw themselves to their deaths from a cliff than submit to the treacherous hands of the enemy men. Britomartis was saved, however. Fishermen caught her in their nets below so she was thereafter called Britomartis Diktayma, "of the nets"—another name of Artemis.[15]

Britomartis of the Nets became a goddess to whom the shipwrecked sailors would call out for help. Legends abound in which Artemis-Britomartis of the Nets would cast down her nets over the cliffs to rescue sailors from drowning after a shipwreck. Artemis, mythology tells us, was known, at times, to give permission to her nymphs for sexuality, and at times not. Likewise, Artemis enjoyed sexual relationships abroad with non-Greeks but at home remained unto herself. This goddess represents the virginal self, an *instinctual* archetypal energy that helps regulate union and preserves the virginal core of being.

The life task of individuating into womanhood—into instinctual care of self and the ability to play and join erotically with another—was not possible for this woman, given the constellation of her personality. This absence brought a crisis to the fore. Without the inner guardian of Self and the trust of true Eros, her life shipwrecked. Indeed, her husband began having affairs and eventually left her for a friend who was "sexy." She suffered from a lifelong, unconscious avoidance/fear of Eros, of passion, sexuality, and life. The larger realms of archetypal experience were mostly blocked out, that is, until the depression set in.

Like Britomartis the nymph and the historical Greek mothers and daughters, as she grew desperate, she literally let go of hope, of control, of knowing what to do, and leapt into the unknown. In a way, her lostness and hasty suicidal urge drove her off the edge of life's stage. An ancient Zen saying, "Leap and a net will appear," rings true in her situation. This web, this weaving, this net to catch her, began her relationship with the dream world and natural world. As she leapt, the divine inner mystery sent help—a net to catch her *and* an erotic helper.

The new presence, her inner guide, brought vitality and Eros into her life and consciousness over the next few years. Learning to discover her deeper instincts (her Artemisian core, where she belonged to the feminine and to no man), she also opened to love, to Eros. Dreams were full of new animals arising and accompanying her; for example, a wolf pup became her constant ally. It is said that when Leto gave birth to Artemis and Apollo, Hera proclaimed that the birth would have to happen at the wolf hour, the hour before dawn, when only wolf eyes can see in the dark. The fresh core of psychic energy—both spiritual and instinctual—that this young woman tapped initiated her into the wellsprings of her own instincts, slowly over time, so that she could see into her inner darkness. Here, discovering the resources in the larger personality, she learned to penetrate the problem areas in her life, where libido had previously frozen. These resources helped to raise her, taking her through the developmental stages of life she had missed earlier on because of her severe wounding. Her connection to the self and her erotic core invigorated her.

She learned to court the living dynamism of this lion-man in active imagination. He opened doors in her psyche and body, and even taught her trance dancing. Her meditations became spontaneous bursts of dancing that brought the life force up her spine and chakras and through her whole being. Her fear and her mind learned to trust the flow of libido from the larger personality.

Two years later she developed a loving relationship with a younger man. They seemed to discover a core of passion and also had tones of the brother-sister dynamics one might expect for one of Artemis's women. They playfully enjoyed many competitive sports together, and happily, he was not excessively threatened when she continued to take the room necessary to care for her inner core. Her relationship with the lion-man on the net, which first appeared in this dream at her darkest hour, created the bridge to healing and an opening to life. She also learned to let this presence recede when it was time for that to happen, and she discovered other helpers over time.

Jung took great care in his life's work to convey the living reality of the psyche. In his own life, he discovered a living relationship with his guide, Philemon, and others, and taught us about the ability to bring energy to the inner characters we meet by carrying on a relationship with them in active imagination and meditation. Shamanism shows us the ancient roots of participating with the inner guides, or *ayami*.[16] Helper spirits open us experientially to the larger psyche and personality in myriad ways. This young woman found remarkable courage through her connection with this ally-spirit to discover the Self, which brought the flow of Eros and healing necessary for her to become more fully human, more fully woman. Her journey encourages the rest of us to find that helper spirit who comes to us when we authentically reach out or leap, as the case may be.

The Divine *Anthropos*

The Fourth nature leads straight to the . . . idea that stands for man's wholeness, that is, the conception of a unitary being who existed before man and at the same time represents man's goal.[17]

I would like to close this discussion of the transforming god and goddess in the vessel of the human soul by directing our attention to the divine

Anthropos, to the mystery of the Great Human Being. If you watch for her and him in your dreams, you will see that Anthropos often appears as a huge human (and sometimes as a tiny human or *homunculus*). In the big version, the large human is often so big that it is trying to find room to dwell among ordinary mortals. I have seen this image portrayed in my own dreams and the dreams of others:

> This giant, ancient human, who is also a planetary star-being, comes to Earth and . . . looks about for a place to rest. Then I see there are two of them, a male and female. As the beings lie down, they discover they both need more room for their heads, so they scoot around until they can get comfortable. A few humans see them, and try to get something to make a pillow for them to rest their heads on, so that they can stretch out, have a place to rest, a place that is comfortable for their heads.

This image is so reminiscent of the Christ image, when Jesus remarks, "The son of man has no place to lay his head." I think that the question is: Do we have room for this cosmic couple and their *coniunctio* of cosmic consciousness among us? Can we stretch with them from the Earth to the stars and make room for the span of being they emanate? Here is an example. One woman dreamed:

> I am standing on the border of two countries, high in the mountains. The sky cracks open just slightly above me. Two guides standing with me go up to the crack to help the sky open. They have to pry it open to let the god, who is curled up and rather cramped above this sky, to come onto the earth plane and visit me. The god descends and I begin talking with him about my life, and how he happened to come to me.

Our fixed thought forms can be just like that sky that leaves little room for the divine—the autonomous otherness of a being beyond ego consciousness's control—to come on in and dialogue with humanity. In contrast to the eventual success in this dreamer's journey, it seems nearly impossible for some people to truly open their consciousness to the possiblity that the divine itself may choose to live close to their humanity, and to open to the possibility that the divine may want to reveal its own nature to a human being, and partner with human beings in individuation. Many experiences of the numinous are missed by people who block out these possiblities.

Our experiences of the incarnating god and of the Anthropos open us to the great cosmic being. Jung said:

> The ancient teachings about the Anthropos or Primordial Man assert that God, or the world-creating principle, was made manifest in the form of a "first-created" (protoplastus) man, usually of cosmic size. In India he is Prajāpati or Purusha, who is also "the size of a thumb" and dwells in the heart of every man, like the Iliaster of Paracelsus. In Persia he is Gayomart . . . a youth of dazzling whiteness, as is also said of the alchemical Mercurius. In the Zohar he is Metatron, who was created together with light. He is the celestial man whom we meet in the visions of Daniel, Ezra, Enoch, and also in Philo Judaeus. He is one of the principal figures in Gnosticism, where, as always, he is connected with the question of creation and redemption.[18]

Sometimes we get in contact with this cosmic consciousness via experiences of other dimensions of time and space. I have worked with people in my practice who dream, for example, of star beings who live under completely different relationships to time and space. Usually, contact with such consciousness does involve experiencing the crack between the worlds. The psychic wound is meant to help us learn to crack, to open ego consciousness to worlds beyond its coordinates. In the preceding dream, the Anthropos figures can be aided in their incarnation among us if we also find means to support their consciousness which is larger than ordinary ego consciousness. Many people are learning this art over time.

Primitive and indigenous cultures that are alive in the psyche also come to us in dreams and visions, asking us to open to their dimensions of knowing that carry ways of opening our consciousness to the larger reality of the Anthropos. Indigenous cultures are mirrors for our need to connect with this indigenous reality alive in the soul. Shamanic reality learns to keep connection with all the relatives, all the minerals, plants, animals, and spirits of the many worlds of which we are a part, and to find means to create harmony between the realms, via participation with those worlds.

For example, a man in New Mexico, a physicist at the Los Alamos Laboratory who worked with the local Tewa tribes for many years, was deeply moved by their intact sacred ways. During the Iraqi war, over which he felt great pain, he dreamed:

> I am standing at Mount Rushmore, and all the presidents' heads are alive and have things to say about the troubles in the world. But then there is a Native American shaman behind them. As he chants and prays he rises up much larger than Mount Rushmore, and his presence of cosmic consciousness reaches way beyond the consciousness of these presidents. His prayer feathers, rattle, and chants take him into communion with the

> heavens and he helps appease the darkness we Americans are part of. With his presence looming up into the sky, the earth feels like it is awakening, and humans are beginning to discover their place in the processes of change by learning to harmonize with the elements, and the heavens. This Native American shaman spirit is capable of making the bridge.

This dream shows how the American psyche reaches to find healing with the shamanic indigenous traditions that live in the soul of the land itself. Dreams often show that the indigenous shamanic cultures are alive in the psyche and available to all, and these cultures can even connect with the psychoid and bring the opening and consciousness helpful to humanity and nature during these troubled times. Practicing shamanic rituals of prayer and connection to all the relatives became a part of this man's life. He sought the help of a local shaman, as well as that of his inner one.

That the shaman in the dream is a being who rises up into the stars and communicates with the vast regions again illustrates the stretch humankind must make—between heaven and earth, between human and divine—as the earth and the original spirit of nature move through these evolutions. The shamanic figure of the dream is an Anthropos figure, too, for he is the original being alive in the soul and capable of providing that bridge. The Anthropos, when it appears, opens us to the divine star indwelling in humankind. Tapping into experiences of the Anthropos brings us that dynamic cosmic opening and realignment. Because it reaches throughout time and space, it can reach into the heavens and into the depths of the earth, into as well as through time.

While I was in the Dordogne region of France, I had a tremendous mystical opening to Original Woman, which caught me totally by surprise. I had driven for hours on the windy country roads with my dear friend, Marcie Telander, a renowned storyteller and mythographer. Not knowing how far we were from the caves we were so eager to see, we finally pulled into a bed and breakfast inn. Tired and hungry, we decided that we would figure it out the next day, after a good meal and a night's sleep. We each headed for our own room. After showering, I stepped out of the shower and looked down: My feet blurred in a subtle-body interplay with a primordial woman's hairy feet. Even now when I write this, I can feel those feet. Primitive, rough, hairy, ancient, knowing, and sensitive. They were larger than my feet but distinctly female. They emanated a felt sense of the original source of being—an experience of the Anthropos.

Wanting not to scare the experience away with the rational mind, I tried not to "question" those feet. I looked down again, dried off, and tried calling my friend over, who never came. Then I looked at those feet some more, appreciating the living qualities of the psychic body in them. Again I experienced the sense of the original source of being throughout time. I walked around the room and did some yoga, breathing, and stretching while these living hairy feet showed through. Finally, I laughed and retreated to my bed. While I was reading Yeats' poetry, my own, normal feet then were all that was visible.

That night after the shower, we drove around the river bend for dinner and ended up in an ancient troglodyte village, which we were not aware even existed. The small people who lived there seemed related to the ancient people who inhabited these cliff dwellings and caves. I knew then that this land carried the essence of original peoples very strongly. When we returned to our auberge, Marcie found out (thanks to the great French she had learned) that the shower and room I was in were directly above the caves we had been driving *all day* to see, and the spirit of the Original Humankind came right into my shower and yoga time!

This experience felt tremendously like the head of the snake and the tail coming full circle. Modern consciousness of an ordinary woman in the 1990s meets with the hairy, gnarly feet of "first woman," or "Anthro-paws," as a friend calls her. The numinous often comes in through our less developed or inferior function, and for a person, such as myself, with sensation as an inferior function that also means sometimes the numinous comes in through the sensate world of earth, body, and such. And so for me the numinous quality coming in though the body-psyche field was particularly meaningful. In fact, it led me to realizing the ways in which I needed to consult with Original Woman more on a daily basis about the ordinary facts in my life, for example, rhythms to daily life that make her flourish, and food that is better for her, and so on.

This opening to these hairy feet, coupled with the descent into the Peche Merle caves was by far one of the most "religious" experiences I have had. An actual ancient footprint remains on the cave floor in Peche Merle, left by a human being eight thousand years ago. It is as though she or he just now walked by. In the psyche, where time is nonlinear, this is so. Original Human Being *is* just walking by, and more, is alive and well, discovering life anew in each modern person.

These experiences of "first woman" or "first man" (as well as their close kin, creation stories) heal the tear in the modern human heart that has severed us from our "beginning." They give us a felt glimpse into the beginnings of the world, beginnings not necessarily located in literal time but present all the time. Jung and the alchemists knew this principle of omnipresence. For them, the goal of the work was to discover this *Adam*

Kadmon, Original Human. When we are blessed with a whiff or glimpse of her or his presence, we also may feel that first spark of existence, that divine core of life that is attempting to incarnate itself in each of us *for the first time*. At these moments, we drop into the creation matrix informing all life.

Contact with Original Woman and Original Man moves us beyond fixed thought forms and our compulsory sense of linear "time." Such contact opens us to the vast, paradoxical marvel that life is—a myriad of mysteries of which we are miraculously a part, and an important part at that, particularly if we can bring the tail of the snake around and learn, for the sake of all life forms, to live with the spirit in nature in renewing ways. Only then is the ouroboros mystery—the crown of creation—able to incarnate.

REFINING THE RELIGIOUS ATTITUDE

Though we seem to be sleeping
there is a spirit that directs the dream
that will eventually startle us back
to the truth of who we are.
—Rumi

Why do we seek the divine water, the flow between the human and spiritual worlds? Jung thought this a worthy question for all pilgrims who sense the religious function in their lives. He also saw humankind's longing for redemption as universal and therefore having "an ulterior, personalistic motive only in exceptional cases, when it is not a genuine phenomenon but an abnormal misuse of it."[19] If grace and relationship with the divine are sought for a wrong reason and this goes unchallenged, our work and the transcendent bridge fade away over time. We cannot approach the numinous for long without being confronted with who we are.

We benefit from asking ourselves not only why we seek the experience of the divine, but how we seek, and how we do not enter into the dialogue with the divine. Tending to these issues, we may realign in a more centered relationship with the living spirit and with what the dialogue requires of us.

Serving the font and participating in the alchemical changes may, at times, mean learning the art of discerning genuine from fake. In the context of refining the religious attitude, we take another look into the illuminating dream of von Franz, who has one last task, after death. In the dream, she reaches into the compost heap (of the "Jungian world"), the *putreficatio*, the *prima materia*. She locates a plastic vessel first and says, "It is time to sort genuine from fake." She throws it out, recognizing that it is not valuable, and then discovers a glass vessel that carries the living waters. She takes in a deep, satisfying drink.

The inner attitude this dream sequence represents is capable of facing and reaching into what has gone rotten in our life, in our psyche, and in the life around us. This attitude is capable of discovering what is plastic, or false, what is incapable of carrying the divine waters. This inner attitude is also capable of sacrificing the vessel that does not carry the mystery and of moving on in search of the simple vessel carrying living water, the rebirth mysteries. This is the religious attitude: (1) the courage to admit when our consciousness is not connecting to the living mysteries, (2) the sacrifice of attitudes and values that do not seek the waters, and (3) the knowledge of how to plunge deeper into the *prima materia* to locate the true spirit of the autonomous psyche, where the living waters are alive and well. This attitude is also capable of partaking deeply of the waters.

To be penetrated by the truth, we must take in the messages of life, and of the dream spirit that pierces our blindness, our "off" state. Then we gain truer human ground, uncontaminated by the ego problems or complexes that serve false gods.

Before going into analytic training, I dreamed the following, with an image similar to the von Franz dream appearing at the end:

> I am visiting a graveyard and being guided underground by a barefoot man with a lantern who is wearing only tattered, three-quarter-length pants. He lives on the edge of the forest in a rustic cabin next to the graveyard. Underground, he points to several transcendental poets—Whitman, Emerson, and more. One is holding a staff and pounding the top of the grave, the earth above his head. They are chanting, "The grave cannot hold back the poets!" Jung then meets me on a fence, and leaving the graveyard, we walk into a field together. He says he wants to build an engine. Then Jung takes me to the banquet table, where there are many analysts gathered. A spirit being alongside me says, *With your Jungian heritage, what will your politics be? Whatever you do, do not take the food that is in the plastic cups! The earth cannot take them back!*

Plastic is a petroleum product that has been so overprocessed that Nature Herself cannot recognize it and take it back in the alchemy of dissolving again into organic matter.

Likewise, some of us are called to sort out that which the earth, our ground of being, can and cannot recognize as organic. We then can learn to release overprocessed forms in our own consciousness. Because oil is thought to symbolize the soul in the psyche's language, originally soulful material is of no further use after it is rendered into plastic. We frequently describe things we experience as inauthentic as "plastic." Relating to the unconscious, without distorting living mystery, means staying with the genuine oil.

Many attitudes, hidden operative frameworks, and expectations can lead to a consciousness that is like the plastic vessel, devoid of the living waters. Manipulation, overprocessing with the mind, or complexes change the genuine substance of the soul into a substance of the ego world. And it is an easy thing for many of us to fall into. Plastic results from unconscious fear-safety issues, power drives, and an overexertion of the will upon the soul. Marie-Louise von Franz hones a remarkable parallel between oil and soul life:

> Oil represents the life substance of the psyche, in its aspect of ultimate spiritual devotion, devotion with complete awe. By anointing their statues, the Egyptians gave their Gods the best they could, i.e., unconditional awe and reverence, which made them alive. And it highlights that one may turn everything wrong by not giving unconditioned and loving respect, a recognition that a living mystery within their own souls has to be kept alive, not for any other purpose than its own sake. [20]

From its ancient uses, oil carries with it the heart's devotion to a living mystery within the soul that is to be kept alive for no other purpose than its own sake. It seems that the psyche values our containers if they can return to the earth, into dissolution, into the alchemical round of death and rebirth.

Unlike plastic, glass is made with little processing. It is composed of the most common material on earth—sand, heated by fire. In its simplicity, glass does not leach into what it holds and can be taken back into the earth. This tells us that the inner attitude for the waters is readily available, simple, nonleaching, and noncontaminating. Also, glass is transparent matter that can be seen through to the spirit it carries. It is not static but subject to dissolution, released back into the great round of life. The forms we create are not for immortalizing. Our vessels, our love relationships, our creative projects, our associations with the mysteries are part of the round of death and rebirth. The hallmark of genuineness, in this regard, lies in the ability to submit the conscious attitude to this continual round of renewal.

Can we handle the scathing honesty of the unconscious toward the conscious self? Can we pick up the challenge and develop a living relationship with this spirit of rebirth and renewal? This exploration identifies subtle attitudes that serve the relationship with psyche and unconscious attitudes that may get in the way of living with the spirit of the inner spring, and examines how the dream spirit brings to our attention what is required for a fruitful life close to the font.

Devotion, honesty, and learning to walk the changing razor's edge come as we tend the spirit of the spring.

Love of the Infinite, Love of the Soul

Windows to the mysteries open between the larger realms of psyche and psychoid and our personal lives, the realms of the personal unconscious, and provide the means for alchemical rebirth. If the larger "wilderness of being" (the psyche and psychoid) is not allowed and invited to wash into the smaller dimensions of our personal psychology, all we are left with is a stagnant pool cut off from the source, from renewal and individually-held meaning. Here no individuation, no alchemical rebirth occurs. On the other hand, without enough human ground and connection to personal soul and daily life, we may be pulled into the unconscious and fail to bring the fruit of the journey back into human life.

Along the way of individuation that opens to the larger psyche, where we meet forces that assist in the alchemical rebirth process, we learn the task of the ego. The ego must discover means to enlarge perspectives, relatedness, and experiences of the realms of existence. Over a lifetime, the ego's task in individuation is to work with forces of both expansion and contraction and ultimately be expanded and more humanized in the process.

Joseph Campbell contributed a potent notion about this goal of life. Asked about the actuality of reincarnation, he replied that he did not know the exact realities of what comes after this existence but that he saw reincarnation mythology as a vital, symbolic expression of the goal of this life. He believed that the bounds of the ego, in this lifetime, would constantly be challenged to enlarge in relationship with the mysteries. Conscious participation in a cycle of psychic death and rebirth in this lifetime results in ever-expanding boundaries of consciousness. Life lived with the mysteries deepens experience of these borders. Such a goal requires travel into and beyond the boundaries of the personal unconscious and the concrete storyline of personal history, and bringing the boon of the journey back into mortal life. This entails following the Tao, the ever-changing energy flow in our lives. At times, our consciousness misses the changing inner way or, in fear, may refuse consciously or unconsciously the invitations to follow the Tao.

Where does the water of the unconscious come washing into our pools, into our life and consciousness? Responding to the invitation and the flow in our daily lives opens us to the mysteries. How do we block out or run from the invitation? How do we lose our connection to the waters of renewal? Do we refuse the invitations consciously or unconsciously? Growing awareness of how we answer these questions on a daily basis makes us better able to walk the changing razor's edge that is individuation. Sometimes the difficulty comes when we do not recognize the psyche's invitation for renewal. Living out of ego desires and fantasies, we may remain unaware of the invitation and miss the daily opportunities to die to the ego's fantasies, projections, and personal unconscious and to be renewed in evolving contact between human and divine. When Jung said that it is contact with the numinous that heals, I believe that this is what he meant. The personal self and life heal when we live closer to the evolution of the human-divine relationship. To do this, we must also watch the ways we fear or sidestep the mysteries and realities of the psyche and psychoid.

When we lose sight of our connection with the divine (whether that connection is found in fiery passion, earthy devotion, watery care, or airy appreciation), we risk the death of something in the soul. In a sense, the divine's ability to incarnate into our lives also dies.

In the poetic dialogue between the Sufi Ibn Arabi and his visiting angel, Sophia, the poet-seer asks if the visitations are real, or if they are just part of his essence. When she reprimands him, her direction of consciousness is profound. She tells him that the question is not whether the visitations are alive but whether he can permit them to invest his being.

The question is: Is each of us alive? Can we each "answer for" our divine visitors and permit them to invest our being? Sophia's response, written down by Ibn Arabi in the 1200s, is an enduring question I believe each of us answers on an ongoing basis in subtle ways. If we can still permit the mysteries to invest our ground of being, to answer this question freshly, from inside, requires devotion to cultivating a renewing relationship with the subtle realms. It also requires walking that changing razor's edge of honesty with ourselves when something in us either blocks or defends against the mysteries, or treks off into some repetitive compulsive relationship with the archetypes without bringing that back into service of the incarnating Self. This changing razor's edge is the life lived close to the heart of the divine and demands remarkable tending. The rewards bring us toward our pearl of great price. Yet the possibility of getting lost is always present. Inner humility and heartfelt attention to the changing path are vital.

To hone the religious attitude means to keep an eye open for the subtle ways in which parts of our inner community resist or defend against the evolving *coniunctio* between human and divine in the psyche and psychoid. It is natural for the ego and regressive sides to cling to safety, or what is known, or what once brought nourishment, love, meaning, adventure, or comfort. And it is human to enter into relationship with the *mysterium* and get lost or off track. However, life with the mysteries requires that we acknowledge when the evolution of consciousness within us has grown stale and we have lost fresh experience of "the moist connection with the divine dew of being" mentioned in the dream in chapter 2. Jung addressed this point in the most moving passage I have yet encountered in his writings:

> So, as soon as we feel ourselves slipping, we begin to combat this tendency and erect barriers against the dark, rising flood of the unconscious and its enticements to regression, which all too easily takes on the deceptive guise of sacrosanct ideals, principles, beliefs, etc. If we wish to stay on the heights we have reached, we must struggle all the time to consolidate our consciousness and its attitude. But we soon discover that this praiseworthy and apparently unavoidable battle with the years leads to stagnation and desiccation of soul. Our convictions become platitudes ground out on a barrel-organ, our ideals become starchy habits, enthusiasm stiffens into automatic gestures. The source of the water of life seeps away. We ourselves may not notice it, but everybody else does, and that is even more painful. If we should risk a little introspection, coupled perhaps with an energetic attempt to be honest for once with ourselves, we may get a dim idea of all the wants, longings, and fears that have accumulated down there—a repulsive and sinister sight. The mind shies away, but life wants to flow down into the depths. Fate itself seems to preserve us from this, because each of us has a tendency to become an immovable pillar of the past. . . . Everything young grows old, all beauty fades, all heat cools, all brightness dims, and every truth becomes stale and trite. For all these things have taken on shape, and all shapes are worn thin by the working of time; they age, sicken, crumble to dust—unless they change. But change they can, for the invisible spark that generated them is potent enough for infinite generation. . . . [E]very descent is followed by an ascent; the vanishing shapes are shaped anew, and a truth is valid in the end only if it suffers change and bears new

> witness in new images, in new tongues, like a new wine that is put into new bottles.[21]

We experience this truism of change in our lives as certain relationship constellations between us and the numinous undergo alteration, for change they must. In life lived close to the divine, there is no place to drop anchor in static identity. Experiences, constellations, and images of the incarnating Self continually transform in our lives. If we do not attend to the intricate transformations between human and divine realms, we may lose the way. In fostering the psyche's continual rebirth in our lives, we discover means to attend to its movements. Our images of the divine die, and when they do, we can either live dried up and lost or find our way back to the well of renewal by assisting the divine and ourselves in the changing way.

A woman author and poet who worked with me for a time dared to meet the psyche in a *nigredo* experience that outlines this rebirth process and changing way. Her writing and perspective had gone flat; she could not find her way. She experienced severe writer's block and feared that her well had run so dry she would never be with the muse again. She fell into a depression. Then came the following dream:

> I am standing with two other women in an ancient cavern, a crypt for women only, beside a large sarcophagus. In the dark, our hands are touching the carvings of the sarcophagus. The carving on the top is clearly the figure of a woman lying on her side with a piece of fabric draped over her hips. She is leaning toward us and has come to life. She is writing to us about the mystery of her death (in the late 1200s) and her coming resurrection. The secretness and sacredness of the experience are beyond words. She writes out a message like a chant, which we can hear echoing in the cavern and inside us. It goes round and round:
>
> By god, of god, for god, in god, through god
> By god, of god, for god, in god, through god

The dream window opens her to experience the force of rebirth present in the feminine in the underground core of her being. We are witnesses here to the mystery of how the feminine value of relationship to the god is working toward resurrection, toward a new life, a rebirth amid human consciousness. In her down-going, the dreamer connects with the death and rebirth mysteries at the core of the human soul. The personal sufferer descends and connects with ancient, timeless mysteries alive in the bedrock of being. The window between the earthly personality and the medicinal movement of the divine opens, and healing begins.

The by-of-for-in-through chant expresses the medium through which the divine moves and infuses. It is process-oriented; the chant points to the movement of *chi*, the life force. Importantly, the one who is resurrecting and bringing in this chant is the woman on the sarcophagus—with the pen! For a writer in trouble, without the juice, the sap, the living core of herself or of life, the flow of *chi* and divinity is perfectly to the point. The writing comes from the underground feminine who is discovering the chthonic god. The ink calls up the rebirth with the chant and directs consciousness to what is true. Namely, the core force of renewal is making itself known, and the writer, as part of the ceremony, will learn to access and serve this force with her pen, her voice, and her life.

This dream has universal meaning as well. If we think back a few centuries ago to the era in which rationalism became the dominant value in consciousness, it is no wonder that "devotion to the infinite, the unnamable" was sent underground. As a collective, we are witnessing this growing presence of renewal as it appears deep in the caverns of the psyche of many individuals. We are witnessing this growing recovery of feminine dimensions of being that have suffered a death with our overvaluation of rationality, domination over nature, and materialism. These rebirth mysteries and religious attitudes of devotion to all that lies beneath the thin veneer of rationalism are now gaining strength. Yet, our human lives must access these mysteries for the divine to incarnate among us.

Vessels we create via creativity, dream work, shamanism, and so on, are of value to us and the world soul to the degree that they give form to the religious instinct that connects us with the original spirit, the mediator of the opposites, the god of change and renewal. How we hear and choose to answer the god's or goddess's call of by-of-for-in-through defines our lives. And that call and the means to answer it are also ever changing, like the flow of the Tao.

The value of the religious function cannot be "exported" out to others. In that direction lie futility, dissipation of energy, and usually fundamentalism. The way of soul ignites from within, but human connection with others on such paths can bring a quickening of the inner fire, an awakening within, as refinement of soul and relational life. Exposure to the mysterious processes and domains of being (often initially via recognition, reflection, resonance, and promptings from a guide/teacher/analyst) helps give form to the religious instinct. Cultivation of psyche and the skills with which to tend a living relationship with the autonomous spirit may take hold.

And these cultivation skills should grow through the ages and find new derivations and expressions in each person. We can learn to draw forth the light in our life through individually-honed media (for example, dance, poetry, art, play, chant, active imagination, meditation, music, nature, sports, and sexuality) that encourage spontaneous relationship with the Self and the *numinosum*. Then, individual expression of that inner fire, alchemically tended, seeks its way into life in unique ways. Individual expression of the inner spark infuses the world soul, just as refined creative fire expressed in the world around us can spur us on toward discovering our own myths and creative bridges to the divine.

One woman who worked with me began a most unusual practice of singing her dreams out loud in meditation and sometimes in session instead of reading them flatly. The dimensionality of her experience of the realms of existence blossomed from that spontaneous act of singing. It also managed to keep her rational mind from trying to own the last word on her dream experiences. In fact, she began doing this when she found her rational mind was trying too hard to understand and control her inner life with "interpretation."

Through devotion to the psyche, life can be lived in relationship with the center that brings fruit. However hellish or heavenly the experiences may be, their natural outcome is the inner kindling of love, gratitude, and wisdom. Out of this wisdom must also eventually come real savvy about the poison and dangers that lie on the path of individuation. As this well-rounded wisdom takes hold, the heart of being learns more and more how to serve and partner these evolutions between human and divine. When we fall short of this, it is usually due to a failure of heart. Respect, fear, and avoidance are all natural, but when devotion—or, as the alchemists called it, "fructifying interest"—is born, it guides the heart toward the new center. If we have been penetrated by forces in the psyche and psychoid, and learn to tend the relationship, the personal heart and transpersonal heart may discover ever-renewing unity and dialogue.

Without a refined love of the infinite, of the soul, in our heart, there is no passion to the work and no fire to help along or mirror the ignition in others. If the soul dies, in a certain sense, God (the mysteries of the divine) dies also.

However, we must watch for those times when this love may weaken, become contaminated by our own devils, or dry up. Part of the journey for the human heart entails discovering where we become lost, dry, or psychopathic. The path of individuation is not a denial of what is so inside. It is accepting what is so and bringing to it the spirit of the font.

A loss of heart along the journey may happen. For example, like Goethe's Faust, we may sell the soul for knowledge and end up no closer to the mysteries. At times, we may not follow the inner lead but go off according to ego desires, repetitive compulsions, or fantasies that don't serve a differentiating relationship between human and divine. Entrenched power problems or laziness may keep us from returning to the well. Sometimes all we do may become tangled with others or in some way become rotten.

Without ears to hear these realities, we may remain hopelessly stuck. Encountering our devils is a given along the path of individuation, so no territory should be judged "wrong." It is just that without consciousness of where we stand and what our part is in the constellation, we can hurt the soul and unnecessarily prolong our suffering and others'.

Fear of the Descent into the Unconscious

Unconscious fear of the chaos present in the psyche may affect our relationship with the divine numen. Some fear is natural and warranted because the power of the mysteries, particularly when we are uninitiated, can potentially kill us or bring madness. Only a fool would not know the fear appropriate to the way that, as Jung says, would even daunt the gods. However, when that fear is unconscious, our relationship with the numen may be hindered.

After Marie-Louise von Franz's death, an analyst shared reflections on a dream he had in which *his* analyst, Frazer Boa, had taken a dream to von Franz: In the dream, the dreamer is standing on the shore of a lake on a darkly clouded night. A few beams of moonlight shine down on the water. A man in a small boat is rowing about fishing. He is aware that a two-headed serpent lives at the bottom of the lake.

When von Franz heard the dream, she reportedly said, "The dreamer is a man who is immersed in rational psychologies. What does he think will happen if he ever hooks that serpent? It will pull him under!"[22] The image of the moonlight and the two-headed serpent carries the feeling of the dangerous and chaotic forces present in the psyche that require genuine respect beyond the realm of rational conceptualization.

This perspective is reminiscent of Guggenbühl-Craig's statement that anyone who can say that God is love must not know God. He goes on to say, "I assume that an encounter with god or with the transcendent, per se, can only occur when we experience the violent side of god." From this perspective, no wonder our ability to relate to the religious function may fall into peril, for its very source is the chaotic, potentially dangerous aspect of the psyche's depths. Guggenbühl-Craig notes, "We are living in an age of secularization—or, we might say, of repression of the divine." Repression of the divine happens in everyone to a degree. By its very nature, the ego limits consciousness to the realities with which it is comfortable and tends to remain blind to the largeness of life and its mysteries. Thankfully, consciousness can learn to connect with the mysteries, turning toward the divine and bowing. It accepts the reality of dimensions beyond itself, relates to those dimensions, and as it changes, it can discover depth, mysteries, joy, relationship, and union.

Yet, because of this unconscious fear of the psyche, many do not consciously risk the descent and consciously make the sacrifice of differentiation. They choose to live dried-up lives, devoid of soul's succor, or are eventually forced into a descent experience via destructive processes. Understandably, Jung says:

> No one should deny the danger of the descent, but it *can* be risked. No one *need* risk it, but it is certain that someone will. And let those who go down the sunset way do so with open eyes, for it is a sacrifice which daunts even the gods.

Who casually chooses to relate to this reality? Only the uninitiated or unwise. Yet, the Fool's attitude can viably land us in such territory as well. With the Fool's gift of openness, we learn to acquire wisdom from the initiation. Some individuals discover an underground power of renewal, a reality promising to counter this "repression of the divine" and bring them into relationship with its rebirth amid their rebirth.

A natural question emerges here: When making a descent or reestablishing the bridge with the psyche becomes necessary, how do we make the sacrifice conscious? When it is not conscious, the "daemon" may trip us, as Jung states:

> Nevertheless, the daemon throws us down, makes us traitors to our ideals and cherished convictions—traitors to the selves we thought we were. That is an unmitigated catastrophe because it is an *unwilling* sacrifice. Things go very differently when the sacrifice is a voluntary one. Then it is no longer an overthrow, a "transvaluation of values," the destruction of all that we held sacred, but transformation and conservation.

To make the sacrifice conscious, we must discern what in us needs to descend, what is worn out and no longer serving life. In the parable, of The Wise and Foolish Virgins, illustrated by William Blake (see figure 21, page 207), the kingdom of heaven is "likened unto ten virgins, which took their lamps, and went forth to meet the bridegroom. . . . five of them were

Fig. 21. William Blake, "The Wise and Foolish Virgins, " watercolor, c. 1822, Tate Museum, London.

wise, and five were foolish. They that were foolish took their lamps, and took no oil with them: But the wise took oil in their vessels with their lamps. While the bridegroom tarried, they all slumbered and slept. And at midnight there was a cry made, Behold, the bridegroom cometh; go ye out to meet him" (Matt. 25:1-6).

Blake depicts the scene just after the good news of the bridegroom's arrival has been announced by the angel. The foolish vestal virgins, out of oil and with no light in the darkness, are crying out to the wise ones, and the wise ones are telling them to go buy oil. The tension depicted between those with oil and those without and the call of the angel toward conscious union with the beloved bridegroom in the dark forms a mandala.

Blake's image captures both sides of our being: that which has oil—soul fuel—and a light to find our way toward the divine, the beloved in the dark, and that which has no oil and is inattentive to the inner marriage, unprepared for the angel's visitation. A central means of traveling toward the religious function is the ability to hold the opposites, both-and instead of either-or. The medicine of paradoxical psychology emanates from Blake's illustration. When we open to the particulars of how we are both, Mercurius is freed and can move the relationship between conscious and unconscious into a new union, prompting changes in our inner and outer lives. When our individual connections to the core of our lives go through stages of death and rebirth (which, indeed, they will), we owe the spirit of life and those we love the honest attempt at a conscious sacrifice and a descent of some sort. We owe the sacrifice of tending to the soul with particular care, of locating the dream spirit's help and the help from others with what is descending—with what in us specifically is seeking the god of renewal in the core of our being—and then going there.

Conscious Sacrifice and Discovery of the New Center

Renewal and sacrifice—the release of an old way and the discovery of a new way—go together. With wisdom, we learn to notice which specific beliefs and values are outdated and of no use to us. Dead wood is a great metaphor for that which *formerly* carried the life force. Dreams bring this theme to light, often using the dead wood metaphor. For example, when I hurt my back, I dreamed of the irrigation canal by my cabin that waters all the nearby horse pastures. In the dream, I was instructed to get into the flowing water and pull out the dead wood so that the water could flow more freely. As the dream ended, I was getting in and clearing out the dead wood. I felt a direct correspondence between my hurting back and the image. Turning to my inner and outer life, I began to recognize and clear out old ways of thinking and communicating, and so on. The flow of life increased and moved more freely, and my back also received support by my lessening the load of "dead wood."

Sometimes the growth, or wood, in our inner or outer life is not dead. We may be asked to cut what is still alive. This theme is often evident, for example, when someone needs to leave a form of love relationship, such as marriage, when love is still present or when someone needs to leave a career that could continue to limp along with some signs of life.

This theme can emerge on the inner plane, too, when we are still identified with a pattern we think brings life, but from the inner world's perspective, it does not. A classic example is the man or woman whose clinging fusion dynamics push away the loved one rather than create more closeness. Recently, I witnessed this pattern in a woman in my practice. The dream world supported her to see it in herself and to pull back her victimization projection at the outset of a new relationship. Then she became increasingly aware of the energy pattern, from inside herself, of the clingy communication and merger that she gets into. By being willing to hear the tone of her communications and realizing the part of her that pulls and tugs, she eventually stopped the pattern. She found new ways to express herself, to reach out to her beloved from new inner ground. With self-directed compassion, she was able to contain the needy one inside her who would skew communications with cloying manipulations. The needy one inside in turn led her to discoveries of her early wound and soul pieces in her history where the pattern began. But it took recognizing it in the outer pattern first, reining the dynamic in there, and then following the thread down inside to the source.

Breaking these entrenched patterns can be particularly difficult if we are attached to the old pattern and cannot see how little life it engenders. If we have a highly developed and cherished emotional style and "drama set" around these infantile needs and we believe that the other person ought to fulfill these needs, outside help is often necessary to get inside ourselves and see what we are doing. (The opposite problematic pattern of course also happens when people fall into completely denying emotional needs and don't allow the natural flow of give and take to happen in their relationships, thereby freezing the relational dialogue.) If the inner world is prompting the change, it can also support us through the change before it becomes an insurmountable crisis of losing the partner. This way takes care and consciousness from within, along with sacrifice of the old pattern. Seeing specifically what needs to transform or be sacrificed comes with help from the dream spirit and attending to relationship patterns with one another.

However, when we naïvely hack away at our lives, with the ego's ideals in charge, thinking that we know, on our own, the sacrifice needed, we are usually off the mark. Guidance from the inner center about what specifically seeks transformation is crucial. At these times, the inner way often provides tremendous insight into the constellations operating in our lives and can instruct us on how to make the sacrifice in service to a truer way of living. During a time of profound change requiring tremendous conscious sacrifice, a woman dreamed:

> I am standing with a woman and am packing my belongings, about to move with my lover to some new home. We are deciding what will go and what will remain. She is the great teacher for whom I feel complete respect. She shows me a tree that is in a pot amid our things. She is saying, "Yes, of course, you will be taking this . . . but what you need to do is cut the tree back down to the ground" (at which point, we are now looking into the center of the tree stump now cut back!). And looking into the tree's rings she is saying, "See, now the beetle emerges out of the middle of the tree. Where it moves from the center will determine where the new life will begin." We see the beetle emerge from the center of the tree stump. It crawls slightly off center to one side and settles. It is here

> the new life will emerge. We put the tree with the beetle in the back of the vehicle amid our belongings, ready now to move.

The woman teacher's instruction on how to make the sacrifice shows the grace and guidance available within the dreamer's core when the dream ego is willing to listen. The dreamer's respect for the teacher heralds the relationship between the dream ego and the inner center and relates to the beauty of what unfolds in the dream. The instruction about cutting back the tree's growth directly mirrors the dream ego's path for living a new life from a new center. The dream ego and the Self figure find connection, respect, sacrifice, and a new center from the forces of renewal.

The dreamer, caught in many outer relationships founded on duty, obligation, and pity (and projection of her own needs onto those around her), could feel her soul's need for her to direct her attitude inward in order to sacrifice the old form of her living tree. Her trust in and cooperation with the teacher to cut back the old life forms to the ground was a healing salve. The new ground to which she must cut back her life's tree is the ground of being in which the ego listens to the Self.

In the dream, we see that after the sacrifice, the dream teacher shows her to look for the beetle coming up from the center. The scarab beetle in Egypt has long been a key symbol in the renewal mysteries. In the night sea journey, the sun seeks its renewal in the underworld. At the last hour of darkness, the dung beetle pushes up the sun into the world, the new sun that renews the pupil of the pharaoh's eye. Like the *lapis* (the Philospher's Stone), the dung beetle emerges out of putrefied matter, the *prima materia*, pushing a rotating ball of dung. The "dung roller" and the new sun emerging from the darkness, renewing the ruler's eye, are connected. The beetle brings renewal of life, vision, and spirit. On the phylogenetic evolutionary ladder, beetles are very far from humankind. This distance suggests the depths in creation from which this force of renewal issues. This force does not spring from ordinary modern rational consciousness.

The dream beetle's emergence from the tree's center speaks to the center's regenerative secrets and repositions the dreamer's life and consciousness around the new center—a remarkable Self mystery seeking union with the woman's consciousness. Also, the new divine center is a little off center from where the old life was. This divergence is important for the dreamer, who must learn how the new center differs from the ego-centered consciousness of the past and how to serve and function from the new center.

Instructed into a new life that is eccentric (literally, away from the center), she may find that others view her life as a little odd. Being off center is curious to the collective mentality. In a way, the dream indicates that the new life cannot happen the ego's way, in the (dead!) center. However, if the ego makes the sacrifice of submitting to change, to "relocation" to an off-the-old-center position, it can tap into renewal in a new centering process. The ego now pays attention to what is beyond its solitary sense of center, whereas before, the personality was directed by the ego's unchecked impulses, as though the ego were the guide and true center. The ego learns to move beyond the narcissism of its monologue, into a larger dialogue with the inner teacher, which summons the autonomous force of renewal. Eventually, the individual embodies the new way instinctually.

Extracting energy from the extroverted persona world of relationships left the woman with an inner emptiness, but also with much energy to turn toward the inner world and relationship dynamics truer to her core. She was leaving her position as a physician and director at a medical center, hoping to find a new life with different meaning. She looked toward practicing medicine in a new way, no longer bound to the prestige and power of the university medical center and professorship, which she now found stale. Truly, sacrificing the growth in our life to a deeper calling leads us into the unknown. Mid-life often requires these sacrifices in order for the new way to appear.

The violence of cutting old growth was necessary for her—cutting back energy given out unconsciously, cutting back her old form for work, sending her patients to other physicians, releasing her office and staff, and so on. Most importantly, she had to cut back her ego fantasy of how her life was supposed to go. This cutting back brought her incredible freedom from the tyranny of a fantasy gone stale.

The descent, the shamanic death, the sacrifice, the dismemberment of a life we once knew, shedding an identity that once served us—these often involve violence. Violence may be required in the alchemical processes of change. If we avoid the chaos, the necessary sacrifices for change, and the violence that kills old forms, we risk encountering or creating deadly constellations of energy in ourselves and the world around us. On that path, we also do not learn active love of the soul or the infinite. Although a kind of conscious violence (severance) is involved and often required in individuation, at the core remain the energies of devotion and service to something larger than our ordinary consciousness. In fact, this devotion to the center growing within us (the latent Self becoming the manifest

Self) is the inner religious attitude that is the fruit of life lived close to the mysteries.

We can have all kinds of relationships with the unconscious. When we grow from being mostly unconsciously pulled into its depths to participating more consciously in a dialogue with the unconscious, we discover a religious attitude, an inner devotion to the center that is a reward of dialogue with and between the opposites.

In the world today, deadly polarized opposites play themselves out, for example, between fundamental Islamic traditions and fundamental Western materialism, through terrible acts of violence. Essential now are the awareness and inner agility required to hold the opposites toward their inner marriage, without unnecessary violence via projection. Individual conscious sacrifice, with an ear toward the inner center that helps us hold the opposites within our own consciousness, is crucial. Building life organized from that center is vital.

The archetypal core rage and psychosis present in world war can be healed on an individual level only if we locate these archetypes in our fields of conscious and unconscious awareness and deal with them there. We must humanize and mediate the flow of their energy in our lives. Our interactions with the world around us bring continual invitations to grow more connected to the inner center. As Jung said, it is only connection with the numinous that can protect us from the moral and physical blandishments of the world. The world is a mirror to us as well, providing inroads to where the Self seeks incarnation. This incarnation process does not mean being taken up only into blissful experiences with an inner angel but also accessing and working with the collective problem of evil, by locating the forces present in the depths of the human soul and freeing and mediating the energy therein. Learning to wield the knife through conscious sacrifice to the center minimizes unnecessary and unwise violence in our life.

Often, in the New Age movement, seekers become confused when they experience their ambivalence toward the god Mars, the warrior god. Many, wishing that they could expunge this archetype, attempt to perform upon themselves and the world a "Mars-ectomy." Of course, this is not possible, nor desirable, for this archetypal power vivifies us if we learn to individually hone the blade of decision and action involved in conscious "violence." Conscious violence happens when we hear the call and wield the sword of differentiation with discernment, following inner directives that are not necessarily pleasing to the ego or others.

In case this sounds too abstract, here is an example of conscious violence. A graduate student in physics who had been always pleasing to his professor comes to carry a projection from the professor of the ideal student who will carry on the professor's work. Eventually the graduate student's individuation requires that he stand up and in fact disagree openly with the professor. His own new ideas for research conflict with the professor's, and he must find his own way. This requires he sacrifice the projection, with its benefits of grant money and such. He performs the sacrifice by having a humane, conscious conversation with the professor in which he owns his differences and pierces through the projection by coming out with more of who he truly is and where he is actually headed with his own research. Such a simple act is often hard, but necessary, to do.

Looking at the pattern of conscious sacrifice, rebirth, and descent on a relationship level, it is interesting to note that, if we believe that we are ultimately doing anyone a favor by remaining in our outworn identities or shallow shell without risking descent, we are wrong. When we refuse a sacrifice, a descent beneath our ordinary way of going, we also hold others back.

Once I watched a friend's husband refuse the descent. His career was over; he had no energy for it. Yet, because he had no retirement funds, he went on year after year, with the artifice of being present when all around and within him dried out. When he finally quit after thirty years, he and his wife had very little money in the bank. For years she had recognized how his inner attitude dominated and suffocated their life. His was an attitude similar to the "foolish virgins," who brought no oil and did not tend to the heart of what mattered. Her recognition of what they both would pay if she did not make the sacrifices as well is what brought about the change. They sold their expensive home and reorganized their priorities so that they could live simply and he could seek his rebirth in the solitude of his inner being. Life in and around him began to "green," as the alchemists put it, began to take on the color of life again. Her recognition of the truth, her trust in the descent, her willingness to make substantial financial sacrifices and to stand by him as he sought renewal for the next chapter of their lives emanated tremendous beauty, soul, and a true spirit of marriage. Had they not found their way and made the sacrifices, the old course would likely have taken its toll. It would have dried their life and their love to the point of despair, and a failure of heart would likely have brought some tragedy, pushing them into a descent, one way or another.

Sometimes, when those we love are in trouble, a sacrifice we make may assist us in our individuation, as well as assist them in making their essential descent. (And of course sometimes there is nothing we can do, and that fate then must be carried as well, and is sometimes even more difficult.) In her case, she submitted to a material sacrifice, with a corresponding faith in a renewal process. Sometimes the sacrifices needed are less obvious. In these instances, the dream spirit may target that which needs to die and transform, making possible a willing sacrifice instead of a slaughter and a falling backwards into the unconscious.

To make an offering from consciousness toward the spirit of the unconscious, we must discover honestly where we stand and must own that standpoint, no matter how wounded, shallow, dark, abhorrent, absurd, or lost. Only then can the deep change truly begin. Only then can we locate the living waters of life that revivify our beings.

GAINING HONEST HUMAN GROUND

We are of no use to the powers of transformation, to the divine, or to humanity, if we lose our human ground of being. Individuation means that the divine incarnates into our consciousness and into relationship with our humanity and mortality. Jung wrote:

> God wants to be born in the flame of man's consciousness, leaping ever higher. And what if this has no roots in the earth? If it is not a house of stone where the fire of God can dwell, but a wretched straw hut that flares up and vanishes? Could God then be born? One must be able to suffer God. That is the supreme task for the carrier of ideas. He must be the advocate of the earth. God will take care of himself. My inner principle is: Deus *et* homo. God needs man in order to become conscious, just as he needs limitation in time and space. Let us therefore be for him limitation in time and space, an earthly tabernacle.[23]

Jung values the embodiment of humanity in all its limitations, in dialogue with the powers that be, for how else could "god" be born into this plane of existence? Looking into the etymology of the word "human," the Greek root is *khton* and the Latin root is *humanus*. Human means literally "of the earth" or "earthling." Humid, humus, humility, humble, homage, chthonic, transhumance, exhume, and humanity all share the same root word. Looking into the definitions of some of these words, light inside the root of our human mystery begins to appear. As humans in homage, we seek the humidity of the water of life. We are fortunate to participate in a mystery in which the psyche may exhume deep chthonic presence. This presence resides in direct relation to our humanity.

Regarding the making of a conscious or unconscious sacrifice, the contrast between humility and humiliation is enlightening. Humility, as an inner attitude, means "near the ground" literally; it is modesty, a lack

Fig. 22. "He who wants to enter the Philosophical Rose Garden without a key is like unto a man who wants to walk without feet." Michael Maier, Atalanta Fugiens, *Emblem XXVII. (Oppenheim, 1618). Reprinted from de Jong,* Michael Maier's *Atalanta Fugiens, p. 403.*

of pride based on understanding the truth of existence as close to earth. In contrast, humiliation means being put into a humbling experience or attitude against our will. Again, the options are to fall backwards into the unconscious against our will (unconscious, humiliating sacrifice) or to turn toward the unconscious with humility and live close to the earth (that is, make a conscious sacrifice of egocentric perspectives through knowing our humble yet important place on *terra firma* in relationship with the larger mysteries).

Gaining awareness of the qualities and nuances of our human standpoint, our inner attitudes toward life and the mysteries, is the cornerstone of the dialogue with the mysteries. In the emblem in figure 22, page 215, the seeker stands before the alchemical garden where the multiplying riches of the alchemical process are growing. The entrance is heavily bolted. The seeker, standing in water, where his feet are invisible, has no key. The text accompanying the emblem tells us that the key to the garden, where one could collect the white and red roses, is buried in the place where the "bones of Orestes, the winds, the manslaughter, the reflection and the ruin of men are hiding."

This reads rather like a cooking recipe. What are these hidden ingredients? Orestes was an alchemist; his bones could be likened to his wisdom that remains. Bones are what remain after death. As the inner structures of the body that remain, they point symbolically to the archetypal structures that do not perish in the death and decay processes. Bones of the ancestors in ancient cultures were used to call up the spirit and wisdom the deceased had embodied. Here it is the spirit of the alchemist, the inner bones of the wisdom of alchemical processes in all life, the inner structures he discovered that remain, which, when found, lead to the key. The reference to winds points to an alchemical mystery of the four elements and their interactions.

From this emblem and text, we could say, psychologically, that the process of redemption begins with looking into the inner bones of things, into the alchemical archetypal structures that endure beyond and through the passing of the temporal in our lives. The reference to the winds suggests that we would benefit from studying the interactive processes of the differentiated elements that make up the cosmos. All ancient religions have reflected this truism, as have their means of differentiating the original chaos with the four directions, elements, and such. This theme also runs through alchemy. Thus, equipped with the wisdom of the eternal structures and in relationship with the movement of nature's elemental forces, we turn to digging into the ground of the human soul and its history of death, ruin, and war—the study of cultures and their decay. Individually, it is a digging in the soil of our being, furrowing around in our life myth and inner experiences, where the "ruin of men" also hides—the ancestral troubles, the shadow elements, drama, and the "sabotage" of our lives. Here our life myth also finds a place in the history of the human soul and culture.

Thus begins the recovery of the key and discovery of our feet. As this discovery in the shadow places is found, held, and used, it brings the human being into dialogue with the Self, the garden. For us, discovery of the key in the shadow material, and the location of our feet reside in our ability to gain consciousness of what our standpoint is as we walk through life. Is it reverence for the mysteries and a willingness to engage in dialogue and change in the process? Is it laziness or aggrandizement that gets in our way? Is it convenient, blind adherence to the compulsions of a complex residing in our unworked psychic wounds? Is it materialism, a naïve, misguided wish for happiness through the accumulation of objects? Whatever the standpoint, as soon as we become conscious of what it is, change has a chance. Then we stand at the door to the mysteries, to communion with the divine from a true human standpoint, not with feet buried in the unconscious.

Digging in the "ruin of men" is a powerful motif. As shown in the emblem, the alchemists believed that this digging would lead to transformation. This psychological truism is relevant culturally. So many cultural problems, to which we turn a deaf ear and a guarded heart, carry the same potential for transformation if we but let ourselves see the unconscious standpoint that leads us, collectively, to abnegation of the world soul, such as our crowding out other species, overharvesting (while many populations starve), and dependence on fossil fuels that causes so much unnecessary suffering. If we were willing to undertake the conscious sacrifice and necessary violence required to expunge the glut of materialism in our lives, the richness of the Self imaged in the rose garden—contained, ever-blooming, and ever-renewing—could have more of a chance of incarnating into the *anima mundi*, the world soul, in which we all live.

This is not a utopian, edenistic fantasy but a simple statement of our moral responsibility to awaken and live in growing conscious relationship with all life forms. Not doing so is a reflection of the psychopathic heart dwelling in our humanity. Moral here does not mean "moralistic." It points to that growing inner core of Self that orients us to see vitalizing relationship with ourselves and the world around us as it is. The biggest tragedy of neurotic ego defenses is their "ability" to blockade us from the rich dialogue of I and Thou, the beauty of dialogue with one another and the world. Our "moral" standpoint within ourselves is defined by our ability and inability to be penetrated by the truth of who we are. Acknowledging and owning the full truth of who we are—including our psychopathic splinters—is of utmost importance, the key for individuation and for the survival of the world soul in which we live.

In a visionary poem titled "The Old Age of Queen Maeve," the poet W. B. Yeats deals with the ruin of men, the ghosts of time and culture. A dialogue ensues between the mythic-historic queen (and legendary lover) and the ghost of Aengus, the lover-hero who cannot rest and is "crossed in love." The old queen wanders the castle halls at night, feeling the "many changing ones" and movement among the Sidhe (the spirits of the ancient ones).

Then the ghost of Aengus speaks out of her sleeping husband's mouth. In the dialogue she is instructed by Aengus to go to the foundation of the castle, wake the sleeping children, and dig into Bual's hill, among the layers of history and ruin, to free spirits captured there. She wakes the children, who help her dig, and while they dig, the spirits of the divine lovers are freed. The old queen weeps and is joyous. The spirits of the lovers take shape and join in the dark air with a "murmur of soft words and meeting lips." The queen and the past and the new generation have freed the spirits from the hill of ruin and layers of the past. The spirits find an erotic new unity, a new alchemical bond.

Out of the historic ruin of humans held fixed by the foundation of human culture—the battles of the opposites and mass destruction humans enact—we can, with reflection and transcendent grace, free essential spirits of creation, yang and yin, the masculine and feminine lovers, who want to discover a new unity. This alchemical theme has its cultural and individual applications.

The Metaphor of the Foot Wound

The dream spirit brings reflections, windows into the "ruin of men," where the hidden key is addressed by surfacing the unconscious standpoint—the feet beneath the water. Initial dreams in analysis often carry imagery of the feet and address just what attitude, wound, or unconscious problem stands in the way of individuation and a more fulfilling life.

Wounding of the foot and growing conscious of the wound seem to be part of what provides a new key to a more fulfilled life. Wounded feet are a mythic theme. Oedipus had a wounded foot, Achilles' heel was his mortal vulnerability. Chiron the centaur was wounded when his hoof caught a stray arrow from Hercules' bow. Chiron crawled off into his cave to heal, later emerging with an apothecary of the healing arts, and a mostly healed wound. Working with the "foot wound" leads to gifts, as in the Chiron myth.

Gaining our standpoint can be difficult. It may require that we submit to embodying experiences that are tender-footed, delicate, vulnerable. This world can be nearly too hard for certain sensitive people and for those whose suffering is so great and avoidance so high and for whom help is so scarce. These individuals learn numerous ways to cope that lead to avoidance and maladjusted patterns that can be destructive. Blindness to these patterns is usually part of the problem. They may turn to addictive means to try to block out sensitivity, loneliness, or loss, attempting to fly at higher altitudes above the specifics of real life. The image of feet in water often appears in the dreams of individuals whose feelings and emotions are repressed, unconscious. Grief or loss in life can bring on serious difficulties if our feet remain in the unconscious affect too long. Here are a few examples.

A tender-hearted man in his mid-fifties lost the love of his life. She left him for another man, whom she soon married. Over the next two years he began to drink more heavily. Then he sought the help of AA and an analyst. He dreamed:

> I finally have submitted to a surgery that is essential. My feet are being worked on. Somehow, whatever shoes I put on are now taken off because they were getting me into some kind of trouble. Now I see my bare feet. The surgery will bring out all this vulnerability and tender-footedness in my feet. It is a little scary to me, but somehow I am trusting this doctor, who thinks that the tender-footedness is valuable. This tenderness was in my feet all along, evidently, but I didn't know it, and somehow I kept it in these boots.
>
> Now the surgery is complete, and I am instructed to place my feet on the ground. It is scary, and I have to go slow because my feet feel so much of the ground now. I will get new shoes, but for now, I need to try a little of this barefootedness first. Someone tells me, "Now your friends won't worry about your drinking too much."

Like this dreamer who had the courage to seek help, we most often begin a fertile, life-enhancing relationship with the unconscious when we take an honest step forward to address our brokenness, woundedness, onesidedness. Seeing the ways in which we compensate or need assistance from the transcendent in order to get along in life requires walking consciously with our gimpiness.

The wound in the foot brings us into an experience of humility, a tender way of going. Unlike a heroic attitude or an ego defense of denial or addiction, it keeps us close to the ground of our own mortal lives. As this dream shows, the wound also connects us with powers beyond the ego. Yet, the ego then must learn to bring up from the unconscious, from the soul, the new means of going that brings wholeness in relationship to this maiming, this humility. The "operation" in the dream that brings the vulnerable, sensitive feet to light is a powerful alchemical operation the personality requires. Unconscious means of dulling the pain over time, such as drinking alcohol, are known to deaden the feet, and trouble, such as gout, appears. To escape the ill cycle, the psychological operation of connecting to his earthly vulnerability and sensitivity, to experience his own ground of being, is the prescription.

One young man, a cowboy from a large ranch family, worked with me after his father died. A horse-shoer we both knew had told him to come on over for a few visits and "talk some of his troubles out." After his father's death, he had inherited the ranch, along with a tremendous amount of responsibility, and he felt himself slipping into trouble. Then he had the following dream:

> I have a hole through my foot, and I'm trying to attend my father's funeral without anyone noticing my foot. I'm bleeding. I hope it won't get too bad until after the service, when I can go off by myself and soak it and wrap it. Later, a key that must have been in the bandaging I was holding fell out, onto the ground, then onto my foot, where it stuck in some blood that was clotting.

After telling it to me, he said, "Does everyone have some 'hitch in their get along'?" I said, "Well, pretty much. The problem usually isn't the hitch so much as what happens if you don't know what your own hitch is—and then how to work with it."

This was his first dream in the analytic process, so we began the inner work of soaking the wound (connecting with memories, emotions, and healing dreams, the grace present in the psyche, his personal history and defenses, and so on) and then wrapping it (carrying it along with new inner support and understanding from the work). I could see that he needed deep inner support to move out of a deflated ego, full of embarrassment and humiliation at having trouble in his life and wanting help.

He told the following story. One day, as a teenager, he was cleaning a gun when it accidentally went off and he shot himself in the foot. The bullet hit his boot and grazed the side of his foot. As a result, he missed a horse show in which he had hoped to bring his new horse into the arena for the first time. His father's anger at him for missing this event never left him, and he lived in introjected disappointment and shame that crippled his life. His father's death brought the key of his woundedness to consciousness. The coagulating blood and the key seemed good signs to me that he could see the grief process through and end up with a better connection to his core nature, a "better footing" in his life. The dream pointed out the course of therapy. He did indeed get the blood of life to gel in a new way through his attention to the inner world after his father's death. The imagination opened up beautifully to support him, to help him heal. The key in the coagulating blood pointed to the alchemical process of the coagulation. This image underscored the nature of the psychic wound as one of pouring his life energy, his "blood," into the world unconsciously via the wound. It suggested that if he became conscious of the wound and its manifestations in his life, his unconscious outpouring of himself, via his deflation, could stop and the life force could become more contained, congeal, and heal.

Another man in his mid-forties, in a crisis in which he was about to lose his wife and family because of a grief process that he funneled into incessant overcommitment to work, dreamed:

> I look down and see that my feet and ankles have been amputated somehow, and it is something I am trying to live with. I hope this amputation can remain a secret, for it is really humiliating. I am glad to discover that I have work boots I can put on. I quickly put them on and think, now the amputation is not noticeable.

The dreamer's problem, of course, is that his compensation of overidentifying with work (the work boots) to the point of losing his family life was being addressed by the dream spirit and was no longer "secret." Instead, the truth of his core problem was revealed. He did not have normal human feet; he lacked substantial, experiental contact with the ground of his being. This contact and his standpoint in life had been cut off somehow. It came to light that he had a serious addiction to pain killers, which had begun after a death in the family five years earlier. He had used the drugs to kill off the emotion—the grief and vulnerability—and used the work identity to cover up his lack of humanity. His road ahead was clear: If he wanted to individuate, he would have to find his vulnerable, naked connection to the earth, to life, to his humanity, beneath those "work boots." He would have to grieve his loss and he would have to discover his own masculinity and humanity anew. In addition, learning to value his humanity inside his work and the gifts he did have would help him loosen his fear of life so that vital, instead of compulsive, life energy could fuel his work life.

Turning toward the psyche and accepting the truth of the inner situation and lostness requires a sacrifice of conscious will and of our ego defenses against life. Often the dream world will bring the next steps in the transformation, providing a way where before there was none.

A woman poet in her forties dreamed:

> I am in my childhood home, and the poet William Butler Yeats comes to talk with me. We go to the music room, where my mother taught me piano as a girl. Yeats tells me that there are no accidents, that we are

> born in time and space in meaningful ways important to the soul. He shows me an axis that runs from the heavens above, then down through my childhood home and down into the earth's molten core. The human story of my youth lives along this axis. He then shows me that my music, my poetry, comes as I can tolerate the hole, the wound in my left foot, and bring the threads of creativity up through this wound. Then there are fine threads of each color and possibilities of brocade-embroidered garments. I work with the threads and bring them up and through. I am learning "storying" and poetry.

The dreamer's standpoint with the unconscious is to embody the wound, the gaping hole that manifested in the story of her youth, and through that wound, that empty place, to bring the art form into the world. This gift is not only related to the wound but also must come right through it. The wounded standpoint, when embodied, becomes the healing creative standpoint. For her, this meant that she had to turn to the specifics of how her way of going through life was psychically wounded. Rather motherless in her youth, she had leaned toward the spiritual worlds and the world of nature for containment and nurturing. And becoming aware of the compensatory nature underlying these venues in her life took her down to her wounded foot so to speak, into a discovery of soul via confrontation with the reality of the expression of the wound in her early history.

At times, this wound was so big in her life that it threw her around. The archetypal world came through the wound, and she had to find a way to survive and thrive with an onslaught from the unconscious. When she lost her husband (who was a playmate and a mother to her) to her younger sister, she had a breakdown and nearly died. The crisis took her inward, where there was nothing to fall back on—no source of mothering, of self, to get her through the trauma. The inner world and analysis took on the energy and held her until she could emerge again into life.

The dream points a way of going with the wound now that leads the inner music to the gift, which also connects her to the gifts and wounds of her mother. The dream places the personal history in context: The meaningfulness of childhood soul and experiences are directly related to the wound and the gift.

Facing the "mother-wound," the lack of contact, love, and mirroring, and the ways in which this wound left her with a hole through her psyche, she also discovered the gifts that come from such a painful initiation. But those gifts would be for naught if she didn't integrate them with her honest human standpoint, including the wound. The wound becomes regenerative when we accept the reality of it, and its impact on life, and take responsibility for the ways it also operates in the world around us. Here the dream suggests the wound, when related to consciously, can become a medium of gifts that express soul and vision.

The Scathing Honesty of a Rotten Standpoint, Allowed In

Another man, a Jungian analyst in the Northwest, heard about the project I was working on and kindly offered the following dream and story. As he stated it, he came upon a place in his journey, after his training in Zurich and return to the States, in which he regressed backward into a manic pattern to which he, apparently, was turning a blind eye. He reported that he unthinkingly took on more clients than he could tend. He took on commitments to lectures after his art became renowned, and commitments to his sons' sport teams as well. Overcommitted, he became distracted and compulsive and much more overextended and extraverted than he had ever been comfortable with in the past.

He shared that what scared him most, in hindsight, was that he missed the pain he must have been feeling in his depths. One day, he finally noticed that his voice had a hollow ring, an exhaustion in it, as he talked with clients. That hollow ring penetrated him, and he began to wonder about *himself*. Then one night a dream visited him that startled him so much, his conscious pattern changed. A sobriety began to take hold, penetration by the severity of the message, the truth of who he was becoming, on this unconscious road:

> I am somewhere in the woods with my sister and brother, and we are getting things together so that we can move. I am in an old pickup I used to own, and I am trying to drive it from the back seat. In the dream, I cannot imagine how or why I am doing this. I realize I won't be able to hit the brakes from here. I think to myself, something is weird—everything seems out of control. Then I am out of the old truck. A woman has started a fire nearby, and I am angry with her because it could get out of hand very easily. It was not set in a ring, or for any reason, just burning out in the open. I am furious.
>
> Then I see my dearest dog companion, Panna, lying at my feet—and she is all rotten. Her flesh on the bottom side is gross and decaying all over my feet. I think she might still be alive, because the upper part of her looks okay. I almost vomit in the dream. I wake up gagging.

After his panic eased, he let in the message. He let the slap from the dream world shock him with the truth of his out-of-control life and his role in that mess. After grieving and reconnoitering with the quiet and the dream spirit, he made the necessary changes in his inner and outer life, finding his way back to center. The dreams went on to show his dog well and present in nature with him and in his creative projects.

He reported that the feeling of love for the animal and his apparent neglect of "the one he loved so dearly" shocked him, as did the horror of the unconscious ways that were affecting his inner life. This shock successfully awakened him to the tragedy he was unfolding. The backseat driving of an old vehicle with no access to brakes is a tell-tale sign, a neon sign, that the conscious attitude is in dire trouble—powerless, regressed, and unconscious. The fire starter in the dream, he said, mirrored the compulsive patterns, like an impersonal fire loose in his life, a fire that was not in sync with his center or himself. In fact, it was uncontained and potentially very destructive. The image of the rotten body of his dear dog companion at his feet seems to be a bucket of cold water thrown by the dream spirit into the face of the dreamer. It says, "Your standpoint is all rotten. What you love dearly has gone to shit, into a *putreficatio*." The effect of his unconscious standpoint on the dog said to him that what he was doing was so destructive that the dog, a guide and instinctual presence in relation with the unconscious, was turning rotten. This, beyond all, is what scared him and woke him up. Uncontained fire is an alchemical problem. This motif may appear when "sulphur"—desire, drives, or action—runs off with our life without our consciously holding connection with the center, the Self.

Luckily, he heard this message in time, and the love and devotion the dog represents in his inner life returned to health. If he had not heard the message and changed, a destructive wildfire was imminent and loss of soul dangerously real. He likely would have been engaged in a *putreficatio* of his conscious attitude that might have lasted for years while he searched for rebirth.

Importantly, the religious function by definition brings the energy back into containment and provides the medium of support, along with incredible honesty. The ego, when it discovers the vast mysteries of which it is truly a part, can more easily accept the truth, release defenses, and work with personal shadow problems so that these deeper dimensions can flourish in the fields of consciousness.

Imagination is the key to the work, to the inner garden, to the intermediate realm of symbol that moves and changes us and our lives as it shows us how to unite the opposites. From this alchemical emblem, the key of imagination means becoming conscious of our standpoint, our footing. Our limits, our human standpoint, and our vulnerable way of connecting to life in dialogue with the psyche and psychoid—these make all the difference in the process of incarnating the latent Self. Without the honing of human ground, the risk of being lost in the vast mercurial sea is great. Then, tragically, we are of little use to humanity or to the powers that be.

Our work helps the higher forms of Mercurius take hold in our lives. The "making of the water" and the containment of fire allows this god to abound in our lives and gives us the opportunity to refine collaborative expression. This refined spirit grows in our lives as we lend time and energy to the honing of our skills in our human work with the unconscious. Mercurius's presence can never be tamed. The trickster nature, our constant surprise at what is outside our awareness, always continues, but our receptivity to his presence and ability to work with him create a dance between consciousness and the unconscious that richly permeates our lives. In this dance, the ego learns to become a graceful, fluid partner that holds its own ground of being.

We might expect these processes of refinement to recede if we have been on the road for a long while. On the contrary, the road seems to require increased refinement of the inner attitude and religious conscience. Von Franz discusses this increased refinement in her book, *Alchemical Active Imagination*:

> . . . in practice one sees that the longer people work on this road, the more subtle the indications of the unconscious become and the worse one gets punished or thrown off if one makes a slight mistake. . . . But when the work progresses over the years, even a slight deviation, a hint of the wrong word, or a fleeting wrong thought can have the worse psychosomatic consequences. It is as though it became ever more subtle, moving on the razor's edge.[24]

With work, the unconscious ground or footing can become ground of being that connects us with the living water of the imagination. When we ponder the mystery of Mercurius in his nobler, truer form as a *sapientia dei*, a "spirit of truth," we must also look to this god of paradox and see where his other form may be at work in our lives—where we are untrue, offtrack, slippery, somehow twisted, in need of this god of the imagination who penetrates into the mystery of matter and can help free spirit with its honesty. This requires that our human feeling become completely honest when we are lost in some way.

7

The Invaluable/ Dangerous Heights: Inflation, Integration, and Incarnation

The journey from cloud coo-koo land to reality lasted a long time. In my case pilgrim's progress consisted in my having to climb down a thousand ladders until I could reach out my hand to the little clod of earth that I am.
—*C. G. Jung*

When the alchemical depths of creation reveal themselves, a drama that is both "cosmic and spiritual" unfolds. In this divine comedy, the "rescue of the human soul and the salvation of the cosmos" comes to light. Jung saw it this way:

> Alchemy represents the projection of a drama both cosmic and spiritual in laboratory terms. The *opus magnum* had two aims: the rescue of the human soul and the salvation of the cosmos . . . This work is difficult and strewn with obstacles: the alchemical opus is dangerous. Right at the beginning you meet the "dragon," the chthonic spirit, the "devil" or, as the alchemists called it, the "blackness," the *nigredo*, and this encounter produces suffering. . . In the language of the alchemists, matter suffers until the *nigredo* disappears, when the "dawn" (aurora) will be announced by the "peacock's tail" (*cauda pavonis)* and a new day will break, the *leukosis* or *albedo*. But in this state of "whiteness" one does not *live* in the true sense of the word, it is a sort of abstract ideal state. In order to make it come alive it must have "blood," it must

> have what the alchemists called the *rubedo*, the "redness" of life. Only the total experience of being can transform this ideal state of the *albedo* into a consciousness in which the last trace of blackness is dissolved, in which the devil no longer has an autonomous existence but rejoins the profound unity of the psyche. Then the *opus magnum* is finished; the human soul is completely integrated.[1]

As Jung mentions, there are many obstacles in this work, many dangers. Sometimes the detachment and dissolution of the down-going that the *nigredo* may require can lead to an experience of the *albedo* and *sublimatio*, where consciousness can join with elements of the transformation and experience a rising up into the heights that is ecstatic. Here, our eyes learn to perceive the mysteries with renewed perspective, as if with new eyes, and we may be gifted, for example, with seeing beyond the confines of time, space, and matter. Sometimes the experiences are nearly more than a person can take in. And to come from these heights and return to earth, as the alchemical round requires, can be difficult. Many pilgrims are extra mindful during the ascent in the *albedo* due to the dangers of psychic inflation, of losing their humanity by getting caught in the grip of a psychoidal or archetypal presence that can accompany the activation of the realms of existence.

If going into these realms with protection and guidance from the psyche is our fate and calling, then returning with the boon is required in the alchemical process of our individuation. It certainly was Jung's fate. His remark of descending the innumerable ladders to reach a hand out to the "tiny clod of earth that I am" gives us a mytho-poetic glimpse into his ascent and reintegration experiences.

A dream I had of Carl Jung years ago depicts this same phenomenon of heights and the return to the earth:

> Jung is parachuting down from the sky, slowly and gracefully. Gently he lands on the ground next to where I am standing. He says, "Will you tell them something for me?" (I think I was so dumbfounded to see him, that I never really replied.) He then said, "Please tell them that I *had to* get so high, go so far up; I had to in order to change the gene pool."

For many of us who are drawn to this work, Jung did indeed "change the gene pool" with his own trekking and mapping of psyche, his discoveries in the human soul, which did in fact take him into the heights beyond the personal, into the transpersonal psyche and into contact with the psychoid realm.

Considering Jung's statement in this dream—declaring he had to go so high in order to change the gene pool—to what specific mystery is this dream pointing? The reference to genes leads us to the DNA coding of genetic patterns in all of creation. DNA expresses itself in all living beings, in all of creation. Modern science has found miraculous ways to work with DNA, decoding genes that inform illness and so on. And the DNA pattern is a double helix, like the two snakes in the image of the caduceus, the symbol of healing and interdimensional travel in numerous ancient traditions.

The snake imagery paralleling DNA diagrams points to the original creation spirit.[2] So, if Jung in the dream is saying his penetration of the heights needed to happen in order to change the gene pool—then this dream is depicting alchemical mysteries of the *albedo* and *sublimatio*, of visionary joining with source that can occur in the heights as we are drawn up into the higher perspectives of different realms of being. And in these higher states the relationship between spirit and matter can be discovered in new ways, as in his words regarding changing the gene pool. Here *albedo* and *sublimatio* mysteries are seen as capable of penetrating into the matrix of creation, and generating something new, beyond the fixed genetic inheritance.

The alchemical round itself can take us into penetrating various realms of existence into the heart of the psyche-matter mysteries, where creation itself and the possibilities for creation can change. And we play a role in these possibilities coming to earth.

Now we know this is true in the modern world of science, medicine, inventions, creativity and so on, but the dream is showing this to be true in terms of alchemical rounds—that is, consciousness learning to participate with the cosmic spiritual fields that bring about death and rebirth, new discoveries and new singularities.

Jung in this dream would represent the alchemical pilgrim who can make the rounds, descend into the unknown, the *nigredo*, which activates the many realms of existence. As the realms activate in the depths, the flow of energy circulates into the *albedo*, the heights. Here, as the dream image suggests, is where the interplay between matter and spirit in the creation matrix resides; the gene pool could be contacted and changed and these changes brought back to earth. It mirrors the alchemical round. As the *nigredo* stage moves into the *albedo*, experiences of utter psychological, spiritual, and emotional darkness ease, and in the language of the mystics, a purification of the self begins to happen in which our senses are cleansed and humbled and our energies and interests are concentrated on transcendental things. Psychologically speaking, new processes begin that work to dissolve, transcend, and transmute the images and experiences of our personal past. Energy is freed from past identities, and ways of perceiving and so on. This allows the energy to rise up out of the old forms, and we begin to feel lighter, have new perspectives and experiences.

Sometimes, as in the image in this dream, there is quite an infusion in the heights, more than simply insight or connection with an archetypal presence. The alchemists saw the purified essence rising up to be fertilized by star seeds,[3] and then returning to Earth with that shining renewal able to reside in matter, and form. The DNA changing reference in the dream suggests being altered by something beyond archetypes and ideas of fixed stars—perhaps (staying with the celestial metaphor) into the farther star regions, what we call the psychoid realm. Either way, it points to a fertilizing mutual penetration with the creation matrix.

This penetration into the matrix of course is what brings new creative and destructive possibilities to life. There are many ways to penetrate into the creation-destruction matrix; the invention of nuclear warfare for example, or numerous kinds of healing arts and sciences penetrate into the creation-destruction matrix. The ancient alchemists were not interested in ego consciousness penetrating into the matrix for random purposes or enacting the ego's latest fantasies out on creation, however. They were interested in this *magnum opus*, discovering a new unity between the human and divine as they contacted the inner guide of the work that would lead to "the rescue of the human soul and the salvation of the cosmos." This work required ever more differentiation and sophisticated development of the relationship with the guide, the work, and so on. The alchemist continually adjusts and realigns his or her attitude and heart so that the co-creation of the new unity in the relationship between human consciousness and the divine could occur.

Mercurius, the duplex god of the alchemists, plays with and is capable of helping us discover new unities between the dualities. That is the art of working with the spirit of the imagination as well, so that the development of consciousness can differentiate from creation to such a degree that it can unite with creation in ever-new ways. This way, lesser *coniunctios* evolve into more refined *coniunctios* between heaven and earth, primordial and celestial, human and divine.

In the dream, Jung is standing up for and valuing his experience of the heights, and he wants the dream ego to stand by this medicine. Jung the actual person made his life's work with the psyche and psychoid, which required great courage. We may also require courage to face the fate of needing to trek some corner or aspect of the heights and depths of the psyche and psychoid, and perhaps even find a way to survive and thrive because of contact with these activated realms portrayed in the alchemical round. We each can then work to realize our potential inheritance from the changed gene pool and to help the "gene pool" change.

The necessity of experiencing the borderlands of consciousness is often not only vitalizing to the soul by "changing the gene pool" of possibilities for our lives, it can be a matter of life and death for the soul, spirit, body, relationships and so on. Given the importance both of experiencing the borderlands of consciousness at times and the work with the shadow that such treks involve, differentiating work with psyche is mandatory. This work that values both realities will assist us to keep a "snorkel" of sorts out to the psychoid, bringing back incredible air to breathe way down deep in our humble humanity.

Work with dreams and active imagination helps the specifics of the human situation or condition come into unique singular relationship with the creation spirit or matrix. Bringing the healing wisdom to earth is essential for the wholeness to ensue in the *rubedo* process, a central goal of the work.

The Mingling of Human and Divine

Eating of the fruit of the work, like the alchemist in figure 10 on page 76, brings the work into living embodiment in our life, and is not about inflation. It is about the religious instinct growing in our life and bringing wisdom as we learn to live with the unconscious and become more truly human, while the divine transforms in relationship with our humanity.

There are times for moving away from more direct contact with archetypes, with the Self and psychoidal presences, just as there are times for moving toward them. The religious instinct awakens a self regulation process. It prompts the desire and the longing to move beyond the revealed, the known, and the secure, to that which the ego may at times try tenaciously to hang onto. The religious instinct also prompts the ethical need to embody relationship with the mysteries that come to honor human life and work with the issues of our planet and daily lives. This urge to move beyond the revealed opens us to the deep synchronizing and sympathy with the mysteries of psyche. And this urge to love the world and live in it in ever more conscientious ways helps to bring the wisdom from the experiences all the way home.

So, the wisdom fruit of the soul's alchemical journey makes the ego *relative*, and underscores how important the ego attitudes are, for without the right attitudes life can become hopelessly stunted or stuck. And without the formation of ego consciousness and connection to the particulars of our life, the experiences of the heights of consciousness cannot come to the *rubedo*, the earthy ensouled world.

When I muse over the people, many with life-threatening illnesses, who have come to work with me in these last two decades, a number of different reflections of initiatory experiences with the psyche and psychoid come to mind. It is remarkable how soul is created in holding the *full range* of human experience amidst the initiation mysteries as a person gains relationship with the numinous. As the alchemical round depicts, this full range of experience at times includes incredible suffering, dark physical-psychic aberrations, and a loss of human ground; indeed for many people it also includes encounters with pockets of insanity, where a person "cracks" as his or her old self dies and the new consciousness emerges. It may also involve risking dancing so closely with Self, sometimes when enough human ground of being has not yet formed, that inflationary experiences may be encountered.

Dr. Adolf Guggenbühl-Craig, in his book *From the Wrong Side*, speaks of the god complex and the notion that we mortals must learn not to confuse what is good for the gods and what is good for human beings. As he views it, living inside our mortality pops bubbles of narcissism and self-importance and returns us to our humble humanity as a way to live "close to god." Identification with Self, the seductiveness of the god complex, brings out the dangerousness of the alchemical work. On the other hand, self-effacing therapy will bring one closer to god, but from a human ground of being. When I spoke with him on one occasion about his writing on these issues, and suggested we must take the risk of approaching the gods and take the responsibility for handling the threat of inflation, he laughed and said, "Okay, it is inflated to think one can fight inflation!"

Dr. Guggenbühl-Craig speaks from eight decades of life experience. It may be that it is human to confuse these boundaries earlier in the course of our life and to need to find out what is and is not possible through our own experience. We cannot, it seems to me, establish a relationship with psyche and psychoidal reality without approaching experience of both dimensions, even with the risk of inflation and deflation in the process. We may need to allow them to enter us, to mingle with our consciousness, in order to find a relationship with them that will not be all-consuming in the long run. It is as unwise to naïvely trek into the vastness of the psyche and psychoid, as it is to overly guard against numinous experience.

The mingling of the human and divine abounds in all we do. The symbolism inherent in many traditional rituals expresses this. One example comes from the Catholic Mass. The priest on the altar mixes water with wine as a symbol of Christ as the embodiment of humanity and divinity. The mixing of our mortality with what is immortal, of our finiteness with infiniteness, is vital to building a relationship between the depths of the psyche and consciousness. Alchemy is all about the continual mixing and separating as these new unities among differentiated elements are discovered. Accepting the paradoxical in psychology is helpful; it needs to be both/and rather than either/or.

Because of the necessity for this mingling, people will explore the edges of these borderlands for centuries to come. They will learn about inflation, deflation, possession, and the ground of being and soul that is in humanity along with the fate of mortality. They'll discover in ever new ways, the stolen fire from the realm of the gods, and happen upon sneak peaks from the top of Mt. Olympus where the gods reside. They'll be innocently out picking flowers one day and fall into Hades, and there become initiated in ever new ways, and await the divine feminine with her torch and headdress of stars to wander in the passageways of the underworld and bring them out of the depths to return to the mothers and grandmothers and earth life.

We have a shimmer of nobility perhaps, as Edward Edinger states, in that we aspire to become a little bit like god. Some of us will continue to have horrendous times returning from the journey and learning to incarnate more into the mystery that is human life.

The depth, quality, and necessity toward initiation are unique to each person. The inner alchemical wedding, the *hieros gamos* mystery, is indescribably chthonic and heavenly. In working in partnership with the inner guide as best we know how, initiatory contact comes, but early on in the journey it is rarely "neat and tidy." These initiatory fires can bring heavenly and hellish experiences, and if we survive and gain more human ground in relationship with the mysteries, we become initiated. This territory may require us to encounter madness, inflation, and deflation—all territory present in the wilderness of the psyche and psychoid. To have caution is understandable, for experiences of the opposites bring us into the presence of the numen, the great *mysterium tremendum*, as Rudolf Otto terms it. He paints with his words an arc of this varying territory of the numen experience:

> The feeling of it may at times come sweeping like a gentle tide, pervading the mind with a tranquil mood of deepest worship. It may pass over into a more set and lasting attitude of the soul, continuing, as it were, thrillingly vibrant and resonant, until at last it dies away and the soul resumes its "profane," non-religious mood of everyday experience. It may burst forth in a sudden eruption up from the depths of the soul with spasms and convulsions, or lead to the strangest excitements, to intoxicated frenzy, to transport, and to ecstasy. It has its wild and demonic forms and can sink to an almost grisly horror and shuddering. It has its crude, and barbaric antecedents and early manifestations, and again it may be developed into something beautiful and pure and glorious. It may become the hushed, trembling, and speechless humility of the creature in the presence of—whom or what? In the presence of that which is a *mystery* inexpressible and above all creatures.[4]

Keeping in view the wide arc of opposites with which numinous experience puts us in contact, we see the polarities arise in the embodiment of different traditions in the East and West. Whereas our Western psychology and spirituality generally values an "I-Thou" dialogue with the numinous, Eastern psychology and spirituality brings to life, with greater emphasis, the mysteries of unity and differentiation, of the great Beloved living Itself and Its desires through all forms in the dance of creation beyond and throughout time and space. Both are core realities available to us in the processes of individuation, both are perspectives from which we may experience valuable relationship with the numinous.

In the alchemical concept of the *sublimatio*, after the *nigredo* the spirit ascends and joins with source, true nature, before re-entering the world of forms. Our consciousness and other elements of our being make this same round. We can unify with source and then re-enter our humanity. This can be on a small, digestible level, such as taking in a dream experience in which the dream spirit brings us a felt experience of renewal, and then we apply our renewed selves to life situations in which we have been off the mark. This round can also happen on a larger scale, and the ego can for a time join with source for a more prolonged experience of unity with Self; the ego may even be swept up into psychic processes at high altitudes where rebirth may or may not happen.

The alchemical texts depicted this *sublimatio* process in the following emblem and description:

> Mercurius is begotten by nature as the son of nature and the fruit of the liquid element. But even as the Son of Man is begotten by the philosopher and created as the fruit of the Virgin, so must he [Mercurius]

> be raised from the earth and cleansed of all earthiness, then he ascends entire into the air, and is changed into spirit. Thus is fulfilled the word of the philosopher: He ascends from earth to heaven and receives the power of Above and Below, and puts off his earthy and impure nature and clothes himself in the heavenly nature.[5]

To be taken up into an archetype, or into an experience of Self or of the psychoid and *remain there* is known to be dangerous, psychically contaminating, and can lead to psychic possession. It may also be, however, a valuable experience from which we may recover.

To never dare the dance with the numinous in which these experiences can take place is also a great danger, for then one risks possession by the uninitiated "ego" complex with its psychic poverty and one-sidedness which distorts the quality and depth of life. This fearful, rigid defense against life's enormity leads to repression of the divine, and life becomes bereft of depth and meaning.

Both realities of experiencing different dimensions of the psyche, and the creation of individuality are crucial to healing, initiation, and formation of the manifest Self, the Philosopher's Stone in our life. Manifesting the latent Self into daily life requires we do not vacate the personal dimensions of being, our humanity, for the divine seeks to unite with our humanity in order to incarnate. Being taken into the tidal release of ordinary awareness, of ego consciousness, is vitalizing. Over time, the relational union between human and divine works this out, where the dialogue is between partners and is not an invasion of the unconscious. Ecstatic union with the beloved occurs, while humanity increases.

The Sufi tradition has spoken to the heart of this matter, valuing both the union with the divine, and the creation of the individual. Rather than seeing contact with the inner angel as leading all disciples to the same goal, or absorbing the human being so fully that all traces of humanity disappear, Sufism sees contact with the inner angel as bringing us to the experience and birth of true human individuality:

> He leads each disciple to his own inner theophany—the theophany of which he personally is witness—because that theophany corresponds to his "inner heaven," to the form of his own being, to his eternal individuality.[6]

As the Sufis see it, the great inner teacher's mission is to help our individual soul and voice find the sound, the inner music of our own "Holy Spirit."

Now we shall turn to some of these varying experiences via case examples underscoring this treacherous/valuable territory of the heights, and the essential life processes of psychic energy circulation among the many realms of being.

CIRCULATION OF PSYCHIC ENERGY AMONG THE MANY REALMS OF BEING

As consciousness and the unconscious meet, if they successfully unite, the *coniunctio* takes hold and a new light is born. The newly-yoked sun and moon, conscious and unconscious, ego and Self, then discover fresh relationship to one another. In alchemy, this is the goal of the work, with ever-increasing differentiations in this union. As the sun and moon join, they begin to move together, and their new light circulates through the many realms; the *coniunctio* leads to the *circulatio* mysteries where the movement of the manifest Self enters into more and more of our lives. Marie-Louise von Franz addresses this in a discussion about Arabic alchemy:

> So when the sun and moon unite they begin at the same time to move along a cycle, which has to do with time. This is symbolized in Eastern alchemy through the process of circulation of the light; after having found the inner light it begins to rotate by itself. In *The Secret of the Golden Flower*, and in alchemy, this is called the *circulatio*, the rotation, and there are many different texts in alchemy in which it is said that the philosopher's stone has to circulate. Usually that is connected to time symbolism, for they say the philosopher's stone has to pass through winter, spring, summer and autumn, or it has to go through all the hours of the day and night. It has to circulate through all the qualities and all the elements, or it has to go from earth to heaven and back again to the earth. There is always the idea that after having been produced, it begins to circulate. Psychologically, this would mean that the Self begins to manifest in space and time, that it does not become something at a certain moment with afterwards a return to one's former way of living, but has an immediate effect upon the whole of life; then action and reaction are constantly in accordance with the Self, real and manifest in its own movements. The stone, or the new light, the Self, can itself move. Naturally we have to listen to it, but if we do, then it can move and can produce autonomous impulses.[7]

On the way to discovering this psychic freedom present in the *circulatio* mysteries of the manifest Self coming into our lives, we may be initiated via various psychological challenges in one realm or another. Understandably, sometimes people get stuck in other realms of consciousness. And, unlike the ideal image of Jung in the dream, who after visiting incredible heights comes to earth gracefully and unabated, people often encounter some difficulty returning to earth life, and that trouble is usually an important part of the initiation. Let's look into these occurrences along with wisdom from various cultures that map the rounds and realms of consciousness, and then later explore how the nature spirit in dreams assists us when we get stuck in these unearthly realms.

First of all, these realms are not all gloriously mystical. Discovering this truth leads to part of the boon of the journey. We begin to discover there is an unending path of differentiation of nonrational states and dimensions of experience. If we work with inflation (being "caught up," overly fascinated or mesmerized in some experience of the psyche or psychoid), then we can help differentiate further the domains of being. In the process, most importantly, we can learn to draw closer to the inner guide so that the processes bring the fruit of the journey into the spirit of daily life.

Here we may also learn to respect, recognize, and consciously participate in the *circulatio* mysteries the alchemists knew, where the rounds of change inform and flow and affect all areas of life over time, where dreams address the flow of life force and how one can participate more consciously in its renewing cycles.

The archetypal nature of these alchemical truths is found in mandalas and medicine wheel images and practices from numerous cultures throughout time. These mandalas and medicine wheels make the reality of these domains of existence and the circulation of energy among the realms come alive.[8]

As a meditation, the Buddhist wheel (see figure 23 on page 238) portrays all the realms of being—heaven and ecstasy at the top, hell and the fixed eye of judgment at the bottom, emptiness in the middle. Desire nature and its shadow—the needy addictive regions of the *pretas* ("hungry ghosts") on the left lower side—is opposite the warring, competitive, angry aspects of the *asura* ("demon") region higher on the right side. Next to heaven on the left upper side is the human realm and opposite that lies the animal region, which are the two most valuable places to learn to dwell. The *preta* realm of desire can lead to many kinds of experiences. The danger here is losing our self as the needy, addictive demons take over. Anyone who has spent time in addictive states or has loved someone who has, knows what it is like if the *pretas* take over a human life. It is hell. The *asura* realm of power can be strengthening,

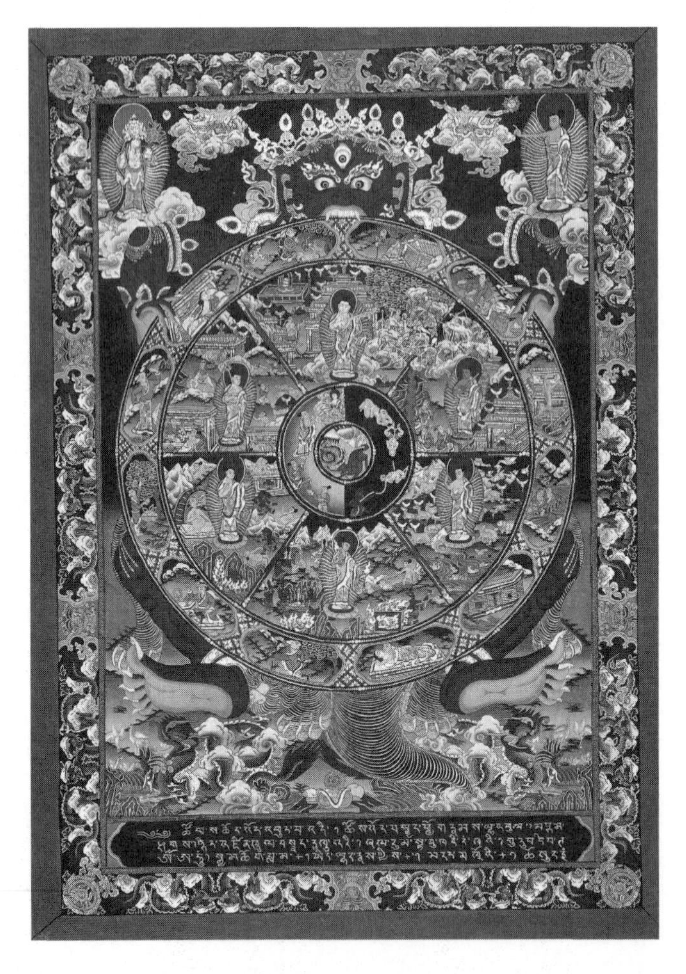

Fig. 23. Tibetan Buddhist tanka depicting the Wheel of Life, from Ben Meulenbeld, Buddhist Symbolism in Tibetan Thangkas, *p. 67.*

but the danger here is that we can be taken over by its shadow, and wield power without humanity, which is always destructive on both the personal and collective levels.

In the animal region we learn to tend and relate with the other species in life and do the simple tasks of earthy survival, like crop tending, cooking, providing shelter, and so on. In the human realm, we discover choice and freedom. Pictured inside the human realm are all the other realms, indicating that all the possibilities in the other realms also exist in the human realm. With an awareness of this energy circulation through the many realms within us, and our humanity intact, our ability to choose different states of consciousness increases. Getting caught or stuck in heaven or hell, the heights or the depths, or getting caught or stuck in addiction or warring energy is natural. But as their wheel teachings illuminate, getting consciousness freed from possession in any of these realms is essential to being human and becoming enlightened. This is also a good image of the *rubedo*; as we come more fully into the *rubedo*, all realms are present and energy flows more freely with human choice and freedom abounding, so that getting stuck or possessed in any realm is less problematic.

Before we learn this fluidity of consciousness in participation with the realms of existence, getting lost or stuck often happens. And of course, getting stuck somewhere in the realms of being and having our earth life suffer is a pretty common human experience. The dis-ease, the imbalance and the illness it may cause in some area of our life, and the need to retrieve soul in order to heal it is mirrored in many healing traditions. This healing work in essence participates in the *circulatio* mysteries.

For example, in ancient shamanic traditions, when a person becomes ill, the shaman goes into the realms of being to locate the person's soul wherever it is stuck and bring it back to earth. Depth psychotherapy in some ways may also participate in this model, although the differences are important. The "shaman" appears in the work as an inner guide, in ritual and dreams, and in the relational field, while the analyst functions as an assistant to the human and his or her own relationship development with the inner guide. As this relationship forms, both the wound and the healing source are often discovered.

In a lively story from the Buriat of Irkutsk in Sibera, the archetypal structures of these healing truths abound, where the realms of existence appear, and the rescuing of the human soul is sought, and in so doing consciousness increases and healing balance is restored between the human and the divine. Shaman after shaman is called in to help a critically ill man. Finally, one shaman with a rare gift of the sight takes on the task. As he chants and sings over the dying man, his spirit enters the realms to find where the man's soul is stuck. He looks around in the human earth realm, sees the relationship world among mortals, the sick man's work life and such. And all is in order. Then he goes to the lower worlds and looks around and sees nothing from the past and no hellish realms holding the sick man down. Stumped, he decides to go into the over-world, into the heavens. There he sees again that everything looks to be in order. The divine beings are all sitting about looking rather peaceful. He is just about to leave when he sees out of the corner of his eye that God has his thumb casually over a bottle. The shaman wants God to let go, but he won't. So the shaman turns himself into a wasp and stings God's thumb. As God screeches and shakes his hand, the shaman goes into the bottle and takes the soul of the man out and brings him back to earth. The man returns to health.[9]

As in this story, illness or suffering in our lives can be linked to libido or life force energy that is not flowing in some dimension or realm of existence. Dreams can address this and begin to help in the process of becoming freed again. In this story, the man's soul is held hostage in the sealed vessel by God in heaven, and it is making the man sick. We could think of this in more clinical language as being in the grip of an archetype. But that language can tend to lose connection with the experiential phenomenon. Therefore, we'll also keep the images and language of the Buriat story in the background as we explore human stories and dreams reflecting the experience of getting stuck, freed, and integration of the experiences bringing wisdom. As reflected in this story, bringing the soul back to earth life can require extra attention and assistance.

Coming Down from the Heavens

A woman who came down with a life-threatening illness turned with what energy she had to the inner world for help, and it met her head on. She began to have daily experiences in meditation and yoga of joining with the great Beloved within. At one point she realized that the intensity of the union could actually pull her out of life, and she knew from her yogic teachings, and heard it in her work with me, that she needed to be sure to ground her energy into the very earthy things in life in order to bring this ecstasy to earth. Then, in the following dream she is faced with this reality:

> An ancient shaman is before me. He is large, with dark hair and skin, and is wearing a loincloth. He motions to the spiral shell I am wearing on my neck. I think the spiral is all right but he mocks it, then pinches it off. As it crumbles, I am certain he has something better to show me. He also pulls the hair on the side of my head. (The thought occurs to me that I have wanted a shaman to train with and he is here.)
>
> I follow him outside to a dance that is beginning. He has me lead the women in the dance while he leads the men. Then we are outside on

> these mesas full of Indian dwellings. The sky has a numinous cast and it is impossible to tell what time of day it is. He motions to the mountain that is the image of their "God." The presence of god is tangible. I approach the shaman and state nonverbally that I wonder, in looking to the mountain, what a marvel it is that humans endure the storms, dangers, and dark times of their lives. He gives the hair on my head a pull and shakes me and sends me up the mountain.
>
> I begin walking but the path is not clearly defined. I walk at first to the left and then get back on the path. The trail heads straight up the mountain and at one point it traverses a ledge that requires the climber to be upside down. I am climbing this part and my lover and partner behind me gives me a push over this ledge. Once on the top of "god mountain," god's view is before us. My lover takes my hand. We can see civilizations of humankind throughout generations, the lights going on in their dwellings all facing god mountain. . . .
>
> The sunset colors sweep over the dwellings and the mountain. I sit down because it is so immense my knees are shaky. There is a permeating feeling of harmony amidst all the cycles of humanity, amidst all the cycles of births and deaths facing god mountain in reverie.
>
> My lover asks the ancient shaman who is with us if he can see the storm in my eyes. The shaman grabs me by the hair and shakes me . . . He says "Once up here you may choose to stay. Or if you choose to come down I'll be there to meet you." I indeed choose to come down and I enter a room where the "teacher" is instructing us on physical exercises for strengthening the center chakra and stomach. I am doing upside-down difficult sit ups and realize this is the instruction from the shaman. Women are with me and are lovingly supportive.

Her reverie and incarnational choice in the dream are clear. The encounter with the psyche and the initiatory teacher in the life and death struggle brings her up to a view of creation and history from "god mountain" where the rounds of life and death all have their place, and her life has a place in these rounds as well. It is an elevated place to be allowed to see into the wheel of life and death, into the dance between the temporal and the eternal. It is a hefty climb up above the daily life stream, and it is part of the map of the psyche she is learning to visit.

This dream suggests that experience of the divine, its heights, and its point of view can be a process from which a person gains the ground of belonging in the human race, the ground of true humanity, and core identification with her or his mortal life. To see things from the point of view of Self, of the permanent and immortal is quite an initiation. In fact, it is one from which we must choose human life or most likely go on and die (or live life in an entranced state, possibly falling into a psychosis of sorts).

Union with the Self at these heights depicts the value of the *albedo* and *sublimatio* processes, where consciousness rises up to join with source and then re-enter human forms renewed. In the dream's chakra exercise scene, we see she will work on discovering a new center in her being as well. The teacher wants to strengthen the center of the body/personality. She will need to embody this new center in order for her renewed life and the fruit of the journey to come into humanity.

The fruit from her experience, revelation, and choice is not about a "mental understanding." Mental understandings are fine as long as they serve to hold the contact with the mystery. If not held carefully, mental understandings can secretly attempt to control or crowd the psyche. The fruit of the journey is instead depicted in the dream as an embodiment of this new center of consciousness that is born from contact with the divine.

The dream teacher-shaman telling her at the end of the dream that he will meet her at the bottom of the mountain in the workout room where he will help her work on her center is important. He showed her where she was trekking, and confronted her with a choice, which, in one direction, would begin the incarnating of the *albedo* into the *rubedo*, into grounded human life, where connection to the guide would continue to flourish and bring her new teachings. In fact, this theme re-emphasized itself in a remarkable dream several months later:

> I descend from a mountain, and stand in a mountain pass looking down into the valley. I say out loud, "But where will the divine eye of god be?" And the dream teacher takes me down to a lake in the saddle of the mountain and asks me to look into the water. As I look in, I see a large, single cell floating up to the surface. A pyramid shape sits in the center of this single cell, and inside the pyramid is the divine eye of god. The dream teacher then answers me, saying, "Where will the divine eye of god be? Why, in every cell of your body!"

The medicine of the dream helped usher the dreamer into the circulation of energy from the heights into embodied life. The incarnated eye of the divine is promised—the divine sight from the heights is now to be found in the valley, in incarnation, embodiment of life. Such comfort came to this woman from the helping spirit guiding her into matter, into her body and into her life issues, and the dance of life between spirit and matter.

Emerging from the Preta Region

A man who deeply worked with me over a decade found his way to an authentic ground of being after a tenacious deflation which lasted many years and nearly choked his life force completely. His ego attitude had been hobbled by a wound in which he was not sufficiently mirrored as a child for the feeling type that he was. He suffered a terrible split from Self; his ego was severely alienated from life-giving energy in his psyche, and thus he was cut off from life ever really touching him.

Luckily, he had a Jewish and Catholic background of religious study from childhood, which served to orient him to the transpersonal dimension for help. Aching for help at his darkest hour, he asked for and received a dream:

> A goddess-like feminine figure is within view. Flowing long hair and dress. I seem to be trying to follow her. We are amid dark corridors, hallways. Longingly I am reaching out to her. . . . (This dream seems to go on all night.) . . . Then there is a chant that begins as I am desperately trying to catch up with her, the object of my longing. The chant goes round and round rather hauntingly:
>
> ISHTAICARAICTOME
> ISHTAICARAICTOME

The dreamer reported the chant without any conscious knowledge of any specific words or names being contained in the chant. Yet, he had a feeling that this powerful chant seemed to be an invocation of the mysteries. He repeated the chant over and over and soon from out of the chant audibly discernible names began to emerge in my consciousness: *Ishtar, Icarus, Ictome!* Looking into these names, we find that Ishtar is the Sumerian goddess of descent mysteries; Icarus, the Greek hero of ascent mysteries and flying into the sun, thus signifying the danger of identifying with the powers that be to the point of destruction; and Ictome is the trickster shamanic god of initiation among the Sioux. With his discovery of Ictome's nature being called up in the chant, it became clear to the dreamer that the painful path of initiation amid the down-going and the up-going was a calling. He drew strength from his sense of the creative and intelligent inner presence leading him. The promise of help emerging from the depths spoke straight to his heart, and his process began to flourish.

Two days after the dreamer shared this dream with me, I flew from my office in California to my home in New Mexico. On my way to a plant nursery the next day, I turned on the radio and happened upon an hour-long broadcast from the Dakotas about the medicine of Ictome! I learned that among the Sioux, Ictome is enacted at the ceremonial dances by a figure who holds a mirror draped with spider webs. The trickster Ictome dances with the mirror, trying to capture audience members who happen to glance at their own reflection in this spidery mirror! No one volunteers to be caught by Ictome's mirror, the Sioux myth states, for once caught, you must go the way of the shaman. You must descend to the depths of hell and suffer afterwards the heights and then come to identify with neither as you emerge from the mirror of Ictome and become a true shaman. Or the other course could be that you end up stuck in the mirror somewhere, in some region you visit. The trek into the mirror can entail a horrendous adventure from which you may not return. If you lose your humanity, that is if you fail to release identification with the regions or the gods, then you may find yourself walking the edge of, or into the heart of, madness. Your medicine for the world would then be weak or nonexistent, or, on the other hand, your medicine ways might fall into malevolent sorcery.

Clearly the alchemical motif of the down-going *nigredo*, and the up-going *albedo* and *sublimatio*, and the *rubedo*, where humanity emerges and grounds the initiatory gifts, are all being named in this archetypal pattern of the Ictome shaman.

The dream's broadcast of the dreamer's initiation was pointing him into archetypal territory. Would he have to make the descent to the human and discover the divine feminine within dwelling like Ishtar at the bottom of the *nigredo*? Would he learn to soar to the heights in the *albedo*, and watch out for the inflation that could make him crash? Then, lastly, could he refrain from identifying with either terrain? Would he emerge from the mirror of Ictome with his humanity and medicine intact? This was such a tall order for anyone, let alone someone as young as he.

Thankfully he had had an analysis with a male analyst before he arrived at my door. (They both had thought that working with a woman might help him into his male-female issues and bring up immediate emotions.) I thought at the time that the desperation of the life force within him was willing to throw him into the flames to get it all to change, for the way he was living was lifeless and on the edge. I would try to help keep the flame at a level he could withstand, and to try to see, hopefully with grace appearing, that he himself did not otherwise destructively burn up in the process.

I also asked myself how would he go into such territory when he had not had enough of this in the personal sphere as a young boy and young man. Jung saw that a premature invasion of the collective unconscious can lead to an inflation, and I kept the danger of that possibility within view. I instinctively drew a deep breath and sighed when I heard his dream. I knew if the work was going to come anywhere near touching what this dream was pointing to, then the analytical relationship would need to become one hell of a strong vessel, able to hold the heat and bring human connection and mirroring to life in order for this work to really take hold. I also wondered at the time of this dream what would happen to him if the libido began to free up memories, feelings, desires, emotional and sexual needs, let alone the religious instinctual needs that seemed to be behind the whole architecture of this dream of potential initiation.

Holding all these questions and concerns in suspended animation as possibilities, I began taking the trek with him as his unique path unfolded step by step, interaction by interaction, stone by stone, dream by dream, struggle by human struggle.

As the process later unfolded, the alchemical structure of the dream chant was an enormous help to me, for it mapped the landscape and its dangers succinctly. I kept it in the background of my imagination as we worked. The dreamer launched into the interior realms and the depths and heights were activated. Between the down-going spirals there finally appeared some updrafts that let us know "Icarus" was nearby. This man so identified with the *nigredo*, with Hades, that appearance of updrafts were initially compensatory. Identification with the heights at first was not nearly as dangerous as identification with death. A watchful eye was kept on these opposites, which he needed to endure to finally (using the language of the dream's mythical allusion) leave the mirror of Ictome and emerge into his humanity with some seeing abilities.

Then the link came to the *puer* through his suicidal streak that emerged. The *mortificatio* and *nigredo* he had been unconsciously living in showed us the youth who wanted to die and get out of life, and had just about achieved this for him by the deadening of Self. And yet the other side of the *puer* then appeared, the part that wanted to be great, soar high, be all he could be as a man, a lover, a musician. Now we were getting somewhere, for the *puer* constellation had illuminated the death wishes as the longing to transform and live closer to life and the soul within him.

The more mirroring that the dream world, the work, and life brought to him, the more his wound began to heal with his sense of self, love, and the flow of life. It took quite a long time, as of course it should.

From enduring the highs and lows in his initiation, he learned to recognize the presence of his inner guide throughout the journey. In fact, the anima that appeared, which had its own host of tricks, led him through such varying inner landscape that the process taught him to become flexible, emotionally expressive, and objective. At one point, the door in him inevitably opened, and the energy in affect and sexuality became red hot. A Dionysian core awakened. He resorted to numerous attempts at enacting the heat, and discovered it fed the fire, and got him involved with chaotically organized people who mirrored these states. It reminded me of the *preta* region on the Buddhist mandala, where the starving desire creatures dwell. So many of his emotional and sensual needs had been blocked, that the pendulum swung for awhile, as it understandably would. He had to discover pig-nature, that snout that can go about sniffing what it loves and what it wants and what brings sensual delight. It was so buried in him that it was difficult when that powerful archetypal force rose up.

Here he came to know important parts of himself as he connected with archetypal dimensions. He discovered the flow of life force with others in ways he had no idea existed, psychically and physically. In these archetypal encounters he made peace with instincts that brought in strength, presence, and life. He also discovered human limitations. Eventually his core communicated to his consciousness that he had had enough of trying to live it out in certain ways, and the wild orgiastic energy found a new seat inside of him, housed by much humanity and wisdom.

This pilgrim, with much grace and hard work, found his way through the labyrinth. In the depths, he did meet the erotic divine feminine who helped awaken him to the flow of life within him. And he encountered his *puer* streak that also awakened, and sent him into some dangerous territory in the outer world, in which he could have lost much of what he held dear. He found his way out of this territory naturally and wiser for having visited it. Over time, he learned to respect the power in the energy his process had freed up and to channel it creatively through music and writing and love relationship.

Getting Stuck in the Asura *Region*

In the *asura* region of the Buddhist mandala reign the warrior beings of power, competition, anger, and violence. It also can be a place where we discover strength, for to find our way out of possession in this realm requires making peace with our power and its shadow.

A woman in her late 50s who had divorced a powerful and wealthy husband, took up a new life as an independent woman. At 55, she got a job as a receptionist, the first she had ever had in her life. She also followed a longtime desire to try her hand at painting and took night classes. Eventually, she gained recognition for her work, to the point where she could not keep up with the demand for more paintings. This success in the world caused her to suffer a bout of inflation, and she became quite off center. Her dreams then were remarkable helpers and teachers in bringing to her both the diagnosis of her condition and the necessary antidote for recovery. For example, during her inflation, she dreamed:

> I am with a few other people in some art gallery and jewelry store at a crossroads. I have been handling the jewels, and suddenly the next place on my journey I am to go is calling, and it demands my attention. I am not sure what to do now with these jewels, since I need to go in a hurry. I know it is not quite right, but I put them in my pocket. It feels sneaky, but I was not sure what else to do. Then I take my hand out of my pocket and see that I am trying to hold a paintbrush and there are these incredible rings on my hand, but my fingers are stunted, kind of blue and strange. I realize I do not have the hands yet to handle and wear such rings. I take the jewels out of my pocket. I am connected to them, but somehow I realize at the last minute that "pocketing" them is wrong. I ask someone to help me.

Here we can see that in order to handle her calling in painting, or to handle relationship with life, or with the Self via her image-making medium, she needs to develop more humanity, and specifically hands. Hands are for holding, carrying, embracing, contact, pushing away—mediating relationship with the world. The fairy tale of the handless maiden comes to mind in which it is her fate as a woman to try to find human hands, not ones of silver or any other material, but human ones for touching life, for relating to life from womanliness. The painter's old self had been living passively and acted in the shadows in manipulative ways. Shoving her anger into the shadows, and unconsciously handling the world around her, the urges for individuation were tied up inside. She had deferred to other people's power (her ex-husband) to take care of her, and the bargain was to serve them so she wouldn't have to individuate. Now the dream seems to be taking an important look at her hands and handling of the jewels.

The dream ego's exploration here in this dream, of "pocketing the jewels" is important. First of all, we don't know if she should have those jewels or not. On a mythological level, pocketing or stealing is a daring act, an amoral thing to do that can bring about change in the world, and so this is not about a moral issue. Considering it one would be forcing the ego's sensibilities upon those of the dream world, which are quite different. It is the *dilemma* she is having that is the key. These jewels she discovers are valuable and lovely, but how could she handle them when her hands are so strange, stunted, and undeveloped? I wondered if it was about her human hands and power drives not yet being differentiated. Said another way, inflation and undeveloped power are just undeveloped human hands not yet able to handle the jewels. The image of "pocketing them" may be compensation for feeling so far away from the jewels and values they represent—being drawn to them, but not yet able to handle them.

If we were to take a Freudian perspective for a moment, and look at the humorous way the psyche plays with words, we could imagine that she served the "family jewels" (attending the husband's needs) outside herself in her past marriage. She was going to have to discover and handle what those jewels once represented outside of her in her own life now. Instead of penis envy, it would be jewel envy. But then the dream world is calling her to the task—she'll need to learn how to handle the high value and beauty of the jewels as they exist in her own life and psyche.

That she asks for help seems perfect! Both innerwardly and outerwardly she seemed to be asking for help. When we first spent time on this dream about "pocketing the jewels" she became depressed. It was very difficult for her to face, own, and accept her power drive. She thought of it as something despicable and abhorrent. Her conscious attitude was that women were not to have such drives. No women in her family lineage had graduated from college or held jobs in the work world. She was the first to graduate from college, live unmarried after a divorce, and to "try her own hand," so to speak, at her own creativity. The lack of explicit power drives expressed consciously in the lives of the women in her lineage helped us understand how deep in her shadow this drive was. Then she dreamed the following dream:

> I am with some Christian man and yet he has done something terrible. He shot somebody in the name of God. Yet I am still lovers with him and I do not know how this can be. There is still lots of feeling for him and yet now I feel ambivalent since he shot someone! Feeling terribly anxious, I do not know what to do. Then a voice in the dream says to me, "You can try to deny it, or hide it, but the body of who you shot will just show up one day!" Then, with this, I see that a huge carpet is unfurling. As it unfolds a woman (who is not dead, but clearly who the man thought he killed) steps out of the carpet. It is Cleopatra of Egypt!

I must admit that when she related this dream to me, I spontaneously laughed out loud! Practically no woman in history can rival the power that Cleopatra carried. Her role as leader of Egypt and her marriage to Marc Anthony from Rome held enormous cards of fate that were played during the fall of both kingdoms. Most interestingly, this woman painter-dreamer did not consciously know the story of Cleopatra's power, nor that Cleopatra is said to have sneaked back into her father's kingdom—after having been sent away—by being rolled up in a rare carpet that was brought into the palace as a gift. In the story, when they placed the rug down and unfurled it, out stepped Cleopatra, to take her rightful place as the daughter of the Ptolemaic-Egyptian king, and heir to the throne.

The power or inflationary complex that is viewed as "abhorrent" to the painter's Christian animus and dream ego is pushed of course outside consciousness even further. Her struggle highlights the very human, psychic reality of the old double-faced god, Janus regarding the ego's position with such forces. We have *disidentification* with a force on the one side (the "Christian" man who wants to kill off chthonic power), and then *possession* by that very force on the other (like "Cleopatra" taking over the house). Amid the struggle, if we kill off the power drive then, as the dream voice says, "The body of what you thought you killed will just turn up later."

The *autonomous quality* of such complexes and archetypal energies makes them all the more important to relate to, or else we suffer possession by them (and then suffer the alienation these forces bring about interpersonally). Regarding the autonomous quality and the numinosity of such forces, Jung states:

> Now it is a fact amply confirmed by psychiatric experience that all parts of the psyche, inasmuch as they possess a certain autonomy, exhibit a personal character, like the split-off products of hysteria and schizophrenia, mediumistic "spirits," figures seen in dreams, etc. Every split-off portion of libido, every complex, has or is a (fragmentary) personality. At any rate, that is how it looks from the purely observational standpoint. But when we go into the matter more deeply, we find that they are really archetypal formations. There are no conclusive arguments against the hypothesis that these archetypal figures are endowed with personality at the outset and are not just secondary personalizations. In so far as the archetypes do not represent mere functional relationships, they manifest themselves as [daimons], as personal agencies. In this form they are felt as actual experiences and are not "figments of the imagination," as

> rationalism would have us believe. Consequently, man derives his human personality only secondarily from what the myths call his descent from the gods and heroes; or, to put it in psychological terms, his consciousness of himself as a personality derives primarily from the influence of quasi-personal archetypes.[10]

Wonderfully, the actual story of Cleopatra and the rug shocked the woman painter and made her laugh, too. She could then see how psyche was asking her not to kill off her power drive, or even her inflation, but to separate the ego from it, and learn to keep conscious relationship with both this fundamentalist Christian animus and this "Cleopatra" essence she also carries. Getting a relationship going with these sides of her personality has brought her great humor. Having "fallen asleep in the castle," as she described her marriage, and awakening at nearly 60, she came to feel the pain and urgency within to live the life she had previously left unlived. Connecting with these emotional truths within, she came to appreciate the fire that drove her work, and both her fundamentalist and Cleopatra sides eased up. Power became less of an autonomous unknown force, and the drives differentiated behind her art work as she also enjoyed the success of dialogue with the world via her work.

The *asura* region, the fighting, competing, powerful yang energy, was so out of her conscious identity that it came in with a bang after the divorce. We could say that she was working with an oedipal wound, where loving someone meant that value and power were perceived and experienced as outside of herself, and in this passive receptivity without any penetrating true yang, the unseen Self was drowning within. The wound and grief from early life and her way of being married and then suddenly divorced opened the door. I felt as if I witnessed the very young feminine come to life in a 60-year-old woman and work to grow up and resolve this oedipal problem. The way it took shape in the world was via learning to find the power and true value from within and get that going in dialogue with the world through her creativity and independence.

The power and strength that rose up in this once passive woman was stunning. Of course, for a while, it left her possessed with archetypal rage, hate, and competitiveness—caught up in the *asura* region—but that was an important part of her initiation.

This dream story has relevance beyond the personal, and into the collective. On the one hand, we have the puritanical "Christian" ethos that would like to "clean up the psyche" and kill off the power drive (and all autonomous activities of the psyche). And on the other hand we have the figure like "Cleopatra" queen of Egypt, whose personal power drive was renowned during the fall of history's greatest empires. It mirrors the collective problem in the United States these days, with the war on Middle Eastern countries and the fundamentalism of Christianity that makes America as a collective blind to its power shadow, its *asura* possession.

Getting caught at either pole of this tension distorts the soul's life. Cutting off the autonomy of psyche leaves us bereft, and unconscious, self-serving power gained in relation to the mystery leaves us tangled up in fundamentalism and inflation, and of no use in serving psyche. Between the two polarities, amid this tension born in the psyche, is the necessary human ground of being where we can live more freely in relation with the infinite and the mysterious.

A Message from the Animal Realm

In reflecting on the difficulties of either identification with or alienation from the divine, other constellations of "the god problem" appear. The mystery we are swimming within at times wants to reveal itself, and this causes shifts in our psyches and especially in the "god complex." We noted earlier that Jung saw his work as aimed at melting down the historically fixed thought forms of dogma and pouring it into the molds of individual experience. The psyche, with its raw material in our lives and in the world around us, works toward this.

I have seen in clinical practice that the most common adjustments of the god complex occur when the dream world addresses fundamentalism and collective ideas in order to free up more genuine experience of the numinous. This can be shocking for many people whose faith is completely based in fundamental collective religions.

I remember a young woman of 23 who entered analysis after reading some of Jung's work. She came to session with me one day and announced that she would be willing to change anything except her relationship with God, her marriage, and her schooling commitments. After she let these words out, a strange feeling hung in the air. It was as though she had given the prescription for exactly what needed to change. We said nothing else about it for months.

One day, a week or so after she made this pronouncement, she took a nap on the beach and when she woke up she realized a bird was on her blanket, pecking at the wedding ring on her hand! The synchronicity of this and her statement days earlier about not changing her marriage scared her.

Anyway, months later she began the work of accepting that she needed to look into the nature of her marriage as her emotions, long held in check, started to erupt. Meanwhile, her dreams addressed the nature of her faith and helped her refine and individualize her connection to the divine. One dream early on, began to prompt her instincts to awaken: *I am outside my childhood church, in a lot covered in devil's grass. And someone standing barefoot on the grass says to me, "You should read more Kierkegaard and stop being a dumb sheep."*

After this dream, her anxiety rose tremendously. The ground of being she was now on had changed from her childhood ground. Now her ground of being was covered in "devil's grass" where a Hermes-like character stood with a new, challenging point of view that would play with what she thought of as the "devil" and wanted to challenge her out of being a sheep, a follower. The challenge to individuate came from within, and the reality of the unfolding relationship to the divine prompted along by the dream spirit shocked her.

Later she did read more Kierkegaard and was deeply comforted to discover he was a unique "Christian" philosopher who was not a fundamentalist, but related to the movements of the soul in original ways. A light in the darkness of her faith crisis appeared, another way began to emerge within her. She began to think and feel for herself and her religious instincts toward the soul slowly awakened within. The nature spirit that manifested in the dream wanted more room, more development in the relationship between her conscious self, the god complex, and the unconscious itself. The devil in Native American lore is often seen as the force of renewal. And here, the green, growing grass is linked to the devil and to renewal, a living connection with the imagination and spirit within her, and thus less dependency upon undifferentiated, collective religious life. Most importantly, this heralded less of a split between good and evil.

There cannot be fluid relationship between human and divine when we are stuck in fixed ideations, or lost in collectivity. The nature spirit cannot unfold within us as completely when this is so, thus it is invested in shocking us out of our stuck-ness.

The necessity of facing inflation, deflation, or readjustments to our "god complex" in the search for a revitalized relationship between the human and divine may be for some a fateful part of individuation. It is a process that ancient traditions which remain connected to the fluid mysteries beyond dogma have known for eons.

Eros and the Wound: Walking the Razor's Edge between Inflation and Reductionism

The new unity of opposites found emerging amid the psychic tension we carry is capable of, in alchemical terms, calming the evil in the sulfur. Risking the dance with Eros and psyche leads to new amalgams that bring life, chaos, and enduring awareness and wisdom as well.

Without conscientious participation with the evolution of the *coniunctio* (intrapsychically and interpersonally) and its inherent dangers, we can risk cutting off the religious instinct, and eventually limiting our knowledge and experience of the realms of being. Additionally the *multiplicatio* of the Philosopher's Stone, where the activities of the Self operate and generate among us, often requires a field where Eros resides. Eros encourages us to give the process room for the individual, eccentric relation with psyche we may find via growing conscious relationship with our wound. Placing normative, "preconceived" ideas and forms over individual lives and personalities like a cookie cutter over dough stunts the discovery and development of the inner guide and the divine child. The divine child, the *filius* of the alchemists is conceived in a very different ecosystem than this. It requires tolerating and containing chaos, discovering Eros, enduring the tension of the opposites each of us holds uniquely from within, with more honesty about the complexity and paradoxical nature of the psyche than a normative approach can avail.

An analyst from California brought this phenomenon to my attention. At an annual conference several years ago, I heard him speak on Jung's early life. Part of his message was that if Jung had had better object relations with his mother, he would have found Emma Jung to be "all women to him." And then the women around him who had close relations with him would not have suffered so terribly.

When I first heard this, something in me revolted against the spirit of normativism in his statement. Who knows? Perhaps these women went to their graves feeling the most profound experiences of their lives were heightened or came to light via the encounters they had with Jung, not excluding what they may have felt that was wounding or terrible in their contact with him. Perhaps, for them, it was rather like a true encounter with the Self—marvelous *and* terrible. More importantly, Emma Jung may have not been, nor wanted to be all women to Carl Jung. What woman is all things to any man? Why should or would she want to be? But this rebuttal of his point isn't really the ultimate issue his comments raised.

The issue is that *this strange kind* of application of object relations theory negates the reality that the wound and the gift are intricately interwoven, and this kind of reductionism and cause and effect thinking is lethal to soul. This analyst is not the only one to fall into this kind of thinking. We all can be subject to pushing for normativism at times, without being conscious of it. And it is strangely contagious! The fact that it rubbed me the wrong way also made me want to watch parts of my own undigested shadow aspects that could fall into such an attitude.

This kind of problem certainly is not limited to the use of object relations theories; any theory that attempts to explain the ever-complex human condition can be easy prey to normativism. It is the nature of ego function and its tendency toward reductionism that does this. We all have to be so careful with all theories, for they are only as good as they are helpful to living with the mysteries and discovering rich human lives. No matter the theory, as Henry Corbin states, it always boils down to "untying the knot of dogma" in order to open the way to a "science of vision."[11] The religious function is ultimately about new perception. How psyche lives in the facts of things and is also the spirit of things is mysterious. Splitting from humanity and the facts of things into inflation is fruitless, as is reductionism that can limit our ability to track the life of psyche. Between these two poles, every human life must find its most fruitful livable path.

Without Jung's psychic wound, what could have possibly compelled him to trek so far into the psyche? Had this terrible, perfect crisis of a wound in his psyche not happened just so, Jung might well have been a modern-day medical doctor who worked within the bounds of known experience and whose work might have stopped right there. This is not about denying or defending his "poor object relationships," his shadow, his limitations, elements of his unworked wound, or his trouble with women, or, most importantly, what all of that speculation means as we apply it in each of our own lives. Instead, this is about the danger inherent when we put these normative ideations out onto the life of *anyone* else. This, I believe, is often the other side of the coin of inflation, and just as perilous. When our projection of our moralizing about the ideal way to incarnate is left unconscious, it weakens our ability to truly tolerate and carry the opposites in an inner ecosystem, where the *filius*, the divine child, the alchemical Stone may be born.

Perhaps instead we can seek room to dance with the wounding shapes of our early life, and work with the demons and the gifts in ever more honest and fluid ways. Risking a dance with the chaos and fine tuning our differentiation of Eros *and* coming to work with our own wound, shadow, and limits is essential in order to foster deep work with psyche.

There are times when the experience of "moral torment" accompanies the tension between the opposites. Sometimes adopting the normalizing influences mentioned above occurs as we unconsciously attempt to spare ourselves from having to carry our truer guilt and "moral torment" present in the tension of the opposites uniquely inherent in each incarnation. This accompanying moral torment, if held consciously, heats up the alchemical furnace and here our ethical values are often most deeply truly crafted. The absence of a map with black and white dichotomies between good and evil is often a fact, and it can mirror the depth of the place in the psyche that we are trekking. For example, as Jung states in pondering the incredibly shady character of Mercurius:

> The contents of the unconscious are indeed of the greatest importance, for the unconscious is after all the matrix of the human mind and its inventions. Wonderful and ingenious as this other side of the unconscious is, it can be most dangerously deceptive on account of its numinous nature. Involuntarily one thinks of the devils mentioned by St. Athanasius in his life of St. Anthony, who talk very piously, sing psalms, read the holy books, and—worst of all—speak the truth. *The difficulties of our psychotherapeutic work teach us to take truth, goodness, and beauty where we find them. They are not always found where we look for them: often they are hidden in the dirt or are in the keeping of the dragon.* "*In stercore invenitur*" (it is found in filth) runs an alchemical dictum—nor is it any the less valuable on that account. But it does not transfigure the dirt and does not diminish the evil, any more than these lessen God's gifts. The contrast is painful and the paradox bewildering.[12]

Jung's ability here to point to the ever-widening complexity of the unconscious is striking. It highlights the need for our deepest attention to the nuance of experiences in the psyche in order to withstand the heat of the opposites.

When the dream world and guiding spirit of Mercurius is active—and with the help of analysts who know the territory and have some honestly gained human ground and humor—integration of inflation and narcissism can be addressed from within. It can also be honored and recognized from without when psychic constellations in the relational or natural worlds are telling us that we still need to return to earth and develop more differentiated humanity. Regarding reductionism, the loss of soul that results as we cut ourselves off from the vastness of the psyche when we fall into these attitudes brings pain and one-sidedness. Yet, life, imagination, and dreams can eventually restore our soul connection.

ASCENT, INCARNATIONAL CHOICE, AND ARCHETYPAL DEFENSES

People do hide in inflated or narcissistic attitudes, attempting to live falsely at high altitudes. These can be attempts, consciously or unconsciously, to avoid suffering their bits of humanity. And people hide in normativism to rid themselves of the guilt of individuality and the moral tension of the opposites. Both reasons carry their own curses, for they each limit the dialogue between human and divine; they can each stultify the spirit, and will soon return a person to the alchemical rounds of rebirth—i.e., a *putreficatio*.

As is most likely apparent by now, in my mind "inflation" is not *visiting* the heights or depths, nor even getting taken up into some constellation of energy in the psyche or psychoid for a time. These nonordinary states of consciousness are just a fact; they exist. Inflation involves getting *stuck* there, *identifying with the terrain or the experiences* and not returning to the work of becoming a fully individuated person. We can become stuck in any realm, not knowing how or deciding, consciously or unconsciously, it's too painful to come back again into daily life.

In my research, I have seen individuals who, through an illness, were unconsciously leaving life due to some block with which they could not deal. Their dreams relentlessly portrayed the incarnational choice, and yet pointed no blame on them for consciously or unconsciously choosing out of life. Some of these individuals could not see the psychological constellations behind their illnesses, though the dreams seemed to portray them clearly. Some could see the problem at some level but not see or feel the grace available, or the human warmth to make it possible.

A few men who had just retired from life-long professions and contracted cancer could not feel the meaning in returning to home life and taking on the difficulty of individuation with partners and the value of creating a life without work at the center. Literally their identity and life energy were stuck in the past, which they could no longer have. Without grieving the loss and moving on into a newly meaningful life, they hung in the balance, and the illnesses offered means to leave life entirely if a new way was not discovered. One of the men went into a complicated bereavement process, reviewing over and over in the present tense his work, as if he were still involved in the peak of his career that happened months before he was forced to retire from a company that went broke.

The grandiosity he tried to hold on to kept him completely stuck, and the ground of grief underneath him gave way in the illness. Another man left a career in which he had traveled around the world teaching music. The loss of energy was so great, and his marriage so stuck, he literally decided to give up and die. His doctors were stunned, as they felt he was healthy enough to fight the cancer.

For people on the edge of life or death, and the individuation choices ahead of them, it is not a moralistic issue if we do not return to life and find a way. It may be sad and carry tremendous loss, but it is not morally wrong. What it is, is a soulful individuation issue, an issue of whether the human and divine will discover one another, and find means to bring their communion into earthly life in meaningful ways.

These moments of incarnational choice are not reserved for those in dire crisis, or those facing death. Subtle choices about whether to incarnate—and how to incarnate—are made all the time by everyone. The miracle that we can progressively become more whole and more present to the moment of everyday life, discovering renewal and freedom, is the wonder of individuation.

The circulation of life energy through the many dimensions of existence is a profound mystery. Life energy can get repetitive, one-sided or stuck in any arena in life. For example, excessive emotionality can become draining of life energy, or conversely blocked feelings can lead to impoverished relationships and health issues. Excessively ruminating over finances or ignoring limits of finances can reflect stuck patterns that can drain life energy, and, as I described previously, attempting to hold onto a past job identity can generate a life crisis. Not tending to relationships or trying to over tend relationships can lead to troubles. Putting no energy into reflection about life can create a hollow shallow life, whereas hyperanalyzation of life can become paralyzing to spontaneity and joy, and so on. It is a wonder we each discover balance and regulation!

Often some of the worst blocks in life are not situational realities but really have to do with our own one-sided qualities, to which we are blind. Then life crises challenge us to stretch and grow in new ways, which may mean looking honestly beyond our blindness at the defenses in our personality. We actually cannot speak of the phenomenon of incarnational choice without also speaking of the defense against incarnating into the human realms of being.

Some of us tend to defend more against grounding in the facts and feelings of life, and others more against experiencing the uncontrollable vastness of the mysteries beyond ordinary consciousness. This influences all kinds of adaptations and defenses we learn to use to cope with life. These general patterns of strengths in consciousness, and our accompanying defenses in coping styles can be discerned with numerous tools such as personality typology, astrology charts, the enneagram, and so on.

Relationships challenge these patterns. Whether colleagues, friends, or couples collude in the same defense styles, or whether people in relationships challenge each other's different means of defense, life will eventually try to help round out into wholeness the personality, challenging the armor. These collusions only last so long before life challenges both parties to grow.

Getting caught up with "substitute gods" as von Franz called it,[13] can happen when we have not had experiences that help get under our own psychological defenses, these adaptations in personality that protect us from the vulnerability of being human. When we discover the heroic or victim-identified armor we have unconsciously acquired, then we discover means toward more authentic ground of being, and curiously the numinous is freed to be the mystery it is.

What is adaptive for the ego in early life usually becomes defense structures that can keep us from the flow of life, from the totality of being human and discovering wholeness later on. Mid-life often presents crisis that will shake these adaptations and challenge our rigid or dominant means of coping.

If you look at ego defenses in terms of typology, usually the dominant function develops in certain ways to protect the ego from the overwhelming dimensions of life. The ways in which defenses can manifest are as many as there are people, but here are a few illustrative generalizations. Intuitives in early life may learn to wield a wand of visions and answers attempting unconsciously to stay up and out of the overwhelming difficulties or humble details of life, or conversely get caught in negative intuition, fearing the worst for everyone all the time and being unable to find peace and their own center. Thinking types may learn to look down at others who are thrown around by emotion or subjective experience, or they may feel completely inadequate because they cannot locate in immediate ways their emotional responses to things, and begin to feel alien or that something is wrong with them. Sensation types may learn control of daily life to such a degree that they fend off the larger picture, and defend against the flux and mystery of everything that is completely uncontrollable in life, and later in life can begin to feel separate or caged in their constructed patterns of safety, missing the wild abandon into the meaningful mysteries of life.

And feeling types may learn to get so attached to their own felt sense of the world that they stop letting in others or the airy point of view which is impersonal or transpersonal, or on the other hand, they may learn to ditch their own felt sense of the world and try to take care of perceived pain in others as an unconscious defense against embodying their own experience. These are but a few ideas around defenses and the dominant function, but hopefully it will serve as jumping-off place for your own imagination around defense dynamics and the dominant function of your conscious personality. And of course the personality dynamics between children and their parents and the family milieu reflect the coping styles acquired early in life as well. Looking at the dynamics in childhood relationships along with the development of the dominant personality function can be very helpful in tracking the patterns of archetypal defense.

In exploring this topic, we are in tricky territory, because whether we must get under these defenses in our own life or not is a completely individual issue. Does life require it? Does the dream world or suffering in personal relationships require work here? These questions must be asked and answered from within, and then followed through with the help of the inner guide, otherwise we may find ourselves fruitlessly putting reductionistic ideations on life.

Transformaton of the Ego's Unconscious Defenses

A man who visited great heights and depths of the psyche as he struggled with cancer found himself engrossed in a profound initiation with the inner teacher. As he gave himself permission to retreat from the form and shape of his outer life commitments, he gave room to an introverted life with plenty of space and time for working with the inner world.

His body eventually became well and when he was returning to his ordinary life again with renewed vitality from the experiences he had taken in with the inner teacher, he realized he was feeling very defended against entering the "ordinary" in his life. He was afraid to return to his job, afraid he would get lost in the same old 9-to-5 grind, with no time for creative invention among the other overwhelming duties of his job. He also was afraid he would lose something of himself in his family life, as the needs of others would naturally return to a mutual flow of give and take. And he was right, he needed to consolidate in himself where he had been, where he stood now in life, and find the support of the inner world to help him make these adjustments so that he would remain connected to the nature spirit within his life.

He could feel the soul wanting him to come back into his daily life with work and family. But relationships became a tremendous challenge, for those around him were needing him to return to the flow of daily life, and his "specialness" was wearing on them. His wife clearly needed his coping patterns with her to change, for he had been isolating himself from her for months.

At this time, he had a profound dream reflecting how the inner helper needed him to come out of such defended places so that *their* relationship—the human-divine relationship—could also evolve! It led to healing of other relationships as well:

> I am watching two figures in a large body of water. A knight is standing in the water with a man who is shaking, like an uncontrollable shiver, or seizure. The knight is holding him, and helps him. They are face to face, and the knight's arms are around the other man's arms, in mutual embrace, intertwined. The knight has the antidote to the man's seizure. It is a green newt. The knight takes it in his hands and squishes it all over the man's chest and he is cured! The shivering stops.
>
> Then I realize it is not only the man who changes, but the knight also transforms. Large wings grow off his back, and his armor is gone. He is the winged partner, the angel helper to this man. They are now looking at one another with love.

The dream ego is meant to see something very important. His shadow attitude is in fact imaged by the psyche as in a seizure that needs some healing, some shift. This part of him is in the grip of the "knight." We could see the knight on one level as the heroic, armored consciousness that learns to go out and fight the good fight and survive in life. He is a good representative of the unconsciously heroic defended attitudes.

Yet, the shadow and the dream ego facing the embrace with the armored aspect can lead to a healing. His shadow side, which was vulnerable to unconsciously using and identifying with the heroic defenses, had fallen into a power problem that strangled his humanity. In order for him to transform this energy, the dream ego has to witness how this part of him is in a seizure and is suffering.

This man slowly became more attuned to how his defenses against his loved ones' and his own feelings was old character armor that he grew as a boy to protect him from the chaos of an emotionally chaotic family milieu. When his father would drink or his mother would rage, he went off into his tree fort and performed experiments and science projects, successfully blocking out the drama, chaos, and pain. Not surprisingly he became a nuclear physicist with a successful career of invention, including a method for dismantling nuclear weapons. Unwittingly, he was an alchemist who from boyhood learned valuable ways to work with lethal contaminations.

When it came to a number of other areas of his life besides creative invention, he suffered terribly. This takes us to why he got into analytic work to begin with. He began to withdraw from his wife after they lost a child in the womb, and her grief overwhelmed him. He could not find his own grief, and pulled away, as he did as a child, into work. His two children suffered in his withdrawal, and his son began acting out at school. He saw this and signed on as a soccer coach to try to be more present in his son's life.

But then the illness came knocking at his door. He then pulled away into introversion, and there the dream spirit began to help him. Of course, the family had hope that he would find his way and return to health and the give and take of home life in some new way.

Given his defenses learned in early life, it is easy to see how important it would be for him to be able to come out of his thinking tower and enter his own felt sense of life and love and relationships, without having to fear that (using his own life motif) the "nuclear reactors" would go off at any minute and threaten his existence, and the existence of those he loved. It seems natural that the fruit of the alchemical journey for him would need to help him make links with what was thrown into the shadow long ago—the life of Eros incarnating in all the specifics of his interactions in love relationships.

So how could the dream and the work help him do this? Let's return to the dream and what happened next in his work. In the dream, as the dream ego looks on, the embrace transforms from a seizure, where the shadow is in the grip of an archetype, into a healing embrace. When the dreamer can face the reality of the suffering this shadow problem has caused he can discover the grip by which he has been seized via his unconscious wound. And this whole process can lead him to freedom.

This takes us to the newt. The newt is a mythic medieval reference, once commonly used in incantations to create or break spells. The knight and the newt reference are reminiscent of a fairy tale, an archetypal drama the dreamer has found himself involved in. In the dream, the green newt is applied to the body of the human being and this breaks the spell. The psyche produces something green, alive, and capable of breaking the deadlock between the seized humanity and the armored archetypal knight or heroic self. The ability for the dream ego and the shadow to face the specific reality of the suffering leads to the antidote to the illness. The lysis occurs, the spontaneous change in the stuck situation.

The healing life force present in the green newt returns him to freed humanity. Coming into fresh contact with instinctual being, the paralysis ends. It's interesting when you think of it this way, for it reflects how ego defenses cut off the green body—the open field of instinctual being alive in the soul that is unadulterated by these rigid coping styles or defenses. Yet, the psyche is capable of bringing that medicine to light, bringing the body of being back into contact with the life force, with instincts and felt reality more original to humanity than these defensive adaptations.

So, the dream medicine shows a face-to-face encounter with the armored self, and leads to an antidote. The human being is freed, no longer seized up in a possession of deadlock with the archetypal armor, and humanity returns. Importantly, the armored one transforms into the true angel, the true inner friend. Something of the divine is also freed to be what it really is when we stop identifying with it unconsciously. And the two then discover communion.

For this man, the inner angel—the ally—became stronger as he slowly faced his shadow and his difficulties in life. He reported being breathed into by the inner teacher in active imagination, and the more breath was breathed into him, the more he felt his defenses, brittleness, and lies inherent in his narcissism fall away. Unity with his own sense of soul within took hold, and it was beneath the defenses, in compassion and humble acceptance of his own devils. In this ecosystem created in part by his humility and devotion to the process, both his humanity and the divine could discover each other anew.

As the alchemist in him grew in this work, the joy at the insights grew, and so did his genuine interest in the soul of family life. Deep, erotic healing awaited him with his wife, and from the sound of it, that healing was there for her as well.

This dreamer's example shows us that we can learn to see when we step into our own versions of archetypal defenses against our humanity. I believe his alchemical process shows us an archetypal truth about character armor and the individuation of the human and divine relationship. The differentiation of the inner companion may require that we pay attention to these processes so that the inflation that character armor creates can be dealt with, and both human and divine dimensions can be freed to relate with one another in ever new ways.

Importantly, as a result of facing his archetypal defenses, the dreamer becomes more genuinely in communion with the inner angel, rather than farther away.

Encountering the Divine in Matter

This next example comes from the life of a woman who, in beginning her midlife transition, discovered some powerful instruction from the dream world:

> I am walking up a mountain pass in the wilderness. This is a place I associate with the highest moments of my life, and where I have instructed my lover to scatter my ashes after my actual death. Up here I feel utterly free. The vistas of untouched wilderness in all directions as far as the eye can see is as close to paradise as I have ever experienced in life on the material plane. As I am walking up the trail I get to a clearing of trees before the high alpine meadows begin, where the last trek to the top ensues.
>
> Suddenly, here on the path still in the lap of the mountain, is a spirit, a guide who wants to show me something. I would have missed it if he hadn't stopped me and gotten my attention. I was busy enjoying the hike and eager to see the view from the top again.
>
> On the trail in front of us he reaches down and picks up a snake that is lying across the trail, moving from right to left. The snake has a lovely, long body and is wearing seven rings, each of a different metal than the one before. They are evenly spaced and very intentional. The thought runs through my mind, did a king or a Merlin put them on the snake?
>
> Then the teacher wants to show me something about the snake. The tail of the snake is hidden in the grass. He lifts it and brings it in front of us. Both of us hold the snake. I see the tail is a little dry.
>
> For some reason that I do not comprehend, I am not afraid of the mountain pass, or the teacher, or the snake, or the mysterious bands, but the *tail of the snake* scares me. I am afraid to look at the tail end of the snake. I do so as the dream ends, but it is still scary.

The dream opens with her sense of where she was going being interrupted. The dream teacher has a different encounter in mind, and she meets the teacher there. The point for her is not to go to the heights, a place she is at peace with death and with leaving embodied life and the world of form. The snake and the teacher are in the lap of the mountain, at lower altitudes. And this is where the mystery is calling her.

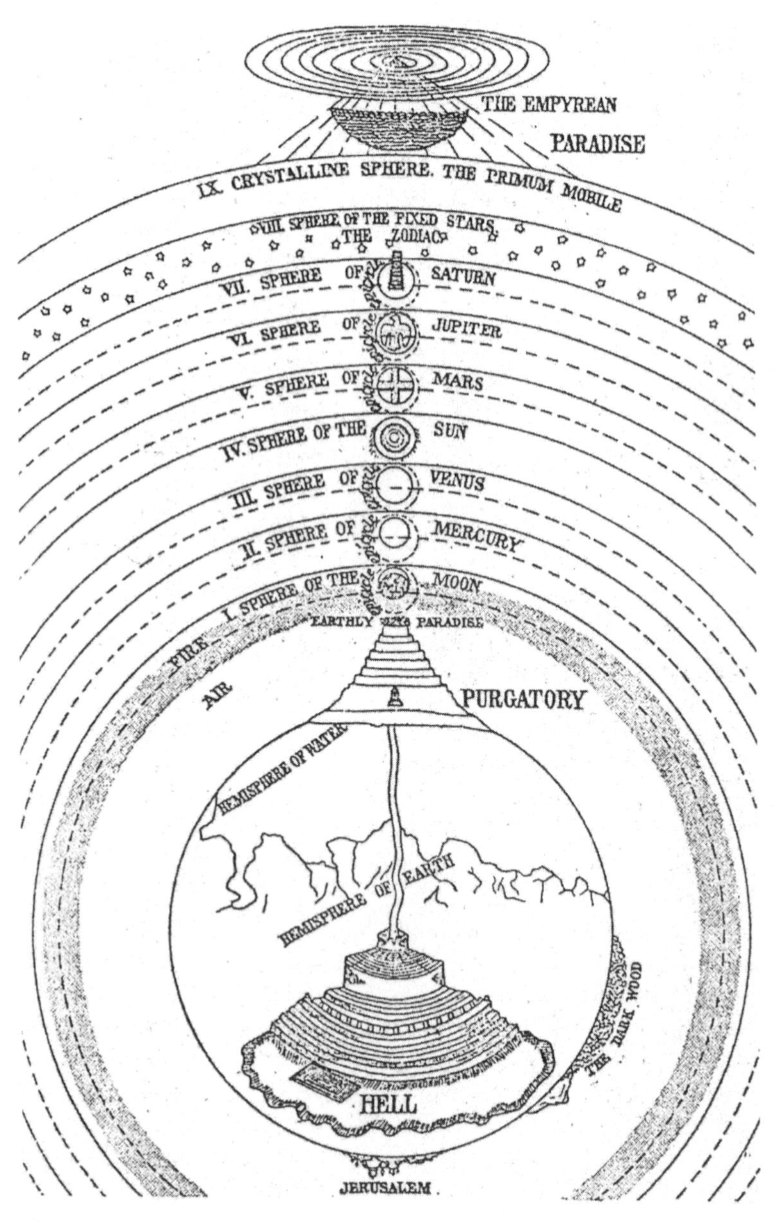

Fig. 24. The planetary ladder. Michelangelo Cactani, La Materia della Divina Commedia di Dante Alighieri, *1855. In Roob,* Alchemy and Mysticism, *p. 41.*

So what about this snake she encounters and its rings of seven metals? In ancient alchemy, the seven metals were correlated with the seven lords or celestial planetary spheres, and in the Hindu concept of physiology the body has seven primary energy centers, or chakras. The mystical number seven is found throughout shamanic culture and plays an important role in the shaman's techniques for ecstasy and transcendence.[14] Siberian shamans have seven bells on their costumes, for the seven heavenly maidens. The seven realms of the shamanic underworld also correspond to the seven heavens. In the underworld, seven lords reign and seven obstacles are put there. Each rung of the planetary ladder, or the shamanic ladder of initiation, or the chakras of the body are said to have "lords" who emanate the energy and the obstacles of each rung. The Altaic shamans call the seven realms of the underworld Pudak and see them as having corresponding obstacles that must be negotiated by the initiate.[15]

Paralleling these motifs we find that the Buriat shaman and the Mithraic mysteries for initiates had similar alchemical motifs—the rungs, the metals, and the planetary ladders. Mircea Eliade tells us:

> The candidate is stripped to the waist and purified by the blood of a goat . . . This ceremony resembles the taurobolion, the chief rite in the Mithraic mysteries. And the same mysteries use a ladder (*klimax*) with seven rungs, each rung made of a different metal. According to the Celsus, the first rung was lead (corresponding to the "heaven" of the planet Saturn), the second tin (Venus), the third bronze (Jupiter), the fourth iron (Mercury), the fifth "monetary alloy" (Mars), the sixth silver (the moon), the seventh gold (the sun). The eighth rung, Celsus says, represents the sphere of the fixed stars. By climbing through the ceremonial ladder, the initiate passed through the seven heavens reaching Empyrean.[16]

Let's look into the imagery of rings and metal for a moment to amplify the dream. To make actual rings like this would require mining the earth, following the vein of each metal as it lives in the earth. Then it would require heating the blacksmith forge, melting the raw materials down to their true essences, and pouring off the dross. When the pure essence of the metal appears, then the liquid would be poured into a mold. These images of course are straight out of the symbolism of ancient alchemy. They sought to discover the god hidden in matter to reveal its essence through a cooking process.

Rings symbolically represent what is eternal, for they have no beginning and no end. Rings symbolize commitment, fertility, royalty, and such. Because of their circular nature they also symbolize the flow of energy, the dynamism of the Tao that is not static. Now, what's strange in this dream image is that these rings of different metals are shown on the body of a living snake. Snake, as we have been exploring throughout this book, is a wisdom bringer, a creation spirit, an initiator, and as Jung pointed out, the snake is "an excellent symbol for the two aspects of the unconscious: its cold and ruthless instinctuality and its Sophia quality or natural wisdom."[17]

Snake, among the Native American Indians is seen as the great teacher. If you go out for a vision quest and return with a dream of a snake, or a skin, or a vision or sighting of snake, that is thought to be the best hope, the deepest medicine. The Greeks also saw snakes as having incredible powers since they could burrow into the underworld; they brought messages back and forth from the earth plane to the depths. The Egyptians and the Mayans depicted the snake as winged or plumed, able to fly into the heights.

So, as this dreamer is hiking along toward the heights, the teacher brings in the snake whose body is bound in metals. This snake is an incarnation of some teaching or revelation that has appeared on the path of this woman's individuation. The emphasis is on the earth. The metals psychologically represent the archetypes mirrored in the heavens and found in the earth, which echoes the law of correspondence: As above, so below. Here on Earth they are mined from the raw material of human experience. Snake lives in these rings here on Earth—amid the pure essence of the archetypes—and unites them with its singular body.

This is reminiscent of the heart of the creation mystery of Gnosticism. God and his feminine half, Sophia, create the world from out of the waters of chaos. In so doing, Sophia falls to earth and enters all of matter. She cries out, helpless, and the being of Light sends a redeemer, Christ, to help her. The *anima*, or soul, of the creator falls into matter and then seeks reunion with its celestial spirit beloved.

Christ mythically symbolizes an awakened consciousness that embodies the mingling of humanity and divinity and walks the path of individuation among the elements, suffering and bringing transformation, transcendence, and redemption.

This snake in the path is rather like Sophia herself, who embodies all the archetypes fallen into matter, into earth and human life. Only here she seems to have developed, for she is not chaotically strewn in raw material. This spirit in matter, this snake, lives in the seven purified metals in the eternal form of the rings. It is as if the alchemical process has been working with the spirit in matter, and it is differentiating and uniting the aspects of the divine, the archetypes fallen into matter, thereby redeeming matter. The dream ego wondered if a king or Merlin did this. This seems to point to royalty, the crowned serpent, and to the element of transmutation that this work would require from a Merlin.

Although nature is crowned and ringed in the purified archetypes as found on Earth, there is still some tension or problem yet for this snake and dreamer. This alchemical encounter with the snake seems to require something of her. The dream says the dreamer would have missed this encounter with this mystery if the dream teacher had not stopped her. This is an important point; her conscious attitude, at home in the heights, is being challenged. The dreamer is ascending the mountain, and the ego attitude is quite happy, even with the reality of the end of life. The infinite heights and the fact of death do not seem to be difficult; it is the snake's tail that seems to bring fear. Whatever it is that this tail is to her, it is outside her comfort zone, outside of her conscious attitude.

She suffers from a split between spirit and matter that the dream world is trying to address. And this is a split mirrored in the Gnostic story, too. Gnosticism grew up under Christianity like a dream, compensating for the splits in the attitudes of the religious dogma. In Christianity, matter became something man was to have dominion over. It was not spoken of as the body of the creator, or as having or needing redemption. The Gnostic myth then said, no, the feminine soul of the divine resides in all matter, and in the chasm between heaven and earth, she needs our help. Sophia is trapped and needs to be recognized and rejoined with the divine, and we can help. And as the alchemical imagery unfolds, they portray the transformations we can participate in. Consciousness discovers ways to participate with the mysteries so that what is matter and earthy is redeemed, is raised up into the spiritual realms and seen for its value, and what is spiritual comes down to earth. (An image in the development of Catholic teachings that parallels this transformation is the Assumption of Mary, Mother of God.)

The dreamer looked down on matter and form from her identification with spirit and the release of form. She thought of the place she was headed up the mountain as a place where freedom is found, and the ultimate place of release of life into the eternal—a spirit place. This snake, by contrast, is on the earth, yet it embodies the gods, the metals mined from the earth that correspond to the archetypes in the heavens. It seems to reflect the mystery of the divine hidden in matter going through alchemical changes, now able to unite the archetypes in one single life.

Her inner guide wants her to recognize the divine in matter and how it is transforming. To do this, she had to change her course, and release her goal of the view from the heights and be confronted with the dry tail of the snake. The dreamer's *puella* attitiude was being challenged.

On the one hand, the snake's dry tail may refer to the alchemical drying out process; after soaking, dissolving, and whitening, there comes the drying out process. Usually this is where energy that has been in certain psychic patterns that no longer serve life begins to dissipate.

Introverted aspects of her connection with the psyche were promoting connection with the Self, and new unity within. It brought her into reverie and ecstatic states that infused her life. Yet, introverted *puella* attitudes can be biased toward spirit, and discovering the *coagulatio* mysteries of spirit indwelling and committing to forms can be difficult. Relationship with spirit came more naturally to her than relationship with form. Coming down the mountain a little and learning the mysteries of embodiment was another story. This began a confrontation with her shadow.

That shadow was impatient with the facts of ordinary life and the slowness of things on the material plane. It also had not let her come into the kind of power that comes from embodying limits. What was calling her now was making peace with the facts and limits of outer life. She needed to die to life, submit to the fact of living in the material world and make peace with form so that her life and work could flourish, and she could find soul harmony. And this meant paying attention to the mysteries of incarnation in the lowlands, in the simplest of ways.

So, as she discovered that some drive in these instinctual patterns had dried out, that the exclusive reliance on introverted, intuitive means of living did not carry soul energy at mid-life, she encountered the tail, the shadow. We can consider the image of the dry tail and her fear of it from another perspective. If the tail is dry and elicits her concern, how would she address that? Perhaps allowing for the dryness to occur is the first step. (Letting the tail end of her own snake impulses dry out, and letting the god incarnating into matter come into view in new ways.)

Then with that awareness, she in effect is performing the act of "getting the head to be aware of the tail." Her awareness is getting conscious of her shadow. This is an old alchemical truth inhabiting the ouroboros. Getting the tail into the snake's mouth would treat the tail's dryness. That is how the alchemists saw it.

The dream snake's medicine is an integration image. It is showing her the numerous differentiated elements, and the living singular life that embodies the spheres. The medicine of the snake is also an incarnation image. The dream snake brings the numerous spheres into a harmonious whole in its singularity. It is in fact mirroring wholeness, the microcosm of a single snake embodies metals of the earth that mirror the lords of the sky, the archetypes. The snake is a living embodiment of harmonious polytheism.

Taking the dream's wisdom to heart, she turned toward her relationships and tried to integrate what had happened in the past and bring more love and care to them. She focused on being in the moment, present to what was right in front of her, while realizing that her inner guide would always be available to her. Feeling *all* of creation awakening, she realized that there was no place that was better or worse for awakening. She dreamed at this time:

> A dream teacher put some kind of special superglue in my eyes. I am trying to open them. When I do open them, one looks into the outer world and one looks into the inner world. The one that looks into the outer world is the one that takes me by surprise. I am told that with this eye I am to look into life in its many forms and I will have to learn to perceive life intricately, and the patterns of pain present there.

This dream heralded a shift in the psyche, for she now was called to look into the outer world from which she had been slightly split off. Her split between inner and outer was trying to heal along with the spirit-matter split. Discovering the god in matter and its processes of change and transformation occurring in the human soul is a good use of both these eyes, and moves toward integration. In her life and work this is exactly what began to happen.

The superglue in the dream deserves mentioning. Jung points out that in alchemical lore, ". . . the life force (*vis animans*), is likened by another commentator to the 'glue of the world' (*glutinium mundi*), which is the medium between mind and body and the union of both."[18] This is exactly how the glue in the dream acts—applied to her eyes, it brings the worlds into relationship with one another.

The duplex spirit of creation is also capable of helping us learn to unify the interplay of the differentiated worlds so that they are no longer split. Contact with the life force substance that is the medium between the worlds and carries their union is the place of healing, the bull's-eye of the creation matrix we have been exploring.

It is interesting to note that at this time, a rattlesnake appeared as her dream guide, which is a good image of working on the tail, integrating fiercely protective consciousness, and relating with greater mindfulness to the poison and destructive potentiality in the Self. This rattlesnake is a great antidote to a *puella* problem that can cling to naïveté or only the ecstatic.

Integrating the tail, the inferior, those shadow aspects of self and life cast into the shadows by the adaptations and biases of consciousness—integrating that which one drags behind one as one plows on ahead in life—this requires a slow careful consideration of where our shadow falls in all arenas of life. We then need to turn toward it lovingly to incorporate those inferiorities into the flow of our life force as it finds new balance and integration. This is not about perfecting the shadow, which is impossible. Instead, it is about accepting it and bringing consciousness to the suffering found there while it may or may not heal.

Mid-life also brought a confrontation with the dreamer's lusty, chthonic nature residing in the depths of being. A great contrast to the airy, intuitive *puella* energy emerged. This lusty side drew her into passionate relationships with people, animals, travel, and dance. Suffering and acceptance of her devils brought a more conscientious spirit that guided her life in a refined way. Devils have a way of changing into aspects of the ally presence over time, and this became true for her as well.

At this time she dreamed a voice said to her, "The way to the San Juans is through the Sangre de Cristo Mountains." The San Juan mountain range of southwestern Colorado is awesome in its jagged peaks and rugged heights. The Sangre de Cristo Mountains, on the other hand, are lower in altitude and very accessible. So the dream medicine seems to be consoling her that the high-peak experiences are now to be found in lower accessible altitudes in life. Both are present, and nothing is lost. This again is an image of recovery from the heights, and of integration of the experiences into life. It also parallels the motif in the Buddhist mandala where the human realm has easy, integrated access to the other states and activities.

As the dreamer learned to dry out runaway impulses, she was able to discern the inflation shadow that her dominant function had cast in her love relationships and her management of energy, time, and money. Integration of these elements that were suffering brought the tail—the shadow—around to the head, to the conscious point of view, and more soul and sustainable energy in her life began to grow. As the ego and Self become partners in this circulation of energy between the realms, new wholeness is discovered. This sense of wholeness beyond and inside time and space is inherent to the ouroboros mysteries, and this is key for any person with strong *puer* or *puella* tendencies. With connection to the inner guide, we can discover, in the *rubedo,* the interplay between spirit and matter informing all of life. The *puer* and *puella* complexes have their deities and their genius, and are to be respected. They are vital for taking us out into adventure and, like the sacred fool, discovering spirit and mysteries. So, it is not that these attitudes are wrong. It is just that in individuation there may come a time where the constellation of the *puer* or *puella* complex changes, and the defense against embodiment lessens. In fact, *puer* or *puella* attitudes can go through deep conversion, in which an individual learns, as the Sufis saw it, that remaining in the heights, or in a state of ecstasy with spirit, would entail fragmentation in both worlds.[19]

Part of the experience of the *rubedo* imaged in the ouroboros is positive experience of what the alchemists called the *unus mundus*. This happens when there is a joining with the collective unconscious where dualism ceases and synchronicity of events brings all elements of life into wholeness. About the *unus mundus* von Franz writes:

> When this happens positively, it brings about an enlargement of consciousness together with a decrease of intensity of the ego complex. When this happens the ego retires in favor of the collective unconscious. To reach that point where outer and inner reality (heaven and earth) become one is the goal of individuation.[20]

And this occurs as the head of the snake is brought around to the tail, for then our work with our own complexes and problems becomes integration, and we can connect with the energy and wisdom in the psyche that flows through the many realms of being within oneself and the world.

The image of the snake with the metal rings contains an incredible calling for the dreamer toward experience of the *unus mundus*, where the worlds unite. It is healing the old splits and initiating her into experience of the worlds as synchronizing rather than dualizing.

Collective Application of these images

On an individual level, the potential for the snake's head and the tail to come around appears in numerous intricate ways in each life. It is up to each of us to figure out how. Collectively, this is of astronomical importance as well, and resounds in many world problems today. This is where we humans hang in the balance of creation. The head of the snake as it enacts itself in collective values has blindly run off into creation and destruction. Consciousness, unaware of its shadow, forgets connection and interdependence with all of life, and in so doing becomes psychopathically driven to its own ends, which also leads to the end of many species, ancient cultures, bodies of wisdom, and so on.

On a collective level, if the head and the tail joined, we would remember and recognize the divine flow of energy between all life forms. All life would take on the sacredness of the divine incarnating into matter. Eros would return between people, plants, animals, weather, food, and life and death. We would live in sustainable ways within the *anima mundi*, and creation's divinity would resonate in our awareness, in all we do. Not that we would not have war and trouble, for these archetypes are also part of the grist of the mill of incarnation. The *asura* and *preta* regions have their places in the wheel. But the current collective possession in these realms, present in the devouring, runaway greed that threatens to capsize the ship of humanity by devouring all the fossil fuels, turning life into capitalism—this spell would break, and soul would be freed and circulate around the medicine wheel, the many realms of existence in new ways. For the shadow this dominant collective zeitgeist casts would come around into consciousness, and the psychopathic heart of modern kind would awaken to erotic felt relationship of the divinity in all things.

Why is this imagery arising in individuals like this so vital? Because by reawakening to the mysteries we begin to address how overvalued and out of balance the human species has become in its own eyes and readjust our consciousness to find our true place within the *anima mundi.*

The divine in matter, like the myth of Sophia, and our work to recognize her within all matter—this is the great resounding mystery we live now as human beings. Here is where spirit and matter mysteries are discovered anew. No few pages of exploration here can touch its vastness, which so many truly religious experiences and religious traditions have touched upon throughout time. But it is an attempt to point to the mystery.

For modern Westerners discovering the flow of the Tao, and means of initiation with the realms, the ouroboros mystery the alchemists depicted is also so profound, it is unutterable. That is why we go back to the medicine wheels, the alchemical symbols, and meditations of divine circulation of energy among the realms—for symbols alone, like the image of the snake with the seven metals, can communicate the paradox, the totality, and the mysteries in which we humans participate.

The Secret Alchemical Stone Has Its Own Properties

Sometimes the only way for the true inner being in us to be protected, is to live as a secret. To even try to talk about the mysteries in a way is tricky, a razor's edge. The wiles of shadow and of ego manipulation cannot be underestimated as we attempt to serve the autonomous spirit of the imagination. Thus, in a way, we might even thank God it has learned to live in the secret recesses of human life. For there it is protected and preserved alive and well, and capable of surprising consciousness again and again.

It is not up to the ego to plot the way. Nor does consciousness have to be hyper-vigilant about all these differentiations, for then they can crowd our mind and inner space, and they can get in the way of fresh experience with the numen. As we experience the *rubedo* mysteries, we may also need to return to innocence and wisdom as the alchemical round embraces daily life.

Sometimes experience of the inner guest doesn't require anything but empty space, a clear or quiet mind so contact can happen. It can also give us perspective on the overactive mind when we discover communion with the inner guest, and bring a peaceful presence into our daily lives. New portals then open between eternity and the moment. Since the Self wants to incarnate in ever more areas of life, the ego can learn to follow and court the process of the union over time, using all parts of our life as the material for the relationship.

This is reminiscent of what von Franz speaks regarding the *unus mundus*, where, in joining with the collective unconscious, the ego complex decreases its intensity, and an enlargement of consciousness happens where *everything* comes into the same contained wholeness. The joining of the worlds, the uniting of heaven and earth come into synchronicity and wholeness, everything contained in the same wholeness that includes all inner and outer events as part of psyche and psychoid.

In alchemy, the creation of the Philosopher's Stone points to the grounding of the union of heaven and earth. Now we will look into a few dream images of the birth of the Stone, and some of the properties of the Stone. The process of creation of the Stone has properties capable of guiding and protecting the experiment of consciousness that nature is performing in each human being. These elements can rise up in dreams and participate in protecting the coming together of heaven and earth. Recognizing this presence and participating with it is the key to living fruitfully with the unconscious.

The creation of the living Stone is in itself a paradox. The alchemists knew that the mysteries are too big for anything but paradox, image, and metaphor to communicate them. Their depth runs so far beneath and beyond the ego and ordinary consciousness that they remain a divine secret, or as Rumi put it, an "open secret."

The alchemists' images and metaphoric language were not an aberration in the process; they were the fruit of the process, for what can communicate the complexity of the mysteries? This language of paradox and the complexity of imagery and mandalas keep us connected to the mercuriality, the mystery and the secret of the Philosopher's Stone.

The unfolding inner secret at the core of individuation is secret in its uniquemess in each human being, hidden from ordinary consciousness, residing in the psychic womb of the soul, seeking to be born into one's life. Like an experiment in the *vas pelicans* in the soul of each of us, it is secretly gathering elements, experiences, beings to itself in order to birth the consciousness it can become in our lives. Our role is to discover and serve this unique secret of nature growing in us and our lives.

STONE AND THE PROTECTIVE SCREEN BETWEEN THE WORLDS: STONE AS THE MEDIATOR

The Stone also speaks to us of the mysteries between impersonal and personal forces in our inner dialogues and meditations with the divine. The personally related activities of the Self incarnating in the life of a woman appeared to her in the following dream:

> I am in a room that is mine somehow—a dwelling with many windows. A meditative home. I realize some man has come in the door, kind of out of shape. I feel fierce protection of this space, and realize he doesn't belong here. I jump up and kick him in the solar plexus and he leaves. (He was busy doing something in here he did not belong doing, tampering with something with his hands. And although he was dumb, his stupid tampering, it was made known, could also become dangerous later.) Anyway, he is out and I lock the door.
>
> Then I wonder about this place and the permeability of the place to spirits. I look around and see an atrium area on a little earthly mesa inside this place, just to my right near the bed. And beyond that is a screen, between this atrium-bed and the woods outside. I think it is good to have the screen and permeability, but I don't want just any spirit to be able to come in. Then I see in front of me—between me and the screen

> to the outdoors—a huge round stone. This stone is somehow alive, and is somehow living protection. With its presence here, only the spirits I need to deal with will be drawn, I am relieved. A deep feeling of devotion and peace permeates. Weirdly, it also feels the stone will not only draw certain encounters, but will help me deal with them.

Let's look at what she does at the very beginning of the dream. She realizes where she is, some room of her own. Then she realizes there is some dumb man whose hands are busy doing something that isn't right somehow. Is he a dumb, overactive, or manipulating attitude she needs to separate from? Anyway, she realizes he does not belong in this room, in this inner sanctum, and she kicks him in the solar plexus, which is interesting as it is an old technique for shocking and awakening Self. Shamans and yogis use this literally to shift the point of awareness and awaken kundalini. But more importantly, it is not time to keep him in there and help him further awaken or develop or work on the animus relationship, so she locks him out of this precious space. There are times for working with the animus, and there are times for getting separate from such tampering presences and finding communion with Self. The dream ego has work to do here, to protect her private inner sanctum, her relationship with the Self, with the Stone. She has to protect the space and connection. The stone, the Self, functions to protect as well.

As the latent Self becomes manifest in time and space in relation to the woman, her dream ego comes to recognize where she is. She is in the inner sanctum in touch with the Self, in relationship with the stone, and learns to protect that relationship and psychic space and center. It is very moving to see what happens to the dreamer in contact with the stone. She does her part (wakes up to her surroundings and gets the dumb *animus* out of this place), and the stone, the Self, is doing its part too. The stone mediates and protects her in connection with the spirit world. It is like a magnet that draws the spirits that would be important for her, and keeps others out. The dream also does not say that all these encounters would be easy, it just is portraying that spirits that would be too much or superfluous are omitted. She is not just a wide open door to the spirit world or outer world without some cohesive meaning and interaction and center. Instead the screen, which is permeable, is there, and the Self functions to mediate and protect the psyche and the center. Though the psyche is quite permeable and open to the flow of air and exchange with the worlds, the large stone and her relationship with it creates a protection.

So to be alone with the living stone, and feel the air that breathes through the permeable screen between the Self and the worlds, and to feel the power of the stone to protect and mediate the worlds—this is where she belongs. And the woman dreamer is waking up to this experience, and learning to recognize animus presences and attitudes that do not serve and do not belong in this communion room. Thought forms and opinions from such an inner character would be disruptive to the newly-found communion with the growing properties of the Stone—the incarnating Self. Contact with the Self in which we learn to consolidate relationship with its growing functions can bring protection and importantly *self-regulation* just as these images portray.

In alchemy, the Stone performs alchemical activities or operations. One is *multiplicatio*, where the Stone relates with the world and grows in the world. It draws people, events and such to a person as It is incarnating. The Stone cannot however do that in a positive way if the ego is not awake. When the ego is not in enough substantial relationship with the incarnating Self and we are therefore too permeable and unintegrated, we can become overwhelmed by an onslaught of psychic material from the unconscious. This can manifest at times (as it did for this dreamer) as a dissociative process, one in which psychic energy both overwhelms the personality, and dissipates in too many directions. In such an experience the psychic container is too weak to hold the energetic processes or nurture self-reflection that could bring attitudinal changes realigning consciousness with Self. The stone dream is working on strengthening that center.

Basically, as is fairly universally true, there must be more and more integration of the psychic wound, so that the wound is not the one giving shape to life. Instead, here the new center is growing, and that new center can positively multiply, become life giving, and affect the world around the dreamer in positive ways. And of course we know the new center and the initiating psychic wound live in ever intricate relationship in the psyche. As relationship with the Stone grows, insight into and freedom from the negative manifestations of the psychic wound grow as well.

This dream medicine speaks to the heart of these issues. It illustrates an antidote to an inflationary process for the dreamer, and gives her perspective from inside her experience of how it feels to be on center.

The development of felt, living relationship between the ego and the Self, where the ego picks up the responsibility of tending to the felt relationship in a daily way, is the bottom line of the *rubedo* process, and the Self has its ways of serving that as well. It is a partnership, as this dream portrays. The Stone often appears and marks where the worlds unite, mediating new relationship between inner and outer, divine and human, Self and other.

Integration Brings to Life the Invaluable Inner Heretic, and the "Orphan Stone"

To meet the divine within the human soul which seeks to fulfill itself, we must discover its unique essence and struggle. As we have seen, the penetrating spirit of Mercurius in dreams can target this core and bring it to light if we bring energy to the dialogue with the unconscious and tend our dreams and live in unison with it.

Certain collective groups have images and growing bodies of wisdom to help us unlock some understanding of our journey, and collectives may even learn to tend the life of spirit and humanity that helps awaken Self. This amounts to little, though, if we do not take the wisdom inward to individual experience of the inner guide. The reverse is true as well. Collectives benefit if we take the inner unfolding of Self and growing wisdom and bring it back to the collective. This can be helped along by gracefulness, relatedness, and at times by discovering and valuing the inner heretic.

In ancient Greek, the word *heresy* came from the verb *hairein*, meaning "to take." This gave rise to the adjective *hairetos* ("able to choose") and the noun *hairesis* ("the act of choosing"). In later times, the noun came to refer to a course of action, school of thought, and philosophical or religious sect. By the 1300s, it took on nonecclesiastical use, applying to any dissenting opinion or dissenting belief.[21] We might again rethink heresy and see it as in the days of old, as our ability to choose, to embody our inner visions and knowing, including the ways we must carry our dissenting sense of the nature of the microcosm and macrocosm.

If we don't value the inner heretic and give it a voice, the problem for us as individuals within collective society may be like that of Niklaus von Flue of Switzerland. When he emerged from his hermit cave, with his deeply unique individual visions of the terrible numinosum, he was tormented about whether he could make his interpretations of his encounter with the divine match the expectations of the Catholic Church. We too benefit from watching this tendency to take inner experiences of the terrible-marvelous numinosum and attempting to make them conform to the consensus of the projected collective structures in the interior *or* exterior collectives, whether a world religion, an inner or outer Jungian collective, or any inner community in us dominated by collectivity.

We might do well to keep an eye on the psychic realities differentiated by the Sufi masters. The Sufi masters have had remarkable success in connecting with the infinite and remaining outside the clutches of dogma. In the words of the poet Junaid of Baghdad, they, in part, humorously honor the heretical: "None attains to the Degree of Truth until a thousand honest people have testified that he is a heretic."[22] Henry Corbin, a renowned scholar of Sufism, describes the relationship of the individual seeker to any collective:

> There is a crucial decision, either a human being is oriented toward a quest for his invisible guide or he entrusts himself to the collective, magisterial authority as the intermediary between himself and revelation.[23]

Of course, tremendous wisdom is embodied in collectives. However, if a projected collectivity remains the magisterial authority between ourselves and revelation, great difficulties with the soul ensue. As the alchemists portrayed it, the living Philosopher's Stone is an orphan. By this, they expressed the reality that the new presence of the divine being born into the human does not belong to any "parents" (to collectives, or even to anyone loving or helpful to you). Rather, each living Self, each honed Philosopher's Stone is unique and in the world as an orphan child would be. There is a quality of aloneness expressed in their orphan image. This is reminiscent of Jesus' remark that he came to set brother against brother, mother against father. A curious remark on his part, but in this light we can see that the indwelling of the spirit brings an eventual uniqueness whose embodiment requires that we become no longer able to remain merged with anyone else. The alchemy of change brings out this unique individuality and humanity, and the Self is most interested in exactly this, for without this it cannot incarnate as fully into the world.

The dream of an elder analyst portrays this theme. At the time, she was going through tremendous psychic separation from her mate of many years. She was also turning toward her creativity in clay work, and moving into semiretirement. She felt an inner imperative that wanted more quiet, empty space and time in her life. This she knew would require stepping back some from the analytic circle she had served and participated in for decades. During these changing times she dreamed:

> I see a young orphan girl. She has just had her first Holy Communion. As a gift, my brother's friend is giving her something—he pours hot metal into a new mold, and this is her gift for her new communion. I can see the mold is made of some unique metal itself, and is in the shape of the

> orphan girl. The orphan girl is lying down next to the mold. She and this unique mold are related.

This is a remarkable expression of the new, unique being this soul essence is becoming. It is a celebration of the young, fresh feminine's communion with the divine. Yet, it contains a peculiar paradox, because usually we think of the first communion as a ritual of the Catholic Church. Here, this initiation communion image spontaneously arises as a reality in the soul. The individuality brought to bear in the image of the orphan and the orphan mold underscore the singular nature such rites require. The dream seems to support her in her decisions toward her creativity and solitude, showing her that her decisions are in fact assisting the formation of the feminine into her unique life. The amount of care the life force invests in each individuating person is stunning. The dreams to portray, guide, warn, and assist the human being can be like this woman's, a true treasure trove that links consciousness to movements and developments between daily life and the soul.

In the image of the hot metal—of all that has been cooking and melted down in the heat of transformation in this woman's psyche—a new shape is taking form. The dreamer thought of this as the melting down of the old ways in which the feminine was in the world. She was sacrificing relationship and daily community efforts of supporting the training of analysands, the energy was being taken back into the psyche, and was taking a new shape, giving rise to new instincts in her life.

Alchemically the "orphan stone" appeared in this dreamer's life when she had the courage to remember her aloneness, to rely on the inner self for directives for creating a meaningful flow of life with the inner and outer worlds. She had to step out of some of the collectivity in herself that was in the way, and in so doing discovered more life energy specific to what her innermost heart needed at this time. She also discovered a more potent concentration of life essence and joy in the process.

Yogic Consciousness, Experience of the *Unus Mundus* Mysteries

At some point along the journey, development of the manifest Self asks that the ego discover new relationship to the totality. Quite literally the inner world may ask us to dance with all areas of life. This can create a fluidity of consciousness, a spirit of Eros and inclusion of all parts of our journey and psyche. Here is one woman's example:

> In a shamanic meditation . . . I [meet] . . . barefoot African women accompanied by a water buffalo who all enter my house and begin going around the room magnetically drawing out each part of my life to come dance. The barefoot women are powerful dancers, the energy in their feet, and the seashell anklets they're wearing rattle, their hips get into the beat in intricately passionate ways. The women convey to me they like creativity, and that they feel honored in one of my projects on the spirit of the buffalo. In their erotic magnetic feminine presence, they also inform me they want the roots of the work to be sure to include these layers of being of the indigenous peoples alive and well in the psychic and spiritual worlds. Each part of my life is then represented by a figure standing around the living room. The most difficult of issues and hard times come out and dance with these African women. I am included in the dance with the African women who teach me to dance with the other characters—each part of life, each realm, each obstacle, each joy. They generate ease in the body with the candid way they inhabit their bodies, and they generate erotic healing with their magnetic, drawing-out power. This has the effect of allowing everything in my life to embody itself *as it is*, in full paradox, and come be part of the dance.

This kind of psychic experience creates acceptance, inclusion, and integration. Integration experiences bring the totality of life together in some new way, and carry an accompanying wisdom that stands in contrast to other inner attitudes. They are different, for example, from turning to the psyche for entertainment, titillation, or escape from individuation and its accompanying pain, or for some unconscious power drive fulfillment. Integration experiences come as fruit of the hard work, and the journey, and stem from a life lived close to the unconscious for the sake of this inner development of unity itself. Integration experiences also stem from weathering the storms of inner and outer life in such a way that instead of splitting between the opposites, a new unity is born.

As in this dance meditation, we are invited into some new embodiment of all the terrain we have encountered in life, all our experiences, psychic states, and manifestations of love, life, and relationship present in our unfolding myth. When the alchemical processes have cooked the complexes long enough into ash, the manifest Self emerges, and acceptance and joy return. We are called to discover a sense of peace in and beyond the trouble of complexes, dark vortexes and difficulties in life to discover what the alchemists termed the "incorruptible," what we would say psychologically is an unbroken connection with the divine that is fulfilling itself at the core of our life.

Here is an example of this calling to discover the "incorruptible" working its way out in an elderly woman's life dedicated for decades to the inner unfolding through dreams and meditation:

> I am with a woman who is pregnant. Standing there, I realize I had been keeping her appointment book, and that I booked two meetings for her in the middle of the day; now her husband is there and is going to keep this appointment book for her. I hand it to him. She needs to be taken somewhere in the car. I realize I have an appointment with her. Perplexed, I go over to the car to talk with her. I am disgusted to see in myself that I have had some sense of false superiority over her. I want to stop this and remedy it. I tell her of my own insecurity about not ever having a child, and I express to her how I see her beauty.
>
> Suddenly then I am with her in a new location and am her midwife. Her husband is beside me. She is new at this too, and needs to breathe. The baby is crowning now. I look over and see a woman beside us is also delivering. We are in a birthing setting, a number of beds for birthing women are set up. It is also outdoors, with a low adobe wall circling the place, and a pool of water nearby. The woman next to us is crowning, now her baby's head pops out.
>
> I return to the woman I am working with who is still delivering. I realize now that we are in a meditation center with yogis of all sorts. They are each grounding their own practices in unique ways. I see someone able to bend in a most incredible way. Nothing I have ever seen before, I am stunned. Out of nowhere a command permeates us and it tells us: Look at where the BABY decided it wanted to be born.

Here we witness the birth of the new religious attitude, the new center of consciousness, which changes this woman's life considerably. Without this new awareness being brought to the fore, which comes leaping out in the dream, this woman would continue to be locked into the dominance of the ego, and miss the true place where the new life wants to come through. It is not through the ego controlling life, as imaged in unconsciously keeping the appointment book and forgetting for whom the "appointment" is arranged!

The new life instead comes as the dream ego awakens to where it has been "off"—in humbling itself and discovering where the new life will come. The dream ego discovers that it has been in the wrong attitude. It has *not* been aware of the "appointment" with the birth of the new way, and it has somehow been standing in a false superiority to the soul's new life. The pregnant woman about to give birth—this part of the dreamer is carrying the new life, not the current ego attitude, so the dream ego needs to get in right relationship with where soul is coming through in the new birth.

As soon as the ego awakens and realizes that it is not appointed as superior, and when it realizes for whom it has been needing to keep the appointment in life, then it has a chance to align with the inner soul-child coming. When the ego then recognizes where the new life is really coming from, it becomes the midwife to this new birth. The dreamer learns to participate consciously in the transformation.

So what is the transformation she is now midwife to? Clues appear in the fact that the new baby coming has chosen where it wants to be born. This means the new life of the autonomous psyche has its own intention and direction that the ego must serve and help bring along. The yogic meditation center where everyone grounds their own unique practices is where this new child wants to be born.

We usually think of yoga as meaning flexibility, breathing, stretching, calming and clearing the mind, bringing awareness to alignment, embodiment, and the flow of life energy. *Yoga*, as a word, relates to *yoke*, to join together. Yoga in this context then could be the fluid participation with the joining together of the worlds, of the opposites within, the *unus mundus* mysteries. The ego learns to find its peaceful place in union with the divine, in the flow of life force among the many realms of existence.

The dream ego is taking in the site of the yogis who are capable of grounding their practices with breath and flexibility she has never seen. Clearly here is an invitation, if not a demand, for the dream ego to learn in daily life to ground her calling, learn flexibility, and for whom she keeps the "appointment" of this calling. Ultimately this is pointing to the ego complex finding yogic consciousness, and grounding on a daily basis individualized means for coming into this *unus mundus* yogic consciousness.

Interestingly this means she will have to put the yogi hand to the earth, as the Buddha did upon his enlightenment under the bhodi tree. For her that will mean discovering on a daily basis what this new child needs, and putting her hand to the earth, to her appointment book, to her daily way of living to give this new presence room.

This new center carries the potential for the dreamer to discover her own yogic freedom. She followed the energy into the various ways it discovers union, and fed this growing center in these activities and meditations. She discovered peace in so doing, giving this new center life as its own reward. Her ego complex decreased its intensity, individuation issues with complexes and problems eased and she learned new means to serve this relationship and come into union and peace with the many realms of existence.

The Rebirth of Consciousness: *Unus Mundus* and the New Fruits of Sun and Moon

Once born, this divine child, *filius*, or Philosopher's Stone, wants to circulate light, life energy into more of our lives. This requires devotion to the *coniunctio*—the continuing dialectic of love between the manifest and celestial realms.

The Sufis believe that, "to be faithful to the angel is precisely to let ourselves be guided by him toward the transcendent he announces."[24] Now this is important when the alchemical child is born, and appears in the dream above. The divine child chose to be born where individual yogic practices are being developed, and the dream ego learns to go where it has chosen, into this yogic birthplace. This dream's truth illustrates archetypal dimensions universal to the birth of the divine child. It seeks yogic consciousness with us in unique ways in our daily lives—between thoughts, under defenses or holding patterns, and in our hearts. It is our job to wake up and discover the appointment and where this yogic relationship wants to unfold, and help give it form. This is the mythic pattern in the *rubedo*. The hand of the Buddha comes to earth; the yogic joining of conscious and unconscious comes into a reddening, while a new flow of energy courses in daily life. Then the *rubedo* and the *unus mundus* windows open together.

Separating from the unconscious allows integration of experience to occur, and assists in the *rubedo* processes. Here, in addition to seeing through our personality adaptations and defenses, incredibly fresh experience of life becomes possible, flowing in and dissolving the need for the old adaptations. For example, the perception of human and divine switches back and forth in the *unus mundus* states. We may get a glimpse of the divine dwelling in a person we love in the core of their life and individuation journey, seeking wholeness among the realms. New instincts and courage may arrive to allow felt experience of life—all the names of the divine as the Sufis see it,[25] sorrow, joy, silence, loneliness, and so on—to flow through us as an offering to life itself, without resistance and prior conditioning blocking their flow. The human appears as the potential vessel of the divine's own flow, as the human is also the necessary, individuated element to carry this flow of life back to the divine. These experiences mark a movement forward into new union between consciousness and the mysteries. This is the goal of the work and the mystery behind the ouroboros moving from its latent to its manifest state. Consciousness has separated and found a way to rejoin in wholeness with the *mysterium*, where it is neither swallowed up nor rigidly defended, but instead is reborn in its strength and ability to participate with the many realms of existence.

In the *unus mundus* states where consciousness experiences this renewing flow of life and union, our sense organs may awaken so we literally see, hear, feel, smell and perceive in brand new ways. Time and timelessness open their doors to one another and embrace in the moment. Matter becomes the transparent, intricate vehicle and expression of spirit that it is. Rock-solid objects in the natural world reveal they are mostly made up of space and moving particles. Cosmic awareness grows, where you dream or suddenly awaken to the feeling of the whole cosmos as one unified being, and your self as an element in, and a tiny mirror of, that cosmic body. This is the fruit of yogic consciousness, of the *coniunctio,* awakening. It initiates us into fuller participation with the fields of synchronicity between the natural and spirit worlds, a participation that is not about inflation, loss of soul, or dropping connection to our humanity and inner work. Nor is it about falling backward into a participation mystique with the unconscious, or about getting stuck in any dimension or realm of consciousness. It is instead about life in which the stone circulates energy among the many realms that are accessible to us humans and can be experienced without our becoming any less human. In fact, humanity grows here as the both-ness of everything prevails and reveals the nature of the mysterious universe in which we live.

Our contact potentially grows with the experiential fields of synchronicity and love found in the *coniunctio*, which transmutes the conjunction between the physical and spiritual worlds. As we work to cultivate this relationship, subtle-body awareness grows and the organs of perception diversify. As new means of perception open, we recognize the feeling and meaning of events as they happen. Throughout her book, *On Dreams and Death*, Marie-Louise von Franz highlights the importance in a number of mystical traditions of experiences in this state, and of building the subtle body before we die, for it is the vehicle to psychic freedom at death. How do we recognize the subtle-body states? Sometimes in dreams we will have an experience of being raised up, or of levitation. In the subtle body state, gravity and density are not experienced as they are in the physical body. The reality of the subtle body is experienced as a third reality—neither spirit nor matter alone. With experience of the inner companion, guide, or ally, we can learn to cultivate this reality with active imagination, psyche-body healing arts, shamanic practices, yoga, creativity, and similar techniques. This is the heart of the sun-moon mysteries, the creation of the third field of being, the subtle-body field of synchronicity between opposites. Many mystical practices worldwide and throughout time discover freedom in these dimensions where utter wholeness and communion with all of nature abounds. Perception among the realms of being is fluid. Here healing occurs, vision and insight arrive, sexuality opens to the vast landscape of the soul, and inspiration and creativity abound. Active imagination is indispensable in growing the connection to the guide who helps us into these subtle-body states.

Sensory organs awaken in the *rubedo*. Many people report experience of the subtle-body state via auguries in nature involving sound, where suddenly all the worlds mingle and ultimate clarity of being arrives. This ties in with the mystery of the *unus mundus*, where lower and upper worlds mingle in harmony with human consciousness. Experiences of the objective psyche and synchronicity often go hand in hand with this interactive field among the many realms of being. Some people in these *unus mundus* states report experiences of an otherworldly smell bringing a felt sense of the celestial, along with some poignant sense memory or fresh feeling of love, all of which are unnameable. Some experience sound that carries an uncanny felt sense of the harmonizing of the realms, where the divine is heard in a wind chime, or a neighbor's bell rings with such clarity that you feel the activation of all the realms present in the moment, and the answer to something you were seeking simply falls into your awareness. Perhaps you see a hawk outside your window as someone is relating to you a dream of the hawk-god Horus, and you feel the harmony between the dream world and the natural world, and it brings peace. Sometimes people in these states spontaneously "see together," as happened to Jung and Toni Wolff when they were in Ravenna and both saw mosaics that did not exist in this world.[26]

Sometimes synesthesia occurs, where senses blend. One man reported that for weeks, whenever someone laughed, his inner eye would see the laughter as a waterfall of music. It is common in the *unus mundus* states for senses to open, switch channels, or blend. The field of synchronicity may help organs of perception not only open but also unify. Teachings may come in which certain organs of perception are trained to harmonize and become one. One woman was shown over and over again, in active imagination, how the inner companion or ally could help her discover the experience where thought, breath, sight become one peaceful unity. This created deeper communion between them and led to the experiential field of her heart door opening to love and connection with the ally and its world. Importantly, as the *unus mundus* mysteries activate, experiential connections with the *mundus imaginalis* and the psychoid may strengthen over time with guidance of the inner beloved. The fruit enlivens life for both human and divine, for manifest and celestial realms.

The whole unfolding of these mysteries depends upon grace and guidance, which each person discovers uniquely. It also depends upon our work and devotion to return to the inner stove daily, see what's cooking, and to help out in life's alchemical kitchen, discovering that each step in the alchemical round, however difficult, is its own reward.

How will this in turn help our planet and the collective? Each person establishing their *axis mundi* between the realms helps the problem of evil lessen and helps restore wisdom and love to its proper place in life. As we alchemically develop open relationship to the energy centers along our individual *axis mundi* ladders between heaven and earth, the hidden realms of the psychoid have greater ease in assisting human consciousness and our planet.

These are incredibly dark times in human history. Our blindness is saddening, for with all our current capabilities and developments as a species, many of us still choose unconscious materialistic values based on runaway power and ego pursuits that rule collective human life and devastate the natural world. As each of us seeks a rebirth of the sun, of consciousness, I believe what Jung felt is true: we help the great human soul, for somehow the balance in the collective unconscious changes to some degree. This is a significant offering each of us can contribute to future generations.

While writing this book, one night on the winter solstice, when the light was at its lowest, and the darkness of the year was at its peak, I skied to a remote valley in the Rocky Mountains to spend the night. I found a ski hut, lit my candle, and waited for dawn. This poem came—an alchemical prayer that the darkness in which we humans find ourselves may indeed become pregnant.

Up Rustler's Gulch: A Winter Solstice Offering

Up Rustler's Gulch
at night
in the dead of winter
our wick burned to its

lowest low,
when this spirit of exhaustion comes
finally the drunkard sun of summer
takes counsel with solstice shadows.

Oh lovely sun before the dawn,
listen in to these dark enlightened ones
and reading between reality
and what should have been
(what the soul whispers
that it longs to become)
you, brightening star,
will find a new way.

Notes

Introduction

1. C. G. Jung, *The Collected Works of C. G. Jung, Vol. 11*, Gerhard Adler, ed., R.F.C. Hull, trans. (Princeton: Princeton University Press, 1970), ¶ 147–148. Further citations from *The Collected Works* will be cited as CW, with the volume number. Full volume details are listed in the bibliography.

2. Jung, CW 10, ¶ 511.

3. Jung, CW 14, ¶ 788.

4. Jung, CW 14, ¶ 129.

5. Ferne Jensen, ed., *C.G. Jung, Emma Jung and Toni Wolff: A Collection of Rememberances* (San Francisco: The Analytical Psychology Club of San Francisco, 1982), p. 13.

6. Jung, CW 14, ¶ 700.

7. Jung, CW 17, ¶ 181.

8. Personal communication.

9. Jalal Al-Din Rumi, "What Is the Path," Odes VI 507-513, in Coleman Barks, trans., *One-Handed Basket Weaving* (Athens, GA: Maypop Books, 1991) p. 112. Used by kind permission.

Chapter 1

1. *Rosarium Philosophorum*, vol. II, ch. XXI, p. 258: in *Artis Auriferae quam Chemicam vocant.* (Basel: 1593). Cited in Jung, CW 14, ¶ 729, n. 182.

2. H.M.E. de Jong, *Michael Maier's* Atalanta Fugiens: *Sources of an Alchemical Book of Emblems* (York Beach, ME: Nicolas-Hays, 2002), p. 67.

3. Jung, CW 14,¶ 182.

4. C. G. Jung, *C. G. Jung Speaking: Interviews and Encounters* (Princeton: Princeton University Press, 1987), p. 228f.

5. Alexander Roob, *Alchemy and Mysticism* (New York: Taschen, 1997), p. 13.

6. See Jeffrey Raff, *Jung and the Alchemical Imagination* (Berwick, ME: Nicolas-Hays, 2000.

7. One of many references to this black light in the alchemical Stone can be found in Henry Corbin's book, *Alone with the Alone* (Princeton: Princeton University Press, 1998), p. 57. The subtle center of the *arcanum*, the "Jesus of thy being," has black as its color. This black light is called *aswad nurani* by Semanani, the great Iranian Sufi of the 14th century who inaugurated an intricate physiology of the subtle body. See also Henry Corbin, "L'interiorisation de sens en herméneutique soufie iranienne," *Eranos Jarhbuch* XXVI (1957): 57–187.

8. Jung, CW 13, ¶ 131.

9. Corbin, *Alone with the Alone*, pp. 222–224.

10. See Monika Wikman, "Reflections on Community Mysteries in the Jungian Lineage," *Quadrant* 33, no. 2 (2003): 6–23.

11. Jung, CW 5, ¶ 672. "[T]he hieros gamos signifies the conjunction of conscious and unconscious, the transcendent function characteristic of the individuation process. Integration of the unconscious invariably has a healing effect." See also C. G. Jung, *C. G. Jung Letters, Volume 1*, Gerhard Adler and Aniela Jaffé, eds., R.F.C. Hull, trans. (Princeton: Princeton University Press, 1992), pp. 336, 355–356. Jung's experience of the *hieros gamos* can also be found in C. G. Jung, *Memories, Dreams, Reflections* (New York: Vintage, 1989), pp. 293–295.

12. Roob, *Alchemy and Mysticism* p. 224.

13. Jung, CW 12, ¶ 394.

14. Jung, CW 13, ¶ 186.

15. Jung, CW 13, ¶ 185–186.

16. Jung, CW 13, ¶ 257.

17. Jung, CW 10, ¶ 304.

18. Michael Maier, *Symbola Aurea Mensae*, p. 5: "Sol est ejus conjugii Pater, et alba Luna Mater, tertius succedit. Ut gubernator, Ignis." Translation from Johannes Fabricius, *Alchemy: The Medieval Alchemists and Their Royal Art* (London: Thorsons, 1991), p. 62.

Chapter 2

1. Jackson Browne, title track from *Looking East* (Columbia Records, 1994).

2. Anthony Storr, ed., *The Essential Jung: Selected Writings Introduced by Anthony Storr* (Princeton: Princeton University Press, 1999), quote 256.

3. Jung, CW 14, ¶ 190.

4. Throughout this book, I use the Chinese concepts of yin and yang rather than "feminine" and "masculine" in order to avoid ingrained sterotypes and more accurately describe a wider scope of energetic exchange.

5. We all have experiences where we are on one side of an archetypal phenomenon and then discover the other side a little later in life: the anima woman (*inspiratrix*)/witch polarity, or the eternal youth/crabby old man (*puer/senex*) polarities, and so on. A common example of an archetype that is split in the collective unconscious as well as personal experience would be the virgin/whore split present in Catholicism. Another example of an archetype that is split in the collective unconscious occurs in the hero-saviour ego identity of the U.S. military that is split off from its own warmonger shadow, keeping its own atrocities in numerous countries from the American public. Some people are more susceptible to falling into that split and acting it out in the world on a large scale, however, it is operating in the collective unconscious and needs to be healed and united at the grand scale level as human beings learn to hold the two sides together.

6. Johannes Fabricius, *Alchemy: The Medieval Alchemists and Their Royal Art* (London: Thorsons, 1991), p. 87.

7. Jung, CW 5, ¶ 508–510.

8. From this cave emerge spirits from the other world at key liminal moments in the seasonal cycles. Anne Ross, *Pagan Celtic Britain: Studies in Iconography and Tradition* (London: Routledge and Keegan Paul, 1967) p. 317.

9. Sylvia Brinton Perera, *Celtic Queen Maeve and Addiction* (York Beach, ME: Nicolas-Hays, 2001), pp. 326–327.

10. C. G. Jung, *Memories, Dreams, Reflections* (New York: Vintage, 1989), p. 326.

11. Perera, *Celtic Queen Maeve*, p. 53.

12. W. B. Yeats, "Before the World Was Made," *The Collected Poems of W. B. Yeats, Volume 1: The Poems* (New York: Scribner, 1996), p. 266.

13. Jung, CW 16, ¶ 454.

Chapter 3

1. Jung, CW 13, ¶114, 115.
2. Jung, CW 12, ¶ 23.
3. Jung, CW 12, ¶ 24.
4. Jung, CW 12, ¶ 8.
5. Jung, CW 14, ¶ 319.
6. Jung, CW 13, ¶ 97 cites "Isis to Horus," in Marcellin Berthelot, *Collection des anciens alchemistes grecs,* vol. I (Paris, 1887–1888), xiii, 1f. Marie-Louise von Franz, *Alchemy: An Introduction to the Symbolism and the Psychology* (Toronto: Inner City, 1981), cites "The Prophetess to Her Son (or known as) Isis to Horus," in the *Codex Marcianus,* 1st century, A.D.
7. Von Franz, *Alchemy*, p. 45.
8. Jung, CW 13, ¶ 97.
9. Jung, CW 13, ¶ 97 cites Helmuth Jacobsohn, *Die dogmatische Stellung des Königs in der Theologie der alten Aegypter* (Hamburg and Glückstadt: J. J. Augustin, 1939).
10. *Rosarium Philosphorum*, in *Artis Auriferae*, II, p. 214, cited in Jung, CW 13, ¶ 90.
11. Dr. M.-L. von Franz articulates these four main problems in her book *Psychotherapy* (Boston: Shambhala, 2001), pp. 188–189.
12. Von Franz, *Psychotherapy*, p. 188.
13. Von Franz, *Psychotherapy*, p. 189.
14. C. G. Jung to Rev. H. L. Phillip, *C. G. Jung Letters, Volume 2: 1951–1961* (Princeton: Princeton University Press, 1972), p. 370.
15. Paracelsus, *Philosophia Sagax*, cited in Jung, CW 8, ¶ 388.
16. Von Franz, *Psychotherapy*, p. 189.
17. Jung, CW 10, ¶ 304.
18. Gerhard Dorn, *The Speculative Philosophy or the Seven Degrees of the Work*, in *Theatricum Chemicum*, vol. I, Elias Ashmole, ed. (London: 1652), pp. 228–276.
19. Neither Eastern nor Western adaptations mentioned here are exclusive, right or wrong. Indeed, many individuals experience both these adaptations over the course of individuation, depending on the unfolding of their own myth.
20. Jung, CW 7, ¶ 360.
21. Jung, CW 14, ¶ 688.
22. See Jung, CW 14, ¶ 41, for the *humidum radicale* reference.
23. Marie-Louise von Franz, *Aurora Consurgens: A Document Attributed to Thomas Aquinas on the Problem of Opposites in Alchemy* (Toronto: Inner City, 2000), p. 133.

24. De Jong, *Michael Maier's* Atalanta Fugiens, p. 221.

25. Alexander Roob, *Alchemy and Mysticism* (New York: Taschen, 1997), p. 199.

26. Marcel Griaule, *Conversations with Ogotemmeli: An Introduction to Dogon Religious Ideas* (Oxford: Oxford University Press, 1965). Thanks go to Eva Wertenschlag, whose lectures on the Dogon tribe have brought these myths alive, for pointing them out to me.

27. Jung, CW 16, ¶ 398.

Chapter 4

1. Jung, CW 14, ¶ 9 n.44.

2. Easterners and peoples with intact ancestral shamanic means for living are not in the same boat as most Westerners in this regard, for the former don't suffer the split that the overvaluation of rationalism has caused in the modern Western world.

3. Interview, 1955. Unpublished audio tape.

4. Jung, CW 6, ¶ 78.

5. W. B. Yeats, "The Song of Wandering Aengus," in *The Collected Poems of W. B. Yeats* (New York: Macmillan, 1956), p. 57. Reprinted by permission of Macmillan.

6. Jung, CW 12, ¶ 207–208.

7. Jung, CW 13, ¶ 139, n.2.

8. Monika Wikman, "If I Could Wake the Dead," copyright © 2004.

9. For a rich discussion on Hestia and her connection to groups, see Ginette Paris, *Pagan Meditations: Aphrodite, Hestia, Artemis* (Putnam, CT: Spring Publications, 1991).

10. Ad De Vries, *Dictionary of Symbols and Imagery* (Amsterdam: North Holland Publishing Company, 1976), p. 26. De Vries attributed these images to Ovid, *Fasti* 3, 750ff.

11. Kabir, excerpt from poem 25 in *Kabir: Ecstatic Poems*, Robert Bly, trans. (Boston: Beacon Press, 2004), p. 33. Used by kind permission.

12. John G. Neihardt, *Black Elk Speaks: Being the Life Story of a Holy Man of the Oglala Sioux* (Lincoln: University of Nebraska Press, 2000), p. 170.

13. Robert Graves, *Greek Gods and Heroes* (New York: Dell, 1965), p. 59. See also Larousse, *World Mythology* (London: Hamlyn Publishing Group, 1965), p. 139.

14. Edward Edinger, *Ego and Archetype* (Boston: Shambhala, 1992), p. 21.

15. Annemarie Schimmel, lecture, March, 2000; see also *A Two-Colored Brocade: The Imagery of Persian Poetry* (Chapel Hill: University of North Carolina Press, 1992), p. 194.

16. Henry Corbin, *Alone with the Alone* (Princeton: Princeton University Press, 1998), p. 124.

17. Personal communication; this renowned horse trainer is Leslie Hammel Turk of Turk Arabians in Las Vegas, New Mexico.

Chapter 5

1. C. G. Jung, CW 9i, ¶ 212–215.

2. Jung, CW 14, ¶ 219, 223. Brackets are mine.

3. See Erich Neumann, *The Origins and History of Consciousness*, R.F.C. Hull, trans., Bollingen Series XLVII (Princeton: Princeton University Press, 1995), pp. 152–168.

4. This is a revised version of the poem "27, To Artemis" in the *Homeric Hymns*, Apostolos N. Athanassakis, trans. (Baltimore: Johns Hopkins University Press, 1976), l. 1–10, and is not the original.

5. Astrologically, 51 is the Chiron return year, where the wounded healer archetype comes full circle in our lives and the reality of our wounded/healing myths circulates energy through the larger psyche, hoping to bring us into greater depth of soul. A lovely synchronizing appears for this dreamer as she discovers a new way during this cycle in her life.

6. Robert Graves, *Greek Gods and Heroes* (New York: Dell, 1965), p. 20.

7. Hugo Rahner, "Das christliche Mysterium von Sonne und Mond." In *Eranos Jahrbuch* X: 1943 (Zurich, 1944), p. 400. Cited in Jung, CW 14, ¶ 174, n. 275.

8. William Mennens, "Aureum vellus," *Theatrum Chemicum*, V, xliv, p. 460. Cited in Jung, CW 14, ¶ 174, n. 276.

9. Jung, CW 14, ¶ 219 cites *Gloria Mundi*, in A. E. Waite, *Museum Hermeticum*, vol. I, p. 225. Readers can find this book in print as *The Hermetic Museum* (York Beach, ME: Weiser, 1999).

10. Marie-Louise von Franz, *Alchemical Active Imagination* (Boston: Shambhala, 1997), p. 42.

11. Jung, CW 14, ¶ 186 cites *Philaletha*, in *Museum Hermetica*, vol. II, p. 169. This work is in print as *The Three Treatises of Philalethes*, in A. E. Waite, *The Hermetic Museum* (York Beach, ME: Weiser, 1999).

12. Ibid.

13. Jung, CW 14, ¶ 218.

14. Jung, CW 14, ¶ 193.

15. M. Esther Harding, *Woman's Mysteries: Ancient and Modern* (Boston: Shambhala, 2001), p. 114.

16. Harding, *Woman's Mysteries*, p. 34.

Chapter 6

1. Jung, CW 13, ¶ 322.

2. Jung, CW 12, ¶ 457, n. 79 cites "Super arborem Aristotelis," in *Theatrum Chemicum, praecipuas selectorum auctoram tractatus . . . continens*. (Ursellis [Ursel], 1602), v. 2., p. 527.

3. Jung, CW 16, ¶ 398.

4. David Whyte, excerpt from "Faces at Braga," in *Where Many Rivers Meet* (Langley, WA: Many Rivers Press, 1990), p. 42. Used by kind permission of the author and publisher.

5. A treatise of Arabic origin, printed in *Bibliotheca Chemica*, vol. I (Reprint, Whitefish, MT: Kessinger, 1998), p. 400ff.

6. Jung, CW 14, ¶ 8, 9.

7. Jung, CW 14, ¶ 8, 9, n. 42 cites *Tractatus aureus Hermetis*, in *Bibliotheca Chemica*, vol. I, Joannes Jacobus Magnetus, ed. (Geneva, 1702), p. 408b.

8. Jung, CW 14, ¶ 9, n. 44.

9. Marie-Louise von Franz, *Alchemy: An Introduction to the Symbolism and the Psychology* (Toronto: Inner City, 1981), p. 116.

10. Personal communication.

11. Marie-Louise von Franz, *The Golden Ass of Apuleius: The Liberation of the Feminine in Man* (Boston: Shambhala, 2001), pp. 186–187.

12. Jung, CW 14, ¶ 257.

13. Jung, CW 11, ¶ 147–149. Italics are mine.

14. See Jeff Raff and Linda Bonnington-Vocatura, *Healing the Wounded God* (Berwick, ME: Nicolas-Hays, 2002), for a courageous and thorough exploration of these issues.

15. Nor Hall, *The Moon and the Virgin* (New York: Harper and Row, 1980), p. 119.

16. Mircea Eliade, *Shamanism: Archaic Techniques of Ecstasy* (Princeton: Princeton University Press, 1972), p. 73.

17. Jung, CW 12, ¶ 210.

18. Jung, CW 13, ¶ 168.

19. Jung, CW 13, ¶ 142.

20. Von Franz, *The Golden Ass of Apuleius*, p. 104.

21. Jung, CW 5, ¶ 553.

22. Douglas Cann, stated in memoriam for von Franz via Internet group communication between Interregional Society of Jungian Analysts members.

23. C. G. Jung, *C. G. Jung Letters, Volume I*, Gerhard Adler and Aniela Jaffé, eds., R.F.C. Hull, trans. (Princeton: Princeton University Press, 1992) ,p. 65.

24. Marie-Louise von Franz, *The Alchemical Active Imagination*, revised edition (Boston: Shambhala, 1997), p. 88.

Chapter 7

1. C. G. Jung, *C. G. Jung Speaking: Interviews and Encounters* (Princeton: Princeton University Press, 1987), pp. 228f.

2. Jeremy Narby, in his remarkable book *The Cosmic Serpent: DNA and the Origins of Knowledge* (New York: J. P. Tarcher, 1999) brings alive the discoveries of shamanism and science and how they meet in the same place with different means of accessing information (i.e., the creation spirits giving information to shamans and scientists discovering coded information from the double helix of DNA).

3. Jung, CW 13, ¶ 186.

4. Rudolph Otto, *The Idea of the Holy*, John W. Harvey, trans. (Oxford: Oxford University Press, 1958), pp. 12–13.

5. *Theatrum Chemicum Brittanicum*, Elias Ashmole, ed. (London: 1652) quoted in Johannes Fabricius, *Alchemy: The Medieval Alchemists and Their Royal Art* (London: Thorsons, 1991), p. 140.

6. Henry Corbin, *Alone with the Alone* (Princeton: Princeton University Press, 1998), p. 61.

7. Marie-Louise von Franz, *Alchemy* (Toronto: Inner City Books, 1981), p. 166.

8. I am gratefully indebted to Ralph Metzner for introducing me to this medicine wheel, an extraordinary meditation tool.

9. Another telling of this story can also be found in Joseph Campbell, *Hero with a Thousand Faces* (Princeton: Princeton University Press, 1972), p. 199.

10. Jung, CW 5, ¶ 388. Brackets are mine.

11. Corbin, *Alone with the Alone*, p. 205.

12. Jung, CW 16, ¶ 384. Italics are mine.

13. Marie-Louise von Franz, *Psychotherapy* (Boston: Shambhala, 2001), p. 185.

14. Mircea Eliade, *Shamanism: Archaic Techniques of Ecstacy* (Princeton: Princeton University Press, 1972), p. 194.

15. Eliade, *Shamanism*, p. 279.

16. Eliade, *Shamanism*, pp. 121–122. "Celsus" in this quote refers to Origen, *Contra Celsum* VI, 22.

17. Jung, CW 13, ¶ 448

18. Jung, CW 12, ¶ 209.

19. Idries Shah, *The Way of the Sufi* (London: Penguin/Arkana, 1991), p. 99.

20. Marie-Louise von Franz, *The Alchemical Active Imagination*, revised edition (Boston: Shambhala, 1997), p. 115.

21. *Webster's Dictionary of Word Origins* (New York: Smithmark, 1996), p. 217.

22. Shah, *The Way of the Sufi*, p. 268.

23. Corbin, *Alone with the Alone*, p. 33.

24. Corbin, *Alone with the Alone*, p. 134.

25. Corbin, *Alone with the Alone*, pp. 118–123.

26. Jung, *C. G. Jung Speaking* (Princeton: Princeton University Press, 1977), p. 184. Jung and Wolff saw mosaics through a blue light and discussed them for hours, thinking they were real. Then, when no one else could find these mosaics, they realized the mosaics did not exist in this world. Years later, they discovered a story about a countess who vowed to make these mosaics if she was rescued from a shipwreck. She had the mosaics made but they were later destroyed in a fire at a nearby church that Jung and Wolff had never entered.

Bibliography

Auden, W. H. *Collected Poems*. New York: Random House, 1976.
Barks, Coleman, trans. *Like This*. Athens, GA: Maypop Books, 1990.
———. *One-Handed Basket Weaving*. Athens, GA: Maypop Books, 1991.
———. *The Soul of Rumi*. San Francisco: HarperSanFrancisco, 2001.
———. *Tentmaking*. Athens, GA: Maypop Books, 2001.
Barks, Coleman, with John Moyne, trans. *The Essential Rumi*. San Francisco: HarperSanFrancisco, 1997.
Boehme, Jacob. *The Signature of All Things*. Reprint, Kila, MT: Kessinger, n.d.
Browne, Jackson. *Looking East*. Los Angeles: Asylum Records, 1998.
Burt, Kathleen. *Archetypes of the Zodiac*. St. Paul, MN: Llewellyn, 1989.
———. "The Beauty of Lakshmi Devi," in *The Light of Consciousness Journal*, Summer, 1999.
Cheetham, Tom. *The World Turned Inside Out: Henry Corbin and Islamic Mysticism*. Putnam CT: Spring Journal Books, 2003.
Chittick, William C. *The Sufi Path of Knowledge*. New York: State University of New York Press, 1989.
Corbin, Henry. *Alone with the Alone*. Bollingen Series XCI. Princeton: Princeton University Press, 1997.
———. "L'Interiorisation de sens en herméneutique soufie iranienne," *Eranos Jarbuch* XXVI (1957): 57–187.

Duncan, Robert. *Roots and Branches: Poems by Robert Duncan.* New York: Charles Scribner and Sons, 1964.

Edinger, Edward. *Anatomy of the Psyche*. La Salle, IL: Open Court, 1985.

Eliade, Mircea. *A History of Religious Ideas*, vols. I-III. Chicago: University of Chicago Press, 1978.

———. *Shamanism: Archaic Techniques of Ecstasy*. Bollingen Series LXXVI. Princeton: Princeton University Press, 1970.

Fabricius, Johannes. *Alchemy: The Medieval Alchemists and Their Royal Art*. London: Thorsons, 1991.

Graves, Robert. *Greek Gods and Heroes*. Garden City, NY: Doubleday, 1960.

Hall, Nor. *The Moon and the Virgin*. New York: Harper and Row, 1980.

Hannah, Barbara. *The Life and Work of C. G. Jung*. New York: Putnam and Sons, 1976.

Harding, M. Esther. *Woman's Mysteries: Ancient and Modern*. Boston: Shambhala, 2001.

Hartmann, Franz. *The Life and Doctrines of Jacob Boehme*. Reprint, Kila, MT: Kessinger, n.d.

Hillman, James. *Pan and the Nightmare*. Dallas: Spring Publications, 1972.

Homer. *The Homeric Hymns*. Apostolos N. Athanassakis, trans. Baltimore: Johns Hopkins University Press, 1976.

Jensen, Ferne, ed. *C. G. Jung, Emma Jung and Toni Wolff: A Collection of Remembrances*. San Francisco: The Analytical Psychology Club of San Francisco, 1982.

Jung, C. G. *C. G. Jung Letters, Vol. I*. Gerhard Adler and Aniela Jaffé, eds. R.F.C. Hull, trans. Princeton: Princeton University Press, 1973.

———. *C. G. Jung Letters, Vol. II*. Gerhard Adler, ed. Jeffrey Hulen, trans. Princeton: Princeton University Press, 1976.

———. *The Collected Works of C. G. Jung, vol. 5: Symbols of Transformation*. R.F.C. Hull, trans. Bollingen Series XX. Princeton: Princeton University Press, 1974.

———. *The Collected Works of C. G. Jung, vol. 8: Structure and Dynamics of the Psyche*. R.F.C. Hull, trans. Bollingen Series XX. Princeton: Princeton University Press, 1972.

———. *The Collected Works of C. G. Jung, vol. 9ii: Aion*. R.F.C. Hull, trans. Bollingen Series XX. Princeton: Princeton University Press, 1970.

———. *The Collected Works of C. G. Jung, vol. 10: Civilization in Transition*. R.F.C. Hull, trans. Bollingen Series XX. Princeton: Princeton University Press, 1970.

———. *The Collected Works of C. G. Jung, vol. 11: Psychology and Religion.* R.F.C. Hull, trans. Bollingen Series XX. Princeton: Princeton University Press, 1970.

———. *The Collected Works of C. G. Jung, vol. 12: Psychology and Alchemy.* R.F.C. Hull, trans. Bollingen Series XX. Princeton: Princeton University Press, 1977.

———. *The Collected Works of C. G. Jung, vol. 13: Alchemical Studies.* R.F.C. Hull, trans. Bollingen Series XX. Princeton: Princeton University Press, 1970.

———. *The Collected Works of C. G. Jung, vol. 14: Mysterium Coniunctionis.* R.F.C. Hull, trans. Bollingen Series XX. Princeton: Princeton University Press, 1970.

———. *The Collected Works of C. G. Jung, vol. 16: The Practice of Psychotherapy.* R.F.C. Hull, trans. Bollingen Series XX. Princeton: Princeton University Press, 1970.

———. *The Collected Works of C. G. Jung, vol. 18: The Symbolic Life.* R.F.C. Hull, trans. Bollingen Series XX. Princeton: Princeton University Press, 1976.

———. *Memories, Dreams, Reflections.* Aniela Jaffé, ed., Clara and Richard Winston, trans. New York: Vintage, 1989.

Kabir, *Kabir: Ecstatic Poems.* Robert Bly, trans. Boston: Beacon Press, 2004.

Meulenbeld, Ben. *Buddhist Symbolism in Tibetan Thangkas.* Havelte, Holland: Binkey Kok Publications, 2001.

Mueller, Lisel. *The Private Life.* Baton Rouge: Louisiana State Press, 1976.

Paris, Ginette. *Pagan Meditations.* Dallas: Spring Publications, 1986.

Raff, Jeffrey. *Jung and the Alchemical Imagination.* Berwick, ME: Nicolas-Hays, 2000.

———. *The Wedding of Sophia: The Divine Feminine in Psychoidal Alchemy.* Berwick, ME: Nicolas-Hays, 2003.

Raff, Jeffrey, and Linda Bonnington Vocatura. *Healing the Wounded God.* Berwick, ME: Nicolas-Hays, 2002.

Rilke, Rainer Maria. *Selected Poems of Rainer Maria Rilke.* Translation and commentary by Robert Bly. New York: Harper and Row, 1981.

Roob, Alexander. *Alchemy and Mysticism.* New York: Taschen, 1997.

Schimmel, Annemarie. *A Two-Colored Brocade: The Imagery of Persian Poetry.* Chapel Hill: University of North Carolina Press, 1992.

Shah, Idries. *The Way of the Sufi.* London: Penguin/Arkana, 1990.

Trinick, John. *The Fire Tried Stone.* Cornwall, England: Wordens of Cornwall Limited, 1967.

Von Franz, Marie-Louise. *Alchemical Active Imagination.* Dallas: Spring Publications, Inc., 1979.

———. *Alchemy.* Toronto: Inner City Books, 1980.

———. *The Golden Ass of Apulieus: The Liberation of the Feminine in Man.* Boston: Shambhala, 2001.

———. *Psychotherapy.* Boston: Shambala, 1993.

———. *Projection and Recollection in Jungian Psychology: Reflections of the Soul.* La Salle, IL: Open Court, 1980.

Whyte, David. *Where Many Rivers Meet.* Langely, WA: Many Rivers Press, 1990.

Wikman, Monika Relph. "Human Connection and Community Mysteries in the Jungian Lineage." In *Quadrant* 33, no. 2, 2003.

———. "Inner Music, Living Water." In *Psychological Perspectives* 44, Winter 2002.

———. "On the Life and Work of Gret Baumann-Jung." In *Spring Journal* 66, Winter 1999.

Yeats, W. B. *The Collected Poems of W. B. Yeats.* New York: Macmillan, 1956.

Index

About the Author

Monika Relph Wikman, Ph.D., obtained her B.A. from University of California, San Diego, and her doctorate from the California School of Professional Psychology, San Diego. For several years she taught graduate students at California State University, Los Angeles. She graduated as a diplomate from the Jung-Von Franz Center for Depth Psychology in Zurich. Monika works as a Jungian analyst in private practice, and part-time as an astrologer. She lives along a stream under the starry skies of Tesuque, New Mexico with horses and friends. Readers may contact Monika via e-mail: *monikawikman@comcast.net*